NARRATIVE COACHING

Bringing Our New Stories to Life

David B Drake, PhD

CNC Press
Petaluma, CA

Here is what leaders in our field have said about the book

There are very few coaching approaches that are fully theory-based and also serve as a sensitive guide to practice. Narrative coaching as developed by David Drake represents an outstanding example of such an approach. It includes a skilful synthesis of the best ideas in the field of human change, made richer by his years of thoughtful refinement and integration into coaching practice. This book truly extends the knowledge of the coaching field and beyond.

Tatiana Bachkirova, PhD
Co-Director of the International Centre for
Coaching and Mentoring Studies, UK

David Drake knows narrative at its core and has skilfully drawn on his deep knowledge and wide experience to define the field of narrative coaching. I'll keep his volume close by as it is worthy of many slow and thoughtful reads.

Shawn Callahan
Founder of Anecdote, Australia

This book looks to add a critical dimension to our professional development as coaches and provide some wonderful resources for all of us to gain liberation from and through our stories. The true meaning of a gift.

Michelle Duval
Founder and CEO, Equilibrio International, Australia

This almanac of narrative coaching is a generous gift from the heart, soul and mind of a deeply committed and extraordinary coach. David walks the talk and brings together in one place a rich collection of insights and astute observations. Don't miss this opportunity to join David as a guide for truly empowering others.

Terrence Gargulio
President, makingstories.net, US

Wow—it is so good to read something about coaching with this degree of freshness and energy! It offers a genuine and helpful alternative by highlighting narrative as a key way to understand and appreciate one's patterns and life events. Whatever you are doing right now, just stop and read this book; you won't be disappointed!

Professor Bob Garvey
Faculty Head of Research, York St John Business School, UK

David is a global thought-leader in Narrative Coaching and this book will stimulate, educate and provide valuable insights and tools for all coaches. An essential read.

Anthony M Grant, PhD
Director of the Coaching Psychology Unit,
University of Sydney, Australia

David lives, eats and breathes narrative; it's what he does and who he is. It is like he can see into people's soul through their narratives and help them see all of who they are. When we taught together, it was evident how profound and powerful narratives are in revealing and healing our deepest shadows. *Narrative Coaching* illustrates this important work in a way that we can use in our work and lives. Brilliant!

Donna Karlin
The Shadow Coach®, Canada

Most coaches deal with the surface of life, focusing on arranging behaviors and tasks. David has a way of quickly getting to the deeper personal narrative that shapes how we perceive daily life. Once I understood the story I was living in, I had the power to change it. Behavioral changes that had been a challenge seem much less daunting now that they are tied to a deeper intention.

Brian Lanahan
Brand strategist, US

Narrative coaching is fundamentally about helping us change our narratives about ourselves as the rower, our life as the boat, and our place in time and space as the river. This book deepens my knowledge and understanding of David's work, and it will undoubtedly enrich my practice and growth as a coach. It is the perfect companion for all coaches seeking to work in a 'profoundly human way'.

Haley Lancaster
Organisational psychologist and coach, The Netherlands

This is a deeply thoughtful yet highly practical account of narrative coaching. David Drake has made a significant contribution to the field of coaching, not just to narrative approaches. I highly recommend this book.

Professor David Lane
Professional Development Foundation
and Middlesex University, UK

David engages in coaching from a quite different perspective than do many in the field. I appreciate this wonderful text, which brings together many aspects of his work in one coherent narrative! However, what I derived most from this book was some slightly uncomfortable insights into my own practice and stories. I commend this book without reservation to anyone involved in coaching.

Paul Lawrence, PhD
Director, Centre for Systemic Change, Australia

David gives us the inside story on Narrative Coaching and how it brings not only our stories to life but our practice as well. He shares his decades of research and coaching experience and kindly includes the reader in his own journey to better coaching. This is an inspiring and remarkably generous book. I'll be returning to it again and again. Relax, trust and listen. Everything we need is in the stories.

Moya Sayer-Jones
Founder and story activist, Only Human, Australia

David Drake charts the waters for any coach or trainer willing to help a fellow soul change the stories that bind him or her. Wonderful examples and a healthy respect for the diverse and unpredictable variability of two humans talking (or sitting in silence) makes this book entertaining as well as useful.

Annette Simmons
Group Process Consulting, US

This is a book for anyone who is seriously concerned with the business of personal and professional transformation. It is written with great authority—an authority grounded in many years of diligent scholarship and reflective practice. Most importantly it tells the 'story' of narrative coaching in an engaging way, and it is very accessible and practically useful. I can see our students benefiting enormously from it.

Gordon Spence, PhD
Master of Business Coaching, Sydney Business
School/University of Wollongong, Australia

With a passion for narratives and stories that began early in life, David Drake offers an approach to coaching that integrates different theoretical positions—from psychodynamic to social constructionist—into a coherent and striking bouquet. Reflective practitioners will value this book as an inspiring and insightful source for their professional development.

Reinhart Stelter, PhD
Coaching Psychology Unit, University of Copenhagen, Denmark

David has taken his doctoral research and created a globally recognized body of work. It has been a joy to watch narrative coaching evolve and David along with it. His systemic approach to developing people is on the leading edge of coaching. I highly recommend this book for both its scholarship and its profound insights on practice.

Judy Stevens-Long, PhD
Faculty, Fielding Graduate University, School of
Human & Organizational Development, US

This book is a superb guide to narrative coaching and an important and innovative resource. It is a must-have for any coach wishing to develop new perspectives on their skills in helping clients reflect on their experience and test new stories for themselves. *Narrative Coaching* offers plenty of practical advice, underpinned by David's unique and ground-breaking theory about how people develop through coaching.

Sunny Stout-Rostron, DProf
University of Stellenbosch, School of Business, South Africa

David has created a multi-faceted book that offers a scholarly text on narrative coaching, while capturing his own thirty year journey of discovery with the voices and stories of those he has met along the way. It is a lovely book, written as though we are walking with him on a long pilgrimage. The book encourages 'listening' to familiar tales differently and to being open and attentive to the moment when people seek new stories. This book will become a highly valued reference for people interested in narrative work.

Ann Whyte
Managing Director, Whyte & Co, Australia

Based on strong theoretical foundations in attachment, identity and developmental theory, David Drake has crafted a very persuasive case for the narrative approach to coaching. The book is packed with tools, examples and insights derived from thousands of hours of client practice and coach training—all integrated into one model. I found the book hugely inspirational and trust that you will too.

Ian Wycherley, PhD
former Programme Director, MA Coaching and
Mentoring Practice, Oxford Brookes University, UK

CNC Press
Petaluma, CA, USA
www.narrativecoaching.com/cncpress

ISBN: 978–0996356305
Library of Congress Control Number: 2015910045

Cover and book design by Jennifer Omner

To Caroline Tompkins for inviting my voice into the world, Terri Mandler for inviting this work into the world, and my daughter Hannah for inspiring me to get the book done.

ACKNOWLEDGMENTS

In reflecting on everything that went into writing this book, I kept coming back to important people who in varying ways made it all possible. I am grateful for all of them; I am a better writer, coach and person as a result. While I have other books in the works, this one feels personal as the culmination of a long journey. As such, there are people I wish to thank who helped me get to the starting gate and others who helped me get across the finish line. One group that is not named here are those who challenged me along the way. However, our lives are like stories in that they are often defined by conflict and how we respond to it. I have come to appreciate these people as I used these experiences to strengthen who I am, what I write and how this work is done. The book is better for it.

I want to start by acknowledging some people who helped a shy, bright kid find his way early on. I learned the value of resilience and critical thinking from my late father, Bill Drake—both of which have held me in good stead. His untimely death in the middle of my doctoral studies was the impetus for creating narrative coaching. I learned that it is never too late for new stories in watching my mother, Sally (Drake) Murphy blossom later in life—and appreciated her support along the way. I learned that intelligence was cool and that I could lead from Bob Scarola, my marvelous 6th-grade teacher. I learned the importance of defining one's own stories from Wayne Carpenter, a pastoral counselor at my church. I learned to see the world through a systemic lens and the power of purpose from David Oliver, the Chair of the Sociology Department when I was an undergraduate. I developed a life-long interest in the relationship between grief and development when Amy Coffman, a young woman with whom I worked closely when I was in college, was killed in a car accident. I am grateful to my uncle, James Laurie, for introducing me to Fielding and from whom I learned about authenticity and grace.

I appreciate Ghost Ranch where I taught my first Shadow workshops and came to see my gifts for facilitating transformation. I deeply appreciate my experience at Fielding Graduate University—from which the second half of my life, a doctorate and narrative coaching were born. My dissertation Chair, Judy Stevens-Long, was a masterful mentor from whom I learned when was enough and the art of being done. My classmate, Wendy Rowe, is a kindred spirit and one of the most honestly astute people I know. Through faculty member, Will McWhinney, I learned how much we can learn about ourselves through seeing ourselves in others. Lastly, I am grateful to Dianne Stober for encouraging me to present my work in Sydney and rejecting my first academic paper. The first opened up the world for me and the second challenged me to step up my game—both with great success. I am grateful to my core group of friends in Portland, Oregon—Bruce Hazen, Brian Lanahan, Carolyn McKnight, Alex Merrin and Niki Steckler—for their wonderful fellowship and support over the years. You are my home base.

Many of the important steps I took in developing narrative coaching over the years were in Australia. It began at the coaching research conference at University of Sydney where my work had its real debut. Terri Mandler helped me to see how much I had, was my first champion and became a lifelong friend. Sandra Bannister was an early supporter who opened some marvelous doors for me. I appreciate Ann Whyte for our wine and cheese conversations, her advocacy, and her fierce and faithful friendship. I will be forever grateful to the folks in my first Narrative Design Lab in Sydney—it was a raw and generative time without which narrative coaching would not be what it is now. In particular, I want to acknowledge Sophie Francis for her keen insights, hard work and persistent faith and Lucas Finch for his insatiable curiosity and invitations to play. Moya Sayer-Jones has been my muse as the work has evolved, and reminded me (along with Ross) of the importance of the simple things that make people feel welcome. I look forward to our forthcoming collaboration. Lastly, I bow to Leora Krowitz, my yoga angel, and to the waters of Clovelly Bay, my sanctuary, for helping me heal and find joy again.

I want to acknowledge some people in Europe who played an important role in making this book possible. I appreciate Ian Wycherley for our work on thresholds, Tatiana Bachkirova for our lively exchanges and both of them for providing forums at Oxford-Brookes. People who aspire to great things often have friendly rivals who spur them on to be their best; Reinhard Stelter plays that role for me. I want to acknowledge his work on the philosophical foundations of narrative coaching and as champion for its values-based and collaborative nature. I thoroughly enjoyed my time at the ANSE Summer School in Stavanger, Norway. It was where the Four Gateways had its debut; the power and spirit of this process was captured best by the colleague who so beautifully played his saxophone on Pulpit Rock. I am grateful for Haley Lancaster for her diligent efforts in bringing the Labs to The Netherlands and partnering with me to help them grow in Europe.

In closing, I am grateful for Bill Randall and the opportunities to present my first post-doctoral papers at his marvelous Narrative Matters research conferences in the Canadian Maritime Provinces. I became friends with Donna Karlin the moment we met at an ICF conference many moons ago. I learned a lot from running workshops with her and deeply appreciate her witness and humor. I want to acknowledge the guys at WBECS, Leadership Coaching Summit and Het Eerste Huis for helping me get this work to more people this year; I look forward to our on-going partnership. I am grateful for all that my clients, colleagues and participants on this wondrous journey have given me and for the amazing opportunities to share my work all over the world. I am a far better person for it. I offer a big hug to my daughter Hannah who kept asking, "Are you done yet?" with such love. I appreciate Jennifer Omner for her expert help in getting the book into print. Lastly, I want to thank you for buying this book. May you have a rich and rewarding time as you read it, reflect on it and put it to good use. The world needs you.

CONTENTS

PREFACE

Have you ever had that experience when you're driving down the highway . . . and you suddenly realize you've not been fully conscious for the past few seconds? How is it that we can drive and yet have no recollection of how we got to where we are on the road? I think that our lives are often not too different: we find ourselves further down the road over time, but we are not quite sure how we got there. Stories are a great resource because they provide the means to mark what has happened, articulate what sense and meaning we made of it, and deconstruct how we got to where we are. Narrative coaching gives people an opportunity to wake up, imagine a different future, tell a different story and make new choices with greater consciousness. In the process, some of their stories are let go while others are let come. I am particularly interested in what stories can teach us about how to connect with people, listen to them and co-create with them. Otherwise, it is too easy to be asleep at the wheel.

My passion for stories began early in my life through a love for reading. I still vividly recall the sense of anticipation I felt when the books we had ordered arrived in our elementary school classroom. The smell of fresh paper . . . the eagerness to lose myself in the plot . . . the dilemma about which one to read first. I found respite in the richness of these books and their stories—a love that would take me through thousands of books across the decades that followed. As a shy kid, I was particularly intrigued and inspired by characters who 'colored outside the lines'. In seeing the world through the lens of these characters, I became fascinated by the different ways in which people narrate their experience—and the worlds that form around those choices. As an introverted child, reading was central to the formation of a rich inner life that has served me to this day. I also found insights and a certain solace in these narrated worlds as I compared them with my own. It was an early introduction to the role of projection in learning and development.

My love for stories was enriched through epic tales at church and two teachers who introduced me to the marvelous world of classic literature. I remember being captivated by the descriptions of worlds far beyond my suburban American life and the thrill in searching for the deeper meanings within these famous works. There were important mentors as well who helped me start to find my own voice in the process. I went on to get a degree in sociology in which I was introduced to the novel idea (at the time) that reality and stories were socially constructed. This provided the foundation for a lifelong passion and commitment to understand the context for stories and the people in them. Next came a graduate degree in theology and an introduction to the field of hermeneutics, the use of stories to witness and awaken, and the symbolic value of sacramental rituals. I came to appreciate the various ways in which people make sense and meaning of their lives through my study of different religions—sparking a spiritual journey that continues to this day. I was also involved in peace and justice issues, and I saw firsthand the challenges in liberating ourselves and others from challenging social narratives.

Over the next twenty years I supported people through transitions—as a grief educator and counselor, a rites of passage guide, a facilitator of dialogues on difficult issues, a change consultant and coach, and more. This rich background provided a strong foundation for what was to come with narrative coaching. This book traces the path it has taken since its inception in my doctoral studies in 2000. I developed it as an alternative to both narrative therapy and traditional coaching, and I started to share it with others as well as use it in my own practice in 2002. Over the first decade, narrative coaching served as both my muse and my mantle. It challenged me to grow at many levels in order to keep up with and shape what it was becoming. In writing this preface, I feel both grief and joy as that era comes to an end and another begins. I am proud to have established a solid place for narrative coaching (and all it stands for) in coaching, grateful for what I have learned from the thousands I have worked with in this space, and keen to see how this work evolves in the years to come.

I know firsthand how powerful this work can be, as I've used it to help myself through a series of major transitions in my own life. Everything I have written here, taught to practitioners and done with clients I have used to support my own ongoing well-being and growth. Many of the newest and most powerful applications of narrative coaching were developed in my living room overlooking Clovelly Bay near Sydney in the wake of a divorce. Out of this proverbial "dark night of the soul"—and the near daily ritual of snorkeling in the bay—I discovered what this work is really all about. I know firsthand that the literal and developmental thresholds we must cross are not for the faint of heart or the ill-prepared, but are essential for those who are serious about bringing their new story to life. Thresholds call *everything* into question, require us to walk through the doorway of unknowing, and open us in the end to more than we thought possible. I emerged from this time with a much deeper understanding of the power that was within this work and a commitment to develop its full potential as a resource for anyone seeking to make a significant change in themselves and/or their life.

Thresholds call *everything* into question, require us to walk through the doorway of unknowing, and open us in the end to more than we thought possible.

As you can imagine, writing this book has been both a deeply personal process and a demanding professional crucible as I sought to clearly articulate what narrative coaching is all about. As such, this unique book is part history, part autobiography and part professional resource. Like with a great story, the meaning would be otherwise diminished if I attempted to separate the context, the author and the material. I felt that the best way to describe what goes on in narrative coaching was to model it through the way the book is written. It has been deeply satisfying to me personally and professionally to weave together critical elements from my academic studies in sociology, theology, psychology, and systems theory in developing this work. It brings together key elements of what we know about stories at the *cellular* level (our biological narratives), the *consciousness* level (our ontological narratives), the *cultural* level (our ecological narratives) and the *conceptual*[1] level—(our cosmological narratives) to form a truly integrative practice. In completing it, I was struck by how much I have changed since I began and how much the work has matured.

My journey with this book has served as its own rite of passage. It has challenged me to dig deep into both the passion and the logic of this work so that it can evolve and serve at the highest level. As a result, it now incorporates more of its mindful, somatic and spiritual roots as well as new elements from design thinking, systemic practices and transformational learning theory to accelerate people's development using their own stories. Narrative coaching is more fluid than other approaches that sometimes get locked into their 'isms' because it is a naturally human process that is open source by design. It is a way for people to connect with themselves and others in order to awaken and do what needs to be done. While I draw from and greatly appreciate the work of the narrative therapy community (the late Michael White in particular), narrative coaching has evolved to the point where it is a distinct approach and body of work in its own right. It is an established part of the coaching canon and has influenced other key aspects of the broader field of coaching.

This book is the definitive reference on narrative coaching, and it offers both the academic foundations for this work and some of the core practices I use. It is the culmination of the first decade of narrative coaching and the inauguration of its next decade. It celebrates all that narrative coaching has been and all that it will become in the hands of the thousands of people around the world who use this work and will help it flourish even more. In the end, I came to a place where I could say with pride, "Here I stand, I can do no other." While the book provides a comprehensive overview of this work and how it was developed, it also is a generous guide for you as a practitioner. It is a call to reflect on your own stories and a guide on how to

---

1   This term relates to both conception as language and conception as creation.

be with this work and *do* this work. What stories are alive in you and your life right now? What wants attention? What stories in others are calling you? My sincerest hope is that you will use this book to answer these questions for yourself as a way to enrich your practice.

I wrote this book primarily for people who use coaching in their professional practice and who are ready to step more fully into themselves, the moment and the work to be done. For some of you, it will affirm how you have instinctively worked for a long time and give you confidence knowing why it works and how to take it further. For others of you, this book will be a provocative opportunity to expand your beliefs about how coaching works and give you the confidence to let go of a lot of what you thought you needed. Either way, I welcome you to this conversation and to the global community of those who are committed to helping people individually and collectively bring their new stories to life. This book is part of my larger vision to democratize coaching so it is infused in how we connect and converse with others—whether at home or work, in schools or communities. It is an invitation to leave behind what distracts you, drains you, or no longer serves you so that you can show up more fully as yourself in doing what matters most in your life and work.

I believe that the time has come for narrative coaching to really shine. There is a greater awareness of the power of narrative and the need for more advanced and integrative forms of practice. We need a new breed of practitioner who can work with people in a more holistic fashion and contribute to the resolution of the complex and systemic issues we face. I believe narrative coaching will continue to be at the leading edge in rising to this challenge for three reasons:

- It is based on the broader narrative design platform such that it can be scaled to any size, and it connects the deeply systemic and the deeply personal to support more sustainable innovation and change.
- It has a strong foundation yet is accessible to anyone. Learning the methodology helps people integrate what they know but at a higher level *and* feel more at ease because they can let go of so much of what they thought coaching had to be.

- It is as much a way of being human and with people as it a way of doing, if not more. It will make you a better coach. However, I believe its true power is in who it helps you become in the process and what you can do as a result.

A suggestion as you read this book: One of the central images I use to describe this work is that of a bird circling the tree—sometimes rising up for a new perspective and sometimes dropping down for a new experience. In keeping with this approach, this book is not written in a linear or mechanistic fashion as if it were an instruction manual. Instead, it is written as a layered immersion in the foundations and fundamentals of narrative coaching. Its initial aim, like with the work itself, is to help you become more astute in *observing what is true right now* before trying to change anything. You may find that reading the book feels slow at times, especially at the start. Take heart in the fact that it was designed this way as an invitation to slow down in order to have a richer experience, be in a more natural flow and gain more sustainable benefits. Give yourself plenty of time to let the material sink in and find opportunities to experiment with it. Take note as you read these pages: What is stirring inside you? What is it calling you to be or do? Where would you like to begin? Come to one of our Labs or register for our online program at www.narrativecoaching.com if you want to learn more.

One of our Canadian participants, Heather Plett, wrote the following to describe her experience with narrative coaching after participating in one of our Labs in Toronto. I include it here with her permission because it so beautifully captures the spirit of narrative coaching and the sense of 'coming home' this work offers people. Enjoy the parable and the rest of the book.

> Imagine you are a pilgrim on a long journey, gathering stories as they appear and stashing them like gems in your backpack.
>
> Sometimes you pull the stories out, dust them off, and share them with fellow travelers. Sometimes you keep them to yourself, afraid that other travelers will find them ugly or unsavory and you will feel shame. Sometimes you

roll them around in your hands, re-shaping them to better fit with the other stories they share space with.

The stories in your backpack don't look like those in any other traveler's backpack. They have been shaped by the journey through which they've been carried, by the way you've used them to define yourself, and by your assumptions of how other people are judging them.

Now imagine you've been invited by a kind and supportive fellow traveler to sit down on a comfortable park bench along that journey. Your new companion invites you to open your backpack, promising that he will be gentle with the stories inside.

You're a little reluctant at first, but the stories are getting heavy and you'd really like to be free of the weight for awhile. Your backpack hasn't been fitting very well on your back during the last few miles and you wonder whether it might be a good idea to take some time to rearrange the things that are poking you.

Your companion is very good at making you feel comfortable and safe, and it doesn't take long for you to recognize that you trust him. Finally, you sit down and take a few deep breaths. Your companion waits patiently.

Slowly you pull out a story and hold it tenderly in your hand, glancing up to see what response it will elicit. Surprisingly, your companion holds no judgment in his eyes as he gazes down at the story. He simply asks you kind and energizing questions about it, helping you to define it and see it through new eyes.

Before long, you're pulling more stories out of the bag and lining them up on the bench. Your companion doesn't say much, but asks just the right questions for you to know which stories are important right now. He helps you see the patterns arising as you line the stories up. Sometimes when you shift the story and line it up with another story, it takes on a whole new shape. Sometimes a story shrinks in importance once you pull it out and expose it to the sunlight.

Through your companion's questions, you begin to see brand new things in your stories that you never saw before. There are new colors and beautiful patterns emerging. The light touches them differently, and some that looked like lumps of coal now begin to reveal the diamonds underneath. You see how they fit together, and sometimes you could even swear that you see them dance. The new shapes offer new possibilities for how you will continue on your journey. They're even helping you define yourself in a new way that feels deeply right and true.

When the conversation draws to a close, you pack your newly shaped stories back into your backpack. You brace yourself for the weight as you put it on, but now it feels lighter and fits the groove of your back in a much more natural way. It no longer feels like the heavy burden you placed on the bench when you sat down. You look at the path ahead of you, and though the rough spots aren't gone, you can see a clearer trail through it with a backpack that will offer you tools rather than burdens. You have the distinct sense that your path will be much clearer and your strides much bolder. And so you set off . . .

That companion on your journey is your narrative coach. So, have a seat on the bench and let me tell you a story . . .

Welcome.

David

INTRODUCTION

I begin with an experience from my first career as a great example of where narrative coaching came from and what it is designed to do. The story I reference may or may not be familiar to you or speak to you depending on your background. I myself have traveled far on my own journey since this episode took place over thirty years ago, and I am using it now for its narrative implications. My invitation to you is the same I offered to the women that day: focus on the characters' experience *in* the story more than the content *of* the story.

I was talking one day with a group of older, upper-middle class women in a study group at the church about the Old Testament saga of the Israelites escaping slavery in Egypt. I was having a hard time getting the conversation going, so I asked why. They responded that they had heard the story many times before, but had always felt disconnected from it because they could not relate to the life of a slave which was so far from their own. Fair enough . . . In response, I reframed the question I was going to ask next to enable us to explore the topic from a different perspective. Little did I know at the time that this decision was to become a cornerstone of both my doctoral work and narrative coaching.

I invited the women to shift their focus from the content *of* the story to the characters' experience *in* the story. Instead of talking about slaves, I asked them, "Have you ever felt *enslaved*?" With that question the group came alive. Some told stories about following their husband's career path and feeling enslaved by the assigned role of 'wife'. Some talked about being the only woman in their fields at university or when they started their careers— and feeling enslaved by the limitations of working in male-dominated professions (or being shut out of professions altogether). Some talked about feeling enslaved to money given the costs associated with living in the San Francisco Bay Area. Others talked about feeling enslaved within the church, their theological insights not taken seriously, since they were *just* a 'woman's Bible study'— and older women at that. Through this lens, an all too familiar story came alive for them in a new way. That conversation led to a broader dialogue about their place in the church. It illustrates what can happen for people when they are invited to voice, explore and transform their stories in a supportive environment.

Narrative coaching is grounded in this same pedagogical stance and offers a practical structure to work this way with people. It draws on Paulo Friere's notion of praxis as a dialectical process of bringing out people's story *and then* the teaching story in a liberating dialogue that fosters a new level of consciousness and action. In narrative coaching, we work in much the same way by using the coachee's own narrative material as the source of and catalyst for change—not the coach's methodology. It also moves beyond the individualistic and psychological orientation in most coaching to incorporate collective and sociological considerations. As a result, coachees develop themselves and their own stories *and* their ability to engage with their environments and larger narratives in new ways. This introduction sets the stage with an overview of the key theoretical influences that shaped the formation of narrative coaching, a comparison of narrative coaching to approaches with a similar philosophical stance and related practices, and a definition of narrative coaching.

Theoretical influences

Stories are at the core of what it means to be human and they touch every aspect of our lives. It is no surprise, then, that narrative coaching has a more diverse foundation than most approaches to coaching. It enables coaches to think more systemically and holistically about what is occurring in sessions and with coachees. In so doing, some practitioners have simply adapted narrative therapy practices for a coaching context while others like myself have developed new, native methods built specifically for coaching. I have developed narrative coaching as its own methodology from a diverse set of sources and with its own set of practices. It also has become clear to me that narrative coaching is more than anything else a way of being, a mindset, an attitude. It is grounded theoretically and evidentially in the current literature on human learning, development and performance—and it takes coaching in some exciting new directions. To see how it came to be that way, let's take a brief look at its history.

The groundwork for narrative coaching can be found in my dissertation (2003) and early papers on narrative liminality (Drake, 2004a, 2004b, 2004c, 2005a) and narrative coaching as a psychosocial method (Drake, 2005b, 2007). Two others who contributed to the field early on were Reinhard Stelter (2007, 2009) in Denmark and Ho Law (2007) in the United Kingdom. As the field of coaching has evolved, so too has the depth and breadth of this approach. To secure a place for it in the coaching canon and support its evolution as a 'third-generation' practice (Stelter, 2013, 2014b), I have written introductory chapters (Drake, 2008b, 2009c, 2011c, 2014b; Drake & Stelter, 2014) and made the case in the coaching literature for a narrative perspective on:

- coaching as the first postprofessional practice (Drake, 2011e; Drake & Stober, 2005),
- coaching as an evidence-based practice (Drake, 2008a, 2009a),
- coaching across cultures (Drake, 2009b),
- attachment theory in coaching (Drake, 2009d),
- formulation in coaching (Drake, 2010),
- goals and strengths in coaching (Drake, 2011b, 2012), and
- coaching supervision (Drake, 2014c).

The result is an interdisciplinary body of work and a holistic methodology.

While a narrative frame is relatively new in the fields of psychotherapy and coaching, stories have been an essential component of cultures and communities since the dawn of time. People use stories to structure their experience as events and actions in *space* and as memories and visions across *time*—in keeping with their brain's primary coordinates (see Schank, 1990) and in forming plausible plotlines that help them make sense and meaning. Narrative coaching taps into this ancient vein and also builds on the postmodern "narrative turn" that shifted our thinking from "stories as objects" to "stories in context" (Boje, 1998). It is based in an understanding of stories as a dynamic, relational process that is performed not as a static, isolated commodity that is pre-formed. People can increase their capacity for intimacy (making connections) and agency (making contributions) by telling their stories in new ways. (Bakan, 1966; McAdams, 1985). In so doing, they can live more authentic and fulfilling lives.

Five bodies of work were particularly important as I developed narrative coaching:

1. *Anthropology*: I came to understand how stories are embedded in the very fabric of our communities and cultures and in ritualized processes through people like Gregory Bateson, Joseph Campbell, Victor Turner and Arthur van Gennep. The four phases of a rite of passage became the backbone for my narrative coaching model.

2. *Identity and learning*: I came to understand the critical role stories play in how we see ourselves and others and how we grow through people like Paulo Freire, Tim Gallwey, William James, Roger Schank and Lev Vygotsky. The structure and flow of the model mirrors and supports the four phases of learning and development.

3. *Jungian psychology*: I came to understand the unconscious, archetypal and collective aspects of our stories and our individuation through people like James Hillman, James Hollis, Carl Jung, Ginette Paris, and Murray Stein. Working in third and projective spaces and the psyche's journey toward wholeness are central in the core process.

4. *Mind and body*: I came to understand the importance of mindfulness, somatic work, and neuroscience research for coaching through people like Louis Cozolino, Moshe Feldenkrais,

Gregory Kramer, Linda Graham and Dan Siegel. It has enabled this work to address the whole person in some powerful new ways.

5. *Narrative studies*: I came to understand what to listen for in stories through people like Jerome Bruner, Dan McAdams, Robert McKee, Donald Polkinghorne and Paul Ricouer. The realization that narration, transition and individuation follow the same flow started here and was key in developing the narrative coaching model.

Most coaching models are designed to structure the conversation through a series of steps. In the narrative coaching model, the external process used by the coach mirrors the internal process of the coachee and the process is centered around the latter not the former. Therefore you can facilitate the movement of people through the parallel unfolding of their story *and* their transition and development. The beauty is that either can lead the way at any point and each strengthens the other along the way. Like water that finds its way down the mountain, the conversation goes where it needs to go. In recent years, narrative coaching has been further enriched through the incorporation of non-dualist paradigms such as Buddhism to balance the Western frames that are dominant in coaching. One result has been that suffering is now seen both as the result of our attachment to certain stories *and* as the ever-present doorway to liberation. Given the complexity of the issues coachees face, narrative coaching is well placed with its multidisciplinary background and its holistic approach. It is a layered and spiraling process that is simple *and* powerful, subtle *and* direct.

One of the questions I was often asked, particularly in the beginning, was, "How is this different than therapy?" As coaching psychology has taken hold and more psychotherapists include elements of coaching in their practice, this question has faded somewhat. Still, it is an important distinction as both therapeutic and coaching processes have their place and their requirements. When asked, my answer remains the same: "Done well, narrative coaching is inherently *therapeutic* for people. Otherwise, why bother." Narrative coaching uses some of the same techniques as psychotherapy such as cathartic insight, emotional healing and issue resolution to create a foundation for new actions. However, there is more emphasis in coaching on taking new actions toward the future than you would find in most therapeutic methodologies. The bottom line is that coaches should work at the deepest level for which they are qualified and invited and at the appropriate level for a coachee's readiness and the issue at hand. Beyond that, I am less interested in dogmas and labels and more interested in the rigor of our own development and the vigor of the outcomes for those with whom we work.

The bottom line is that coaches should work at the deepest level for which they are qualified and invited and at the appropriate level for a coachee's readiness and the issue at hand.

Related approaches

Narrative coaching has elements in common with other coaching and therapeutic approaches that are mindful, systemic, and field-focused. In particular, I will look at narrative therapy as well as two experiential approaches (family constellations and psychodrama) and two psychotherapeutic approaches (Gestalt and ACT). The purpose for doing so is to identify the unique features and grounded base for narrative coaching and to position and distinguish it relative to other transformative development practices.

Narrative therapy

Michael White (see M. White, 1988, 1989, 2007; M. White & Epston, 1990) and others in the family systems therapy space led the way by advocating for the externalization of problems, the deconstruction of dominant narratives, the decentering of experts and the contribution of "unique outcomes" to the resolution of people's issues. They helped us see that a story is just 'a story' and the teller, sitting in the protagonist's seat, has more options as a result (Barry,

1997). What was once a totalizing truth could now be seen as simply one of several options to choose from. This involved deconstructing and critically examining people's up-until-then taken-for-granted understanding of life and identity by "exoticizing the familiar" and "familiarizing the exotic" (Turner, 1978) so that a new plot could be formed (M. White, 2004). The narrative therapists lifted up individual stories as legitimate and substantive resources in psychotherapy and championed the notion that any given narrative was just one of many potential constructions from which to choose.

I appreciated Michael White's strong philosophical grounding and thoughtful yet playful approach to his work. He and his colleagues made important contributions on how to frame and address "dominant narratives" and their impact; explore new territories and possibilities; and renegotiate the relationships between identities and stories as well as between internal experiences and external narratives. We were drawn to many of the same sources in formulating our respective body of work, and we share a similar contextual view of identity, development, and behavior. Key to both processes is the observation that the scaffolding for new behaviors can be found in people's own stories (Drake, 2003, 2007; M. M. Gergen & Gergen, 2006). Some key terms and insights from a number of narrative therapists have been incorporated in the book in recognition of their contributions to our understanding of how to work with people's stories in coaching.

At the same time, I see narrative coaching as more than just narrative therapy adapted for a coaching context. Instead, it is a more integrative practice that differs in some important ways in both its underlying assumptions and its approach. For example, it shifts the focus from the implications of the past on the present *to* the implications of the present on the future (and the future on the present). Narrative coaching is distinct from narrative therapy in that it

- addresses preverbal attachment issues using archetypal and somatic practices;
- draws more from multiple disciplines in the social sciences and beyond;

- accesses the personal and collective unconscious using transpersonal means;
- uses the rites of passage framework as a systemic approach to transitions and change;
- pays more attention to the nuances of and points of leverage in narrative structure;
- focuses more on desired narratives and less on dominant narratives;
- relies more on the role of silence, presence, and the field to support change;
- attends to issues of power through a lens of emergence more than justice; and
- uses directive energies judiciously in service of a more overt focus on outcomes.

Experiential approaches

Narrative coaching relates well with experimental and experiential approaches such as systemic constellations and psychodrama because they are philosophies that stimulate deep change, not psychotherapies (Carnabucci & Anderson, 2012). As with narrative coaching, neither Bert Hellinger (founder of family constellation work) nor Jacob Moreno (founder of psychodrama) were concerned with matters of diagnosis. Instead, they too based their work in the primacy of the embodied here–and–now rather than the verbal abstractions of analysis and in the belief that sustained healing and transformation need to be grounded in experience as well as insight. Lastly, all three modalities take a systemic approach to development in keeping with Moreno's observation that:

> the psyche is an open system, constantly influenced and shaped—or misshaped—by the interactional environment in which the human being develops. He knew that to reach this level, words were not enough, that it required action and interaction, that it is in the area 'in between' people that demands our attention. (Dayton, 2005, p. xiii)

Narrative coaching follows a process similar to other experimental approaches, as outlined in Carnabucci & Anderson (2012). However, it does so with more focus on the present and future and a naturopathic rather than allopathic approach. The five phases of the process:

- *attunement*, which involves resonating internally with the person and accepting the person's here-and-now experience [*Situate* phase in narrative coaching];
- *assessment*, which involves seeking the specific issue or pattern relating to the person's distress and where it originated in past experience [and appears in present experience] [*Search* phase];
- *observation*, which involves offering a safe and careful replication of the . . . dysfunctional adaptation [to understand its dynamics] [*Search* phase];
- *intervention*, which involves a new experience that estimates a shift, release, or other expression of what has never been easy or possible to feel or express previously [*Shift* phase];
- *integration*, which involves incorporating new experience into the person's being and positively impacts the person's life [the *Sustain* phase] (p. 20).

Narrative coaching uses the "empty vessel" approach as does constellations in working with what is present in the field[2], and it may use assigned roles as does psychodrama, depending on the needs of the coachee. However, narrative coaching is far less produced or directed than psychodrama or constellation work and is not dependent on expert facilitation in order for it to be effective. This is evident in the fact that I have taught these principles and the basic practices to thousands of professionals, managers, and leaders in organizations. It is only the more advanced practices and complex issues where expertise is essential as the forces in play often require a more robust container, guide for change and duty of care. A large part of what makes this possible in narrative coaching is its emphasis on developing the field in search of transformative experiences not on directing processes in search of transactional explanations.

---

2   If you want to know more about the concept of the "field" in coaching, look ahead to p. 254.

Family and systemic constellations

Virginia Satir (see 1991/2006) and her ground-breaking role-playing work on "family reconstruction" and "family sculpting" can be seen as the pioneer in this space. Later, with the help of German psychiatrist Gunthard Weber, Bert Hellinger (see 1998) brought together existential phenomenology, family systems therapy, and elements of indigenous mysticism from his time in Africa to create family constellation work. He emphasized the role of perceptive intuition, the release of our desire to control the unknown, and the importance of moment-to-moment systemic information as the process unfolds in the 'field'—all three of which are central to narrative coaching. In constellations work, representatives are investigated and moved around in relation to others who are integral to the issue in order to discern the current constellation, what needs to be resolved, and what new constellation would bring about healing and resolution. At the end, the person whose process is being done replaces her representative to sense how it feels to be part of a new constellation.

In narrative coaching, characters are literally and figuratively repositioned in people's stories as needed, but the person being coached is active in, and the focus of, the process. In some of our practices—like with chair work—they are actually guiding the process themselves with peer and facilitator support. The focus is on keeping their felt experience and their narration intimately connected in the moment so that both are available for transformation. This parallel process enables people to see the situation in a new way, develop a new story about it, find a new place in it from which to act and/or enhance their sense of agency and connection as they try it out. While there are principles that guide its core practices, narrative coaching is not guided by a sense of how things are 'supposed to be' in order to achieve resolution as is the case in Hellinger's orders of love, for example.

Psychodrama

Jacob Moreno, in partnership with his wife Zerka, felt that in giving people 'the stage', their life stories could emerge in a space where their memories could be reworked and transformed and their body, mind, and relational ability could heal. They saw it as a safe place and structure where people might freely test out the fears and fantasies that were close to their heart and pressed upon their inner and/ or outer worlds. It was a "therapeutic space where we might meet ourselves, including the parts of ourselves that might be held out of consciousness in daily life, even though they powerfully impact and inform who we are" (Dayton, 2005, p. xxix) through their often invisible scripts and illusory logic. Moreno believed that since we learn and develop in action as we move through life, we must also unlearn and relearn in action. That is why in narrative coaching there is so much attention to working in the moment with what is happening and what people are experiencing. In so doing, you can bring the whole person into the process and they can develop more lasting anchors for their new insights and commitments.

To be able to work this way, narrative coaches tend to focus on one thing at a time—usually what is at the heart of the story and its dilemma— and shifting narrative dynamics rather than relieving circumstantial symptoms. Narrative coaching has other features in common with psychodrama such as using "spatial mapping", inducing mild trance states, working at emotional and somatic levels, and putting people in touch with their own internal healer. There are also differences between the two approaches that are important to note. In narrative coaching, we: (1) invite peers when possible to help one another rather than rely on the expert as the orchestrator, (2) help people connect their body, emotions, and words but generally do so in the present moment rather than searching for their origins in the past, and (3) work with key elements in coachees' stories as they emerge rather than use pre-assigning roles. Even so, psychodrama was an important forerunner to narrative coaching with its use of enacted narration.

Therapeutic approaches
Gestalt therapy
Gestalt therapy and narrative coaching are both based in a paradoxical theory of change (Beisser, 1970) in which change is seen to

occur through fully contacting 'what is'—the truth of our experience—rather than through trying to be different. As with narrative
coaching, it focuses on the individual's experience in the present
moment, the environmental context in which this takes place,
and the self-regulating adjustments people make as they navigate
between the two (Bluckert, 2010). It is defined by three core principles (Yontef, 1980):

- *Change Principle*: It is phenomenological in nature and focused
  on what is happening now rather than what happened 'then'; its
  only goal is relational, present-centered 'awareness'.
- *Process Principle*: It is based in a constructivist, existential-
  ist position and a process of contact and withdrawal in which
  change happens in the crucible of the relational dialogue.
- *Holism Principle*: It locates the dyadic encounter in the field of
  communicative interaction shaped by conscious behaviors as
  well as unconscious projections and expectations.

We must first name our truth before we can change it.

Narrative coaching aligns well with these three principles, though
it focuses more on the field and the coachee's experience than the
coach and the coaching relationship. Both approaches focus on
working existentially in the present moment with what IS—at both
conscious and unconscious levels—so that people can experience and
deconstruct their current patterns and be supported as they begin
forming new ones. We must first name our truth before we can
change it. Threshold moments and pivots in narrative coaching serve
a similar function as Gestalt's "safe emergencies" in which powerful
affect emerges or is triggered so it can be worked through toward a
new resolution rather than blindly reenacted (see Frederick S. Perls,
1992/1969; Fritz S. Perls, Hefferline, & Goodman, 1994/1951). Unlike
most other psychotherapeutic modalities, Gestalt coaches observe
and share their subjective experience of their inner and outer world
as part of an authentic dialogue in sessions (Bluckert, 2010). While
a narrative coach actively participates in the dialogue, they are more

likely to keep the attention on the narrative material and the field. If they are engaged in the reconfiguration work, it is as a mirror in the dialogue or a character in the person's narration.

Acceptance Commitment Therapy (ACT)

The aim of this more recent approach is to increase a person's psychological flexibility by increasing her ability to be present, open up to the reality at hand, and do what matters. These aims align well with narrative coaching's movement from phase 1 (Situate) to phases 2/3 (Search/Shift) to phase 4 (Sustain). Both approaches emphasize contextual and experiential change strategies, the development of more effective repertoires more than singular solutions (Hayes, 2004), and the futility of focusing on symptom reduction. Both approaches help people recognize that "I am not my story," and re-align their identity, story and actions to achieve more of their desired results. This requires what ACT calls 'the observing self', clarity about one's core values, and a commitment to act on those values. They both begin with what ACT calls "contacting the present moment," but differ in some ways in terms of what happens thereafter. In part this is because ACT is expert-driven as a therapeutic modality whereas narrative coaching is more collaborative and facilitative by nature.

The biggest difference stems from the 'glass-is-half-empty' orientation that still lingers in much of psychotherapy as seen in Harris's (2006) article on using ACT to "embrace your demons" and the assumption that "psychological processes [and language] of a normal mind are often destructive, and create psychological suffering for us all" (p. 3). It is true that we are the source of our suffering at a number of levels and we can be destructive of ourselves and/or others. It is called being human. Narrative coaching is no stranger to dealing with challenges from our Shadow and insecure working models. However, I find it more productive to help people release their normative labels, embrace their whole self, tell the whole story, and be more accountable for and constructive with their narrative choices. We help people make room for and be present to all of their experience. It is less about measuring how much water is in the glass and more about inviting people to notice and drink what is there—and trust that there is more.

Other approaches

Gregory Bateson (1972, 1982) was influential in bringing a systemic perspective to psychotherapy and inviting practitioners to think in circles rather than in lines as they approached people's issues. He recognized that problems and patterns were inseparable such that, as Eron and Lund (1996) noted, "serious symptoms could only be alleviated by changing the patterns of interactional behavior that sustained them" (p. 10). The truth in these symptoms—and the problems they are signaling—can often be discerned in the patterns in a person's stories and their relational structure (Mahony, 2003). For example: Which elements are in the foreground or background? How are the elements in relation to each other? Where is the power situated, how is it being used and for what purpose? You can see these systemic principles at work in narrative coaching, e.g., in circling the tree and spiraling through the model; in cycling between the person, the stories and its characters; and in focusing on pattern recognition and sensing the field.

The systemic orientation in narrative coaching is also reflected at the somatic level in that the four phases of the model mirror the four phases of many body-based learning and healing modalities[3]: (1) listening intently and following the person's somatic patterns as the storyteller until they are understood—and deep trust is gained (*Situate*); (2) allowing the body and the story to unravel the past and unveil the truth in the present (*Search*); (3) supporting emergence toward functional integration by reconfiguring the narrative material (*Shift*); and (4) nudging, redirecting, repositioning or disrupting the system to speed change in the story and how it is lived (*Sustain*). Narrative coaching helps people deepen their awareness of the connections between their somatic experience, their stories and the

---

3   Personal communication: (Francis, 2012).

systems in which they operate—and reconfigure any or all of them as need be. As a result, people end up with more touch points to support their growth and more anchors for their new stories in their life.

In my coaching, I often invite people to visualize the scene we are exploring as if it is in the room, to stand beside me and look at it, and notice what is happening for them as the protagonist and in the broader story. It is often both moving and revealing for people to watch these scenes unfold as they witness themselves in action. I then invite them to (1) move between outside narrator and inside protagonist to deepen their insight into what is going on and what wants to happen; and (2) step inside their experiences to get a deeper felt-sense of their patterns *and* step outside their experiences to gain a larger perspective and experiment with new patterns. In particular, I am looking for any patterns that interrupt their inner knowing, outer sensing or authentic expression. Coachees can more fully embody their existential sense of themselves and achieve more of what is important to them if these patterns are addressed systemically.

Definition

In some important ways, narrative coaching is more about a way of Being than about acts of Doing. While it is recognized internationally in the coaching literature, it is also ecumenical in the sense that it can be used in conjunction with other related approaches. Part of what makes this possible is its innately human and open source nature. While there is a deep theoretical base for this work, narrative coaches increasingly find they need less and less to affect positive change with their coachees. This is mirrored in how I train practitioners inside and outside of organizations. We focus first on developing their presence and a narrative mindset—from which they can decide in a given moment in a coaching session how best to apply the model and which narrative practices to use. This is reflected in how I define narrative coaching:

NC
definition

> *Narrative coaching is a mindful, experiential and inte-grative approach to being with people and working with their stories. It enables them to get to the crux of the matter, cross the next threshold in their development and bring their new story to life.*

Narrative coaching is based in millennia of ancient wisdom, a century of social science research, and breakthroughs in new areas such as the neurosciences and design thinking. As a result, it offers an approach to accelerated and transformative development that is fitting for our times. Narrative coaching is unique in that its foundation is systemic not just psychological, and it can be used and applied in a variety of contexts. To be able to work at multiple levels, narrative coaches draw on: (1) *narrative psychologies*[4] to work with people as *narrators* in support of their development and performance; (2) *narrative processes* to work with the material that is *narrated* in support of its reconfiguration; and (3) *narrative practices* to work with the dynamics in the *field* and guide them across thresholds. Stelter (2014b) positions narrative coaching as a "third-generation practice" in which,

> the coach's ambition of remaining neutral is toned down, and the main focus is on collaborative and co-creative dia-logues. The coach and the coachee (or group of coachees) are dialogue partners and have a mutual relationship as reflective fellow human beings in a relationship that is characterized by varying degrees of symmetry over time. (pp. 118–119)

My work with narrative coaching has continually pushed and transcended boundaries to move the broader field forward and to challenge ourselves to keep developing so we can enable coachees to flourish as a result. My ultimate allegiance is to the advancement

---

4   I am using the plural version of the word to be consistent with the other sections and to acknowledge that narrative coaching draws on multiple disciplines from the social sciences.

of this work within a set of principles for the purpose of developing better practitioners and better outcomes for people. For example, my paper on attachment theory (Drake, 2009d) was an important step for the field because it introduced a well-researched body of work to coaching that enables us to better understand how people get caught up in less-than-optimal patterns of narration and behavior. It demonstrated how to transcend the pathological orientation often found in psychological research and how to position this work in coaching in a generative manner. It also legitimated addressing the preverbal and somatic nature of our working models, and it offered insights on how they can be revised as the foundation for new responses. I will continue to develop narrative coaching in whatever ways necessary to increase our capacity to be more radically present with people and to work courageously with their stories.

My ultimate allegiance is to the advancement of this work within a set of principles for the purpose of developing better practitioners and better outcomes for people.

I recommend to my workshop participants inside and outside of organizations that they adopt a set of guiding principles for coaching. Principles provide both structure and flexibility; they allow people to stay focused on what is happening in the session, to adapt to the needs at hand, and make faster course corrections. The beauty of working from principles is that they are immediately recognizable and usable for the beginner, and they continue to add value as practitioners gain experience and deepen their understanding of the nuances of this work. They also act as memorable reminders to keep us in the flow of the coaching process and the field that is constellated. For example, I coached a practitioner who noticed that she is often lost in her head, baffled by the coachee's story and trying to figure out what she should do. We focused on how she could use the first principle below to shift her mindset and bring herself back into the room and the moment whenever she noticed she was too much in her head.

I use the following six principles in my practice and my programs. They emerged from an analysis of the literature upon which the work is based and through deep reflection on how I was being and what I was doing when I was at my best. I offer these six principles to people as when they first learn the work, and encourage them to find the language that works best for them.

> **The six narrative coaching principles**
> - Trust that everything you need is right in front of you.
> - Be fully present to what IS without judgment.
> - Speak only when you can improve on silence.
> - Focus on generating experiences not explanations.
> - Work directly with the narrative elements in the field.
> - Stand at the threshold when a new story is emerging.

Working from principles will help you stay focused on what is happening inside you and in front of you as people are telling their stories in coaching. It gives you more freedom to be present rather than multitasking about what to do next. These principles are very much like *simple rules* (Sull & Eisenhardt, 2012) which serve as a clear guide for practice. Narrative coaching provides a safe and structured space in which people are witnessed in telling their stories, invited to experiment with new ones, and supported to embody and enact them. It does so without the need for standardized assessments, specialized terminology, sequential steps or normative labels. Instead, narrative coaches focus on using the human interaction and the narrative material as the currency of change in the coaching conversation. In part, this is because we recognize that stories do not exist as intact objects in coachees' minds, but rather emerge in a co-creative process between a coachee and his coach (see M. M. Gergen & Gergen, 2006; Kraus, 2006).

This book offers a summary of the past fifteen years of my work in founding, championing, and contributing to the growth of narrative coaching. I hope it inspires you to explore your own stories and consider how you can use this work to do the same for others. While I am passionate about where I have taken narrative coaching, I know there is value here for anyone who uses a narrative approach in their work. We live in a world and a time where ancient narrative battles flare and new narrative dilemmas emerge, e.g., How will we manage hyper-diversity? How will we deal with regressive forces clinging to old paradigms? How will we transition in time to a new economy more in sync with our planet? All the more reason why narrative coaching's time has come. May this book spark your thinking about how you would like to apply this work to help heal broken narratives that divide us and create new ones that inspire and enrich us. I welcome you to the journey . . .

I. NARRATIVE PSYCHOLOGIES

Chapter 1

HOW OUR MIND WORKS
AS A STORYTELLER

Without psychotherapy or a crisis as motivation, the past is rarely recategorized. We might from time to time call upon different episodes from the past to justify a present situation or grievance, but it rarely occurs to us to change the way the events or impressions were initially stored.
Ellen Langer

Introduction

As coaches, we are interested in how our minds compose, remember, communicate, and connect stories in relationship with others. I am using the term "mind" to indicate all of our cognitive (in the most holistic sense of that word) processing faculties, including but not exclusive to the brain. Our mind is a neurobioligical process that enables us to be self-aware, intuit, reflect, mentalize, self-regulate, narrate and more. In this chapter we will look at the cognitive and psychological aspects of our innate drive to narrate our experiences and share them with others. We will explore how schemas shape people's experience, how attachment theory sheds light on their working models as meta-narratives, and why people need their whole brain to tell the whole story. While the focus here is on the brain, it is part of a broader framing of the mind as a whole body system in narrative coaching. It is why we increasingly incorporate somatic activities in our programs to get people out of their heads.

The stories we implicitly and explicitly tell ourselves and others have a significant affect on us at a number of levels. However, it is important to note that all of these stories are ultimately fictions. While some may be 'truer' than others, they are nonetheless the stories we choose to live by. Many of them are invisible to us until they are examined because we have long assumed that this is just "how things are." Many of the issues people bring to coaching reflect gaps or tensions between their stories and their realities, their experiences and their identities, and/or their attributions and their accountability for their choices. Paradoxically, these are also the very openings through which they are most likely to grow. While narrative coaches are committed to increasing people's awareness and agency relative to normative fictions and dominant narratives, we focus more on helping people align their stories with what they desire. We help them explore their current fiction and its consequences, build on stories that work, learn from and release those that don't, and embody new stories that are better suited for achieving their desired results.

The capacity and need to tell stories—and to understand and be understood by others in so doing—is part of our evolutionary and cultural heritage as humans. Our ability to tell stories is one of the traits that sets humans apart from other species. Stories are central to how we identify ourselves and connect with others. In part, this is because their structure matches our brains, which are hard-wired to organize and navigate experiences in terms of time and space (Pinker, 2009). At the same time, they offer the means to transcend our usual sense of time and space in ways that create new experiences and insights. Stories bring together our internal, experiential, subjective mind and our external, observable, objective world in a kaleidoscopic fashion. The stories we consciously and unconsciously keep telling ourselves form memory structures around them and they, not our actual experience in the moment, provide about 80 percent of the neural instructions upon which we base our actions (Graham, p. 37). That is why in narrative coaching we slow the movie down, almost to frame by frame at times, so coachees can reconfigure the relationship between memory from the past, experience in the present and desire for the future.

In helping people to notice and name their experience of the moment, we can help them activate their prefrontal cerebral cortex as a crucial aid for their decision-making (Graham, p. 57). We do so in a nonjudgmental manner because "mindful empathy is the single most important tool for strengthening the functioning of the prefrontal cortex" (Graham, 2013, p. 51). Narrative coaches invite people to experience and reflect on their 'movies', discover that any story they choose is but one alternative, and explore new stories that will enable them to flourish. Narrative coaches help people notice old stories in which they are stuck and reconfigure key elements so they are free to tell new ones more in line with what they want to achieve. We do this by bringing people's attention to the nuances of their narration and the benefits of greater accountability as the narrator of their experiences and their life. This is particularly important for those memories that people select and interpret as self-defining and, thereby, grant privileged status in their lives and identities (McAdams, 2003).

Research by Singer and his colleagues (2005a) determined that self-defining memories have the following five elements: "emotional intensity, vividness, repeated recall, connections to similar memories, and [a] focus on lasting goals or unresolved conflicts" (p. 23). These self-defining memories retain their emotional power because they are generally linked to goals and desires people consciously or unconsciously believe are still important for them. Narrative coaching is designed to help people normalize these memories, de-energize them as reactive behaviors, and de-couple them from their identity. In so doing, they are deconditioning their neural circuitry to create more space for learning, change and growth in support of reconditioning it in new directions (Graham, 2013). You can support their process by creating safe spaces to immerse themselves in guided experiences in which they can: (1) stay in contact with their (often intense) emotions without resorting to their usual reactive response; (2) soften their habituated recall and associations through mindfulness work; and (3) explore new strategies and stories for their current situation.

Look for ways in which coachees are telling the same story and living the same narrative over and over again; e.g., remaining stuck in the same role or response in the misguided belief that *this* time it will get them what they have been seeking. Feeling stuck is often a sign that an underlying pattern has been activated and is, therefore, an opportunity for the coachee to notice the pattern, its trigger, and its alternative. These patterns largely operate at non-conscious and somatic levels, but they can be made conscious and malleable through coaching. One way to do that is to challenge coachees' unexamined assumptions—the gap between *if* and *then*—to open up room for new stories from which new behaviors can emerge.

> For example, I worked with someone who didn't feel heard by her team. After surfacing a self-defining memory when she felt small, I invited her to sit on the floor and talk with me as I stood next to her (and notice that experience), stand on a table and talk with me (and notice that experience), then stand in front of me and talk with me (and notice that experience). With the latter, I then invited her to experiment with how much distance she wanted between us and to notice where she felt the most heard.
>
> She acknowledged her pattern of playing small (and what it costs her), her tendency to lord over people sometimes as a compensatory measure, and her desire to relate to people as one adult to another. She began to feel more empowered to make her own choices as well as get an initial sense of what worked best for her. We identified the relationships in which she felt at ease so she had a baseline; talked through how to build on those to redefine the memory and form a new narrative; and experimented to discover her 'right size'.

We can see this connection between history, memory and story in Freud's realization that the stories he was being told were "psychological happenings dressed as history and experienced as remembered events . . . [and, in saying so, he established] the independence of memory from history and history from memory" (Hillman, 1983, p. 40). Freud also believed that these memory traces and associations could be "retranscribed" in keeping with fresh circumstances, but these memories had to first become the focus of conscious attention. However, as Jung later explored in great depth, they are often more easily and productively approached through tangential, non-direct means (e.g., dreams, nuances of language, metaphors and analogies, shifts in energy or body posture). Otherwise, people's tacit filters and egoic defenses can too easily obscure their awareness and openness. As neuroscientist Norman Doige (2007) noted about Freud:

By sitting out of his patient's view, and commenting only when he had insights into their problems, patients began to regard him as they had important people in their past . . . It was as though the patients were reliving past memories without their being aware of it. Freud called this unconscious phenomenon 'transference' because patients were transferring scenes and ways of perceiving from the past onto the present. They were 'reliving' them instead of 'remembering' them. (p. 225)

Narrative coaches tend to sit within view of the other person, but we share the same interest in their largely unconscious narrative processes projected into the 'field'. We often invite coachees to enact key moments in their old and/or new stories—rather than just recall and reflect on them—so they can discover the deeper narratives at play. In so doing, people often come across aspects of their memory they had not remembered or acknowledged—but which often are the key to their transformation and that of their stories. This is important because the processes by which their experiences are organized and distinctions are made are largely beyond their awareness (Madigan, 1996; Mahony, 2003). As a result, they would otherwise only see and hear what they are open to noticing (Bernstein, 2005) and edit out and effectively forget almost everything else (Kenyon & Randall, 1997). The only way to authentically and sustainably change a person's story is to alter the underlying narrative that supports it.

Often this comes through helping coachees' make new associations, e.g., between two stories, between two characters in a story, between a problem in one area of their life and a solution in another. One of the reasons this is so effective is that it bypasses their taken-for-granted associations to uncover other possibilities—which up to that point have been on the margins of their awareness, thinking and stories. I'm reminded of a conversation with someone who had just become head of her extended family after her husband's sudden death. She was concerned because this role was new for her and she was not yet feeling up to the task.

Early on I asked her what she enjoyed doing in her life outside of work and her immediate answer was "singing." I was curious about what type of singing she most enjoyed. She answered that she especially liked singing in small groups, like *leading a small choir*. As someone who sings poorly, I shared my admiration for her gifts.

I invited her to talk about what it was like for her when she sang and why she loved it so much. I then held out my hands as if one held her story about her dilemma and the other her love of singing and small groups. Pausing, I invited her to imagine what it would be like to lead her extended family as if it were a small choir. With that insight she shed a few tears, then beamed. She realized that it was a role she knew well. She could use many of the same skills, and it would be a great service to her family. She left the conversation with a new clarity and confidence about her role.

The origins of this associative approach can again be traced back to Freud who noted in 1888 that all of our mental associations, even seemingly 'random' ones that appear to make no sense, are expressions of links formed in our memory networks (cited in Doige, 2007). Flash forward sixty years and Hebb (1949) proposes his now famous axiom, "what fires together, wires together," to which was later added "survives together" (Post et al., 1998) and to which I would add "sires together." What that means in a nutshell—largely in ways we still don't fully understand—is that neurons that are activated together (fired) become associated (wired) over time and are therefore more likely to endure (survive) as a result of their frequent use—and in so doing, attract and spark related associations (sire). For example, a difficult experience in a serious relationship may become generalized as a belief system about oneself and/or others that is triggered while dating later and extended as a loss of confidence in other areas. How people respond to events in their lives is based in how they assess the situation, what associations they make, what story they tell, how they cope and what happens as a result.

People are most easily reminded of memories along the neural paths with the strongest impressions, closest ties to core values and the most frequent usage. The stories they most often tell themselves and others—and manifest in their lives—are testament to their most well-worn neural paths. When related emotionally-loaded situations or triggers arise, the bigger and more developed neural pathways and their associated 'stories' have a significantly greater likelihood of being activated rapidly, with predictable effects (Doige, 2007). As already mentioned, this process becomes habituated over time and therefore less visible, and is often in pursuit of needs that are largely unconscious. Ahead of his time, Orison Swett Marden (1894) described it succinctly: "The beginning of a habit is like an invisible thread, but every time we repeat the act we strengthen the strand, add to it another filament, until it becomes a great cable and binds us irrevocably, thought and act." Our habits are further reinforced by the fact that we tell stories in 'shorthand' to express more complex or subtle points. Although this allows us to function in our daily lives, it also obscures the logic (or lack thereof) of our decision-making and storytelling processes.

The stories they most often tell themselves and others—and manifest in their lives—are testament to their most well-worn neural paths.

While the patterns in our stories often fall along common and ancient archetypal lines, they also reflect our particular configurations. These *schemas* can be seen as structures of expectations (Chafe, 1990) a person has learned from experience and stored in memory over time. The result is an organized representation, a set of implicit rules and an accumulated repertoire of tacit knowledge that is used to "impose structure upon, and impart meaning to, otherwise ambiguous social and situational information to facilitate understanding" (Gioia, 1986, p. 56). Russell & van Den Broek (1992) identified three dimensions of schemas that are relevant in working with people's stories in coaching: (1) how events are related to one another, (2) how events and those who are involved are psychologically connected, (3) the style in which the events are narrated—to which I would add (4) the direction in which the events are pointing.

Since schematic representations of events often take narrative form (see Mandler, 1984; Schank & Abelson, 1995), we can access them by unpacking the assumptive patterns in people's stories about how things are supposed to be, why things are the way they are, and what would make them better.

We are all highly selective in what we notice, what stories we develop, and what sense/meaning we make of those stories. This is important in coaching because, as Polkinghorne (2004) notes, how people interpret significant events can limit or expand their possible actions. Their schematic frames shape what is available to them at a given moment and thus influence the rationale, repertoire and range in terms of their available responses. Coaching can help coachees increase their awareness of their habitual narration (including their blindspots), assess how well it is working (and what it leads them to miss), and adopt frames that will yield more of their desired outcomes. Some questions you can ask coachees to help with this unpacking:

- Why this way of seeing things?
- What do you gain from seeing it this way?
- What do you lose by seeing it this way?
- How else could you see it?
- What other perspectives might you take?
- What keeps you from considering these possibilities?
- What might you gain if you did?

As a storyteller, our mind not only helps us to make sense and meaning of what we construe happened in the past but, like all complex adaptive systems, it also builds models that allow us to anticipate the world and the future (Holland, 1995). These systems create "frameworks of expectation" (H. Sherman & Schultz, 1998) which affect our choices as we mine the present for clues to anticipate the immediate future and guide our action in the present (Boyd, 2009). This echoes Kelly's (1955) fundamental postulate that a person's processes are psychologically channelized by the ways in which she anticipates events. This is important because the stories people tell about their lives—and the meanings they draw from them—often end up operating as self-fulfilling prophecies. What we are doing in narrative coaching is unwinding the givens inherent in a person's current narratives to a point where new possibilities become available on behalf of their past, present and/or future.

Narrative coaching is designed to help people externalize their tacit connections and schemas, deconstruct them as if in slow motion, and reconstruct the neural pathways so they can reframe their memories of the past, have new experiences in the present, and express themselves in new ways in the future. We invite coachees to begin that journey with a non-judgmental respect for their current patterns, an honoring of their original purpose, and a release when ready to make room for new narratives. It is like we are working with people to prune a tree to enable new growth to occur. I find that the pruning alone often has a huge impact as it creates more room to breathe freely and see clearly. From there, it is easy to see how the mind's stories start to shift and the narratives people live along with them. Narrative coaching was the first coaching methodology to incorporate attachment theory as a way to address the preverbal nature of people's narrative patterns.

Understanding Attachment Theory

With . . . states of insecure attachment, the mind is 'holding on' to old patterns in an outdated effort to just survive. This inflexible cohesiveness puts the person at risk of chaotic or rigid states. With the movement toward coherence, the system of the person becomes more flexible. . . . The minds of such individuals can be described as having an organized and unimpaired flow of energy and information.
Dan Siegel

Significant experiences that occur when we are young can have a disproportionate impact on our development and identity. In large part this is because we do not yet have the language or a large enough narrative within which to sufficiently process them. It is no wonder, then, that many of our coachees' habits continue unabated when they are only addressed at rational and verbal levels. Attachment theory can be helpful here as it provides a strong evidence base and some useful frames that you can use in your practice (within the bounds of your professional capabilities and client expectations). The incorporation of key elements from attachment theory in narrative coaching has opened up new nonverbal and somatic possibilities for addressing people's issues and reconfiguring their stories at deeper levels. It allows coaches to help people re-pattern their narrative strategies and re-wire their behavioral strategies through small, intentional movements that lead to big changes, similar to somatic learning modalities such as the Feldenkrais method (see 1972).

Narrative coaches pay particular attention to the nonverbal elements and preverbal vestiges in people's stories. This is because the brain is quite adept at deceiving us with its fictions, but the body seldom forgets and often holds clues to greater truths. As Griffith & Griffith (1993) note, "The important life dilemmas are those we feel in our bodies. Closely held, they cannot [easily] be articulated in the functional language of public life" (p. 317). As you coach, notice when insights seem to really settle into a coachee's body before taking action rather than getting seduced by 'aha' moments which often rise up only to dissipate quickly. As you listen to people, try to attune to them with your whole body (Mahony, 2003) so you can more fully sense what they are communicating. Notice the level of resonance in coachees, the field and yourself as they process and communicate their experience and make choices. A strong sense of resonance is generally a sign that their mind is sufficiently aligned around the new narrative, their insights are grounded and they will act on them. This often requires both parties to pause during the session and attune to what is going on at multiple levels. Attachment theory comes in handy as a helpful frame for doing so.

What people are seeking from coaching can be seen, in part, as a largely unconscious attempt to redeem and restore what they sacrificed in childhood, regain a sense of wholeness, and learn more secure ways of relating to others and meeting their needs. The reactive strategies people exhibit or talk about in coaching are often the result of suboptimal attachment strategies repeated and reinforced over time. These strategies frame their experience; reinforce a familiar set of expectations, actions and rewards; and act as defenses against experiences that re-create a sense of anxiety (as overwhelm or separation). Coachees' implicit attachment strategies can be observed and heard in the way they narrate their experiences, particularly when they are describing points that were/are distressing. It is in these places that their defenses often arise. Defenses emerge in the course of early development to protect our differentiating ego in response to gaps in the attachment process. However, an over-reliance on these defenses interferes with the development of more complex neural networks (Dougherty & West, 2007), and can adversely impact people's working models and capacity for secure relationships.

Attachment theory is based in the study of connection and communication patterns between infants and parents or other primary caregivers, and how these patterns shape a children's cognitive, emotional, and social development (Ainsworth & Bowlby, 1991; Bowlby, 1969, 1973, 1988). Siegel (1999) defines attachment as "an inborn system in the brain that evolves [largely in the first two years of a child's life] in ways that influence and organize motivational, emotional, and memory processes with respect to significant caregiving figures" (p. 67). Being able to freely express his emotional state and needs—and have others perceive and appropriately respond—is vitally important for the development of an infant's brain and his ability to regulate his internal states, attune and adapt to various environments, and communicate about and influence his external states (Siegel, 1999). An infant's developing brain instinctively drives him to seek physical closeness and resonant communication with the people who are the most important to him, usually beginning with the mother. Attachment is an evolutionary imperative designed to ensure that the young infant survives and sufficiently thrives in those early, vulnerable years through anticipating and adapting to responses from her caregivers.

This is why children will instinctively do whatever it takes to retain a sense of safety and love—even if they have to sacrifice part of themselves to get it. Bowlby (1969) proposed that the organization of the attachment behavioral system involves mental representations of (1) the attachment figure, (2) the self, and the (3) environment— all of which are largely based on early experiences in a child's life. Bretherton (1991) suggests that these representations result from the scripts formed out of repeated attachment-related experiences. Bowlby's (1982) seminal study of the behavioral consequences of abandonment and loss also led to his theory of the four phases of normal mourning and grieving: (1) an initial *numbing* phase; (2) a *yearning* phase; (3) a phase of *disorganization;* and (4) a final phase of *reorganization.* These phases represent the general flow of response to separation and loss for young children, and they also can be seen in how adults cope with relational challenges. Part of your work in narrative coaching is to help people recognize their preference (e.g., dwelling on yearning) and move on to the next phase (be willing to be disorganized in order to find a better way forward).

This reflects the function of caregivers to accurately read, sufficiently mark, and astutely respond in a way that provides and develops the bedrock upon which the child's Self is built. When children perceive a threat, real or imagined, their attachment system is activated and they seek proximity to and care from attachment figure(s). If the response is satisfying, they gain an increased sense of security, engage in further exploration of their environment, and build working models to suit. If the response is not satisfying, they deploy insecure secondary strategies, engage in less (effective) exploration, and build working models to suit. The behaviors, feelings, and desires that were contained by the caregiver and the relationship will be integrated by the infant in the first instance. Those that were not contained well (or at all) and threaten the attachment bond will be defensively excluded and end up as Shadow in the second instance. Since an infant is unable to regulate himself at first, he learns how to do so through attuning himself with his[5] primary caregivers. His level of success in regulating early in his life often has significant implications for how well he manages himself and relates to others later in life.

---

5   I will alternate between feminine and masculine pronouns throughout the book.

The greater a person's ability to self-regulate, the wider her 'window of tolerance' will be and the less often her secondary attachment strategies will kick in. Graham (2013) describes a window of tolerance as "our baseline state of physiological functioning" (p. 191). Falling between the extremes of hyper- and hypo-arousal, it is a zone within which "various intensities of emotional and physiological arousal can be processed without disrupting the functioning of the system" (Siegel, 1999, p. 253). Within it, we are grounded and centered, neither over-reacting nor failing to act (Graham, 2013). The more secure a coachee becomes, the more she can give herself the space she needs to fully process her experiences and make conscious, self-affirming choices. Therefore, find ways to gauge coachees' window of tolerance related to the issue at hand and provide opportunities for them to experience and explore what it would be like to open it wider. For example, you could invite a person seeking to improve his emotional intelligence to experience and express a wider range of feelings in the coaching sessions so that he can allow himself to remain more open when others do the same.

There are three primary outcomes from the attachment process that children need—each of which has a strong bearing on their level of security later in life:

- **safe haven**—provides a sense of *safety* which enhances our ability for self-soothing and empathy throughout our life,
- **secure base**—provides a sense of *stability* which enhances our ability for self-expression and exploration throughout our life, and
- **working models**—provides a sense of *security* which enhances our ability for self-regulation and engagement throughout our life.

A child gains a sense of a safe haven from the reliable proximity of, ready access to, and resonant responses from a trusted caregiver when the child feels anxious or senses danger. One of the primary ways young children develop a sense of a safe haven, form attachment bonds, and increase their range of tolerable distance is through "contingent communication." This mutual sharing of non-verbal signals and mutual influence through the interactions between children and caregivers forms the basis for healthy, secure attachment (Siegel, 1999). The presence of a reliable safe haven provides a child with the sense of a secure base from which she can increasingly and confidently explore the world with ever widening range—and to which she can return as needed. As children grow, they rely less on external figures for safety and more on the repeated experiences they have encoded in their implicit memory as "working models" (Bowlby, 1988), which they will carry throughout their lives. Mary Main (1995) saw working models as a set of conscious and/or unconscious rules for the organization of information relevant to attachment reflected in patterns of nonverbal behavior, language and structures of the mind.

Working models have much in common with our notions of the schemas and narrative patterns by which people perceive, organize and navigate their world. There is a strong link to narratives in that their working models also have spatial and temporal coordinates. As Bowlby (1973) noted:

> each individual builds working models of the world and of himself in it, with the aid of which he [frames the past,] perceives events, forecasts the future and constructs plans. . . . [Key features include] his notion of who his attachment figures are, where they may be found and how they may be expected to respond . . . and his notion of how acceptable or unacceptable he himself is in the eyes of his attachment figures. (p. 203)

These models shape how people situate themselves and others in their stories, what activates their attachment-seeking behavior, what roles they assign to characters (including themselves) and what they perceive as threats and sources of solace.

Attachment theory offers a useful frame for understanding the cognitive schemas, somatic reactions, behavioral preferences, and narrative patterns that children carry into adulthood. You can use it to help coachees attain more meaningful and lasting change through the evolution of their working model as it relates to their presenting issues. You can also assess people's change readiness in terms of the three key factors—safe haven, secure base, and working model—and adapt your coaching approach accordingly. For example, in coaching someone who is sharing a difficult story for the first time, you may want to pay extra attention to being on time, highly attuned, and compassionate as a way of establishing a *safe haven* for her. In coaching someone struggling to take action you might invite him to do small experiments during the session to increase his sense of a *secure base* from which he can move forward once he leaves the session. In coaching someone who is stuck in a rut in her stories, you may want to invite her to 'circle up the tree' to increase her awareness of the aspects of her *working model* that are holding her back.

Let us look now at the four primary types of attachment orientations and how they shape our mind as a storyteller.

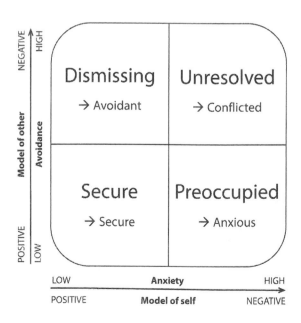

Figure 1. *The four primary attachment styles*

- Children who are seen as *Secure* generally had caregivers who were *secure*: free, autonomous, emotionally available, and perceptive of and responsive to the child's needs, states, and signals. A securely attached child feels safe, understood and confident that most of the time the parent is a reliable source of nurture, protection, and meeting their needs (Siegel, 1999).

- Children who are seen as *Avoidant* in their attachment generally had caregivers who were *Dismissing*: emotionally unavailable, imperceptive and/or unresponsive and perhaps even rejecting of attempts at proximity. As a result, these children tended to avoid dependence by pursuing self-reliance, avoid discomfort with closeness and therefore preserve distance, and avoid their needs by using deactivating strategies (Mikulincer & Shaver, 2007). As Graham (2013) notes, they often develop coping strategies that are stable but not always flexible.

- Children who are seen as *Anxious* generally had caregivers who were *Preoccupied:* inconsistently available, perceptive, or responsive; enmeshed and entangled; and frequently imposing their state. As a result, these children tended to manage their uncertainty about independence by pursuing closeness and protection, and manage their anxiety about their intrinsic value to significant others by using hyper-activating strategies (Mikulincer & Shaver, 2007). As Graham (2013) notes, they often develop coping strategies that are flexible but not always stable.

- Children who are seen as *Conflicted*[6] generally had caregivers who were *Unresolved:* frightening and frightened, disorienting, and alarming. As a result, these children tended to simultaneously approach the caregiver for security and avoid her for safety—resulting in a disorganized or even dissociated state (Cozolino, 2006; Siegel, 2007). As Graham (2013) notes, they often develop coping strategies that are neither flexible nor stable.

You can use these attachment categories to understand coachees' mindsets and predominant patterns of relating and behaving. As

---

6   Often described as Fearful or Disorganized in the literature.

Holmes (1999) noted, insecure representational models interfere with both *story making* (knitting together the events of one's life in a coherent way) and *story breaking* (examining the events of one's life anew in the light of new insight or information). Holmes (2001) later describes three of these attachment patterns from a narrative perspective: clinging to rigid stories (common for those with an avoidant style); being overwhelmed by unstoried experience (common for those with an anxious style); or being unable to find a narrative strong enough to contain traumatic pain (common for those with a conflicted style). People who are secure are more agile with their stories, more resilient in the face of ambiguity or challenge, and more able to engage with difficult experiences.

Securely attached adults tend to have the following characteristics (Drake, 2009d). They

- are sustained by positive yet mature beliefs about themselves and the world (Mikulincer & Shaver, 2007);
- have a greater cognitive capacity for and experience with receiving empathy and, therefore, are more perceptive of, sensitive to, and able to respond to the needs of others (Begley, 2007);
- can organize and utilize their cognitive and emotional memory functioning to a high degree (Cozolino, 2002);
- have a high tolerance for ambiguity and tend to be less dogmatic in their thinking and communicating as a result of their intellectual openness (Begley, 2007);
- can constructively (re)appraise situations so as to maintain an optimistic sense of self-efficacy (Mikulincer & Shaver, 2007);
- are mindful and mature enough to repair ruptures as needed in their rapport and communication with others (Siegel, 2007); and
- can engage in new, growth-promoting, self-expanding experiences and address existential concerns such as aging, love, and freedom rather than having to be perpetually on guard (Mikulincer & Shaver, 2007).

We can see in this list many of the aspirations people bring to coaching. There is a strong connection between the patterns of response in their early relationships, the patterns of narration that shape their identity, and the patterns of engagement in their relations with others. Attachment patterns are reflected in how people move relative to others (with, against, or away from) in their lives and their stories, particularly under stress or perceived threats (Horney, 1945). She also believed that non-secure attachment patterns emerged in children as a result of their frustrations trying to fulfill their need for both safety and self-expression. She believed that these frustrations contributed to their loss of "an ability to wish for anything wholeheartedly because their very wishes are divided, that is, go in opposite directions" (p. 38). Two good questions to ask yourself when you encounter this in a coachee: "What frustrated desire is this person seeking to express and fulfill in this story?" "What need, if met, would end this story?" Resolution and transformation in narrative coaching is often the result of putting the person back in touch with their wholehearted wish.

Resolution and transformation in narrative coaching is often the result of putting the person back in touch with their wholehearted wish.

Narrative coaching views frustration in a similar manner as Gestalt as a generative and essential driver of growth when handled well. We don't rush to relieve people's frustration, but instead use it as an opportunity to explore their wholehearted wish and what stands in its way. The unique constellation of influences that shape a person's early development contributed to a partial, preferential unfolding of their personality and potential. Complicating matters is the fact that attachment insecurities in their working models are often stubbornly stable because they were experienced as critical for survival in their original context. These representations and rules are unlikely to be easily relinquished, in part because they are reinforced by the internally consistent logic within the models themselves (Wallin, 2007). However, if their models are left unexamined, people often will continue to act as if they are still true. Many of us recognize this when we return home to visit our family at the holidays—and marvel at how differently we experience and enact our current selves back in the familial context.

This work on attachment theory is important for those of us who coach because many adults continue to deploy many of their initial schemas and attachment strategies. These patterns often impact their affective styles, narrative themes, and patterns of engagement in interpersonal relationships (Siegel, 2007). Coaches routinely encounter vestiges of these long-held patterns in people's stories and lives. In narrative coaching, it is less about hunting for the sources of these difficulties in the past, and more about experiencing and working with their implications in the present. I have found in my practice as a coach and a teacher of advanced coaching that access to these patterns is most often achieved using nonverbal means. As Wallin (2007) notes, "Given the prelinguistic roots of attachment patterns, and the disavowals and dissociations they may have demanded, we must tune in to . . . expressions of experience for which the person has as yet no words" (p. 4). This is why I increasingly conceptualize my role in coaching as a choreographer and sculptor.

Narrative coaching helps people deepen their sense of security so they can do the following in order to grow. Each of these four capabilities seems to be particularly important in moving through one of the phases in the coaching process. People who are more secure can:

1. Distinguish between their own experience and that of others. *This is helpful in the Situate phase in order to be present to and accountable for their authorship. It is an essential skill in being able to Separate.*

2. Tell the story of their feelings. *This is helpful in the Search phase in order to articulate and explore their inner and outer experiences to ascertain what they want. It is an essential skill in being able to Individuate.*

3. Break up their stories and reconfigure them so they are more in keeping with the flux of their experience, demands and aspirations. *This is helpful in the Shift phase in order to experiment*

with new ways of being and behaving. It is an essential skill in being able to Reincorporate.

4. Continuously enhance their working model in line with the maturing self to reinforce a secure mindset and strategies. *This is helpful in the Sustain phase in order to embed their developmental gains.[7] It is an essential skill in being able to Integrate.*

Attachment theory is integral to narrative coaching because it equips us to work at deeper levels with people's stories and the schemas behind them that began before they had language. The ability to recognize coachees' attachment patterns and working models in their stories is the first step in helping them to develop a more coherent narrative and attain a greater sense of attachment security. The second step is helping them do the same for themselves in order to nudge their working models toward more mature states. With increased security, people can move with more freedom, volition, and efficacy in their lives. Coaching can be very helpful in this quest as a sanctuary in the midst of organizational and civic cultures "with fewer and fewer psychic homes, places and moments, persons and situations where one can take off the armor, put down the defenses" (Paris, 2007, p. 121). It is both a warm refuge for people and a fiery crucible in which to be re-born.

Tips on using attachment theory in coaching

*   Provide a safe haven and a secure base for people so they can more fully experience and explore what else is possible.

    Your ability as a coach to stay in sustained, regulating contact with coachees is a crucial ingredient in their healing and outcomes. Invest in your own development so you can remain compassionate and clear in your reflections to coachees. The more your own security needs are met, the stronger the container you can offer coachees—and the more likely they are to feel understood and have positive experiences associated

---

7   The first three capabilities are from (Holmes, 1999, p. 155); the fourth was added by the author along with the words in italics.

with secure relationships in working with you. As time goes on, help them build on where they are secure and bridge between what goes on in the coaching relationship and what can happen in other important relationships.

- Position yourself as a "good enough" and available caregiver to help people become more proactive and less reactive.

    Regulate your behavior to offer coachees the experience of an appropriately responsive secure relationship. This often involves being resonant enough to be allowed in and make a connection and dissonant enough to break through and make a difference. Make room for experiences their original attachment figures could not sufficiently provide. Suggest assignments to enhance their ability to mentalize, initiate repairs when relationships are ruptured, and stay connected while feeling autonomous. Use people's stories and the relational dynamics in them as a window into their working models and a resource for helping them to shift.

- Reframe what you perceive as defensive or resistant behaviours in people as their attempt to get their legitimate needs met.

    Listen for the defenses which coachees use to stay within the bounds of their implicit beliefs about "what can be known, what can be felt, what can be spoken, and what cannot be contained" (Slade, 2008, p. 773). Help them to recognize how their defenses influence how they form their stories, engage in coaching and live their life. They can then start to notice their attachment strategies and start to question what else might be possible. Bring their words or experiences into the present moment, activate their defenses so they can be recognized and addressed, and invite them into experiences where they can try out healthier strategies for getting their needs met.

- Make room for the feelings, desires, and abilities that a person has denied or inhibited so they are more able to self-regulate and respond from a secure place.

    Invite coachees to examine and adjust their often unexamined, taken-for-granted working models. One way to do this is to listen for any tensions in their stories between their need for safety and their need for self-expression. In the process, help them resolve any "divided wishes" so they can invest more wholeheartedly in their life and work. For example, what unconscious loyalties or allegiances keep them from venturing forth to a new town or career? Help them recognize that their old working models probably seemed better than the alternatives in relating to sub-optimal attachment figures, but they may no longer be sufficient for meeting the demands of their adult life or fulfilling their aspirations.

- Recognize that people often need different coaching strategies depending on their attachment preferences and be willing to adapt your approach to suit.

  People with anxious patterns tend to be overly merged with their story and may benefit from externalizing processes that create more spaciousness between themselves and their stories. Help them fill in the gaps in their stories with the factual information they typically dismiss, normalize, or rationalize. People with avoidant patterns tend to be overly separated from their story and may benefit from internalizing processes that reconnect them with their stories in new ways. Help them fill in the gaps in their stories with the emotive information they typically dismiss, normalize or rationalize.

Working with the whole brain

I know that most men, including those at ease with problems of the greatest complexity, can seldom accept even the simplest and most obvious truth if it be such as would oblige them to admit the falsity of conclusions which they have delighted in explaining to colleagues, which they have proudly taught to others, and which they have woven, thread by thread, into the fabric of their lives.
Leo Tolstoy

Modern imaging technology has enabled us to begin developing a more nuanced view of our inner universe and how our brain organizes itself and fulfills its functions. As a result, the original emphasis on two distinct and separate hemispheres has been enhanced to focus more on how the various elements of the human brain interact with one another and work together. As Cozolino (2010) points out, "When we speak of functions of the right or left brain, we are more accurately referring to functions that are either represented more fully or performed more efficiently in one hemisphere than the other" (p. 94). However, it is still useful to think in broad terms about the two hemispheres given our interest as coaches in how each affects the way people narrate their experiences, engage others, and work with us. It is also useful to acknowledge the significant neurological connections between the brain and the mind, the body and the environment, and the self and others. By understanding how the brain functions, you can better understand what triggers coachees, how and why they respond the way they do, and how best to intervene as their coach.

Although both the left and right hemispheres are developing at very high rates during the early years of our lives, the right hemisphere appears to have a relatively higher rate of activity and growth during the earliest years (Chiron et al., 1997). During this time, "vital learning in the areas of attachment, emotional regulation, and self-esteem are organized in neural networks biased toward the right hemisphere. This pattern of asymmetrical growth shifts to the left hemisphere" (Cozolino, 2010, p. 71) somewhere around age 3, in large part as a result of the rapid growth in our ability to use language. Around the same time, the prefrontal cortex becomes more able to read and regulate the emotions as largely perceived by the right hemisphere (body sensation, affect) and integrate the meaning of those signals as largely perceived by the left hemisphere (language and thoughts) (Graham, 2013). Stories are useful resources in coaching because they draw on the whole brain and also provide a way to understand people's narration style, e.g., which hemisphere's preferences are more dominant in the way they form and communicate their stories.

Although basic language functions are associated with the left hemisphere, recent research is beginning to show considerable involvement of the right hemisphere in the processing of aspects of language such as metaphor—especially when novelty, creativity, and imagery are involved (Wilkinson, 2010). This lends support for a narrative approach which works not only with the cognitive, logical, and literal processes favored by the left hemisphere but also with the images, sensations, and impressions favored by the right hemisphere (Fosha, 2003). Stories provide the brain with a tool for emotional and neural integration because they bring together information and intentions from diverse neural networks (Cozolino, 2006). Helping people to better access and integrate their two hemispheres enables them to "put feelings into words, consider feelings in conscious awareness, and balance the positive and negative affective biases of the left and right hemispheres" (Cozolino, 2002, p. 29). Therefore, listen for any incongruence between their literal verbal story and their emotional nonverbal communication. For example, "I notice that you slouch down when you talk about how much you appreciate your boss."

Understanding the preferences and contributions of each hemisphere will enable you to adapt your coaching style to meet the differing needs of coachees—especially in drawing out narrative elements from their non-dominant hemisphere. You can help coachees who operate more from their left hemisphere to drop down out of their head and into their body as an important source of information about their inner world and the richer, often more emotional, narrative material there. You can help those who operate more from their right hemisphere to rise out of their body and into their mind as an important source of information about their external world and the more factual structure of the story. In general, your first task in coaching is to help people notice the partial nature of their stories as they tell them; your second task is to invite them to bring more of the whole story into the dialogue. For example, connect with coachees who tell stories that are factual, sequential, and verbal at that level first and then invite them to explore the emotional, contextual, and nonverbal parts of their stories.

The following is a summary of the preferences of each hemisphere[8]:

---

8   Primary sources: Cozolino, 2002, 2006, 2010; Siegel 2007.

Left Hemisphere	Right Hemisphere
Form	*Form*
Digital (binary choices (i.e., up/down, yes/no)	Analog (integrated map of the body)
Verbal: words, symbols, numbers	Visual/Spatial: images, patterns, maps
Guided by facts, logic, cause-effect and analysis	Guided by emotions, dynamics, intuition, and non-verbal signals
Processes sequentially, linear thinking, likes lists	Processes simultaneously, parallel thinking, likes big picture
Literal, sees the details to get to the whole	Conceptual, sees the whole to get to the parts
Compartmentalizes, atomizes, categorizes, lasers	Makes contextual, lateral, synthetic connections
Problem defining and solving; goal-directed and solution-seeking	Context-dependent thinking; embraces ambiguity, can hold multiple realities
Function	*Function*
Later to develop	Earlier to develop
Farther from body, explicit memory, slower	Closer to the body, implicit memory, faster
Factual/semantic memory; story structure; acts as narrator	Emotionally rich autobiographical memory; story material; references self
Biased toward and mediates moderate, positive and prosocial emotions; associated with engaging and approaching behaviors	Biased toward negative and/or intense emotions; associated with avoiding and withdrawing behaviors
Appraises opportunity; mediates more positive affective states;	Appraises safety; mediates distress and uncomfortable emotions
More involved with conscious coping	More involved with self-regulation, self-soothing

What is missing from a coachee's story is often associated with one hemisphere more than the other and provides clues to what they are seeking. It is often helpful for a coachee to first quiet the overactive hemisphere in order to create more space in her narration and in the stories themselves. For example, helping a coachee tap the mental distance and language favored by his left hemisphere can be quite helpful as a regulatory resource if he is feeling overwhelmed by emotions. Conversely, helping a coachee map the big picture and ground in his body as favored by his right hemisphere can be quite helpful as a regulatory resource if he is feeling overwhelmed by details. Working with the whole brain enables people to create the spaciousness they need to make more mindful choices in the present and hone new neural pathways for the future.

You can also help coachees develop a greater sense of sustained attachment security by moving between neural resonance and dissonance and back again to resonance in keeping with their developmental needs and trajectory. This flow between the two is what enables any of us, no matter our age, to learn and grow. Again, the more we can do this for ourselves as coaches, the more we can offer this to others. For example, I found that I had a much greater aptitude for and comfort with creating and re-creating resonance, and so I have worked a lot in recent years on my ability to create, stay present to and leverage constructive dissonance. In coaching, you can use this flow between resonance and dissonance to build and repair rapport so coachees increasingly trust you, themselves and the process; you can use the strengthened relationship to help coachees explore new ways of being, relating and acting in their world. Being able to access this flow is the key to self-regulation and maturity as the storyteller of their lives. The flow has three phases and they mirror those of the narrative coaching process: (1) Situate; (2) Search and Shift; and (3) Sustain.

1. *Build rapport by matching hemispheres with coachees to create resonance.* This mirroring will generate a sense of neural resonance and sufficient attunement as well as elicit more of the story. It will increase people's sense of *safe haven* in the session and dampen any unproductive limbic responses. It provides a "holding container," a safe place where they can adopt less defended positions. In my experience, most coachees appreciate right hemisphere to right hemisphere resonance at some point early in the coaching relationship and at critical moments, such as when they feel vulnerable.

2. *Connect with their non-dominant hemisphere to create the neural dissonance necessary for change.* By shifting your attunement, you create the conditions for people to increase their window of tolerance and build a stronger *secure base* from which they can explore openings for development. Help them address the strong emotions that often emerge, experiment with new ways of framing and responding, and develop the inner resources to return to a balanced state. This aspect of the work is based on the need for an increased testing and facing of reality as the basis for change.

3. *Match their dominant hemisphere again (though now at a more integrated level) as the foundation for a new story and the new actions to bring it to life.* Re-creating resonance enables coachees to operationalize and anchor their gains before moving on from the session and back into their relationships in the world. In the end, it is about modeling a secure relationship by deepening your empathy for them, sensing their emotions, sharing their states, and imagining the experience of truly being in their shoes *while* remaining grounded in your own experience, adept at managing your own state, and flexible in your engagement with them.

I am reminded here of a memorable quote from W.I. Thomas in my undergraduate sociology program: "Things perceived as real are real in their consequences." It highlights why narrative coaches take people's stories so seriously. What they see is often what they get. Therefore, consider asking questions such as the following to help coachees observe their narration in action through both hemispheres: (1) What are the consequences you are experiencing? (2) How did your story contribute to these consequences? (3) How does your story differ from the reality in this situation? (4) If you want different results, what about your story and/or your behavior needs to change? Invite people to incorporate the hemispheric information they often overlook in telling their stories so they can discover and tell more of the whole story as a whole person. This will serve as a new foundation for making choices. Otherwise, it is like trying to paddle a rowboat with one oar—and traveling in circles as a result. Narrative coaching helps people paddle with both oars, with a greater sense of flow and in a direction more in keeping with their current conditions and desired destination. It is fundamentally about changing their narratives about themselves as a rower, the boat as their life, and the river as their journey.

What they see is often what they get.

Chapter 2

HOW WE FORM IDENTITIES

Those who do not have power over the story that dominates their lives, the power to retell it, to rethink it, deconstruct it, joke about it, and change it as times change, truly are powerless, because they cannot think new thoughts.
Salman Rushdie

In the previous chapter we explored the notion that our minds are perpetual storytellers. The stories of who we think we were, we are and will be are the most elemental of these narratives. Narrative coaching works at the intersections of people's identities, behaviors and stories. How does each keep reinforcing the others? Where are there disconnects that undermine the person's power? While much of the focus in coaching is on changing behaviors, we ultimately need to address people's issues at all three levels if their changes are going to stick. Narrative coaching is about working with people to reconfigure how they define themselves, narrate their experience and live their lives. The aim is to help people develop an increased sense of agency and accountability as an author of their stories and an increased awareness and agility as an actor in others' stories. Working at the level of narrative and identity in coaching results in a stronger foundation for people's progress after their sessions.

In this chapter, we will look at the social and narrative nature of our identities and the tensions between (1) how we experience ourselves and how we express ourselves and (2) how we see ourselves and how others see us. In particular, we will look at the contribution of social constructionism to our understanding of narrative identity, the useful distinction between *I* and *Me*, and the role of imagined selves in shaping the person we become. The following framework (figure 2) depicts how people's identity can shift through coaching, the temporal and spatial points of reference, and the thresholds they will cross.

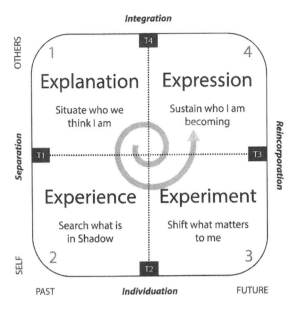

Figure 2. *The flow from explanation to expression in identity re-formation*

The four phases in narrative identity re-formation
1. *Situating* themselves in the current *explanations* of who they think they are → *separating* from certain aspects of their identity, often internalized from others;
2. *Searching* their *experiences* for what holds the key to their growth → individuating through (re-)claiming aspects of themselves previously held in Shadow;
3. *Shifting* what matters through *experiments* with how to be and act → reincorporating with what is necessary to fulfill what they set out to do; and
4. *Sustaining* their new identities through new *expressions* of themselves → integrating what works as part of who and how they are going forward.

Identities are critical in making and sustaining change because so much of what we do in our lives is based on the story we tell ourselves about who we think we were, are now, and should/could be. Growth often comes when a core aspect of our identity is challenged and we are compelled to allow in new stories and other aspects of ourselves. For example, some years ago I lived for a number of weeks largely from a sensory and emotional place while I recovered from a concussion and rebuilt my cognitive capacities. During that period, I came to see how much I had over-identified with my thinking function. Through this experience I gained a more expanded sense of myself by moving through the 4Es above as well as a healthier respect for the long arc of change and what it takes for people to truly heal and develop. We often underestimate what is truly at stake for people when we ask them, often blithely, to undertake a change in their identity or behavior. We take this seriously in narrative coaching by focusing on one dynamic at a time so that coachees can sufficiently invest in what is truly required and the benefits can extend to other areas of their life or work.

> We often underestimate what is truly at stake for people when we ask them, often blithely, to undertake a change in their identity or behavior.

We are guided by a belief that identity is more of a verb in process than a noun in place. While most of us experience a sense of coherence and continuity to our identity most of the time, we are forever engaged in a dance with our environment. You can see this in Singer's (2005b) definition of identity as "the psychosocial construct that meaningfully locates us in a sociocultural niche and unifies our lives temporally by finding continuity among our previous experiences, present concerns, and future aspirations" (p. 11). Similarly, Stryker (1987) defines identity as an internalized role designation corresponding to people's social locations in their various networks of interaction. I would suggest[9] that we speak in terms of "identities" rather than

---

9   As they both do in later writings.

the traditional notion of a singular identity because each person is a portfolio of the "individual and the collective, the relational and the volitional" (Bernstein, 2005, p. 25). People tap into various identities in the course of their day and across time to keep pace with their internal and external demands and personal and shared aspirations.

Our identities are formed in the continuous interplay between our needs for stability, consistency, familiarity, and continuity as the basis for safety and security *and* our needs for agility, adaptability, novelty, and discontinuity as the basis for exploration and growth (Drake, 2008a, 2009d; Penuel & Wertsch, 1995). The former is informed by our need to preserve and protect who we think we are, and it helps us retain a sense of a coherent whole with a center that holds. The latter is informed by our need to advance and enhance who we could become, and it helps us increase our capacity to flourish as we push out from the center. People tend to see themselves largely based on the meaning they (and significant others) give to the events in their lives, and people generally act in ways that are consistent with their familiar or desired identities. Many of their actions can be seen as attempts to optimize their environments in their favor and re-create situations that call upon their favored identities.

However, many of the issues people bring to coaching are related to actions that have not yielded the desired results. In part this is because they have created—"both in their minds and in the actual environment—a social reality that verifies, validates, and sustains the very conceptions that initiate and guide these processes" (Swann & Read, 1981, p. 371). The more salient a particular identity is to a person, the more often situations will be perceived and structured according to this identity (Cross & Markus, 1991). In addition, the more important an identity element is to her, the more she will seek to have it validated by her significant audiences (Oyserman & Markus, 1993) and the more her behaviors will be in service of confirming these identities (Markus & Nurius, 1986). Again, we can see the interconnections between our realities, our stories and our identities—and the self-fulfilling prophecies that tend to keep it all in place. Narrative coaching is about stepping into these spaces with people to increase their awareness of their current reality and open up possibilities for another way.

Narrative coaches think about these issues through the lens of identity performances (Mishler, 1992, 1999) through which people are trying to keep a particular narrative going (Giddens, 1991). This strong correspondence between structure and identity can be leveraged in working with people's stories in coaching. Openings for growth occur when there is an internal or external interruption in the usual performance and gaps appear between their expectation and their reality. It is hard for most people to do this through direct reflection, so it is often more fruitful to indirectly approach their identities through exploring their interactions, communications, and actions (Ricoeur, 1992). It is about inviting them to be a keen observer of themselves in motion. Stories are perfect for this as they make visible people's largely invisible identity processes and, thereby, provide access to the narrative mechanisms by which they define themselves. A critical piece of the process is helping people see themselves as both authors *of* and actors *in* their performances, recognize that these are just performances, and make new choices about how they want to be present to themselves and with others.

You can gain a sense of their narrative identities by listening for these five elements (see Botella & Herrero, 2000):

- events they include (or exclude) in their stories,
- main themes around which they organize them,
- characters they regard as significant (or non-significant),
- voices they privilege or silence when telling their stories, and
- genre into which they place their narrative material.

For example, do they tend to favor positive or negative events? How do they tend to position themselves in relation to other key characters? Do they tend to talk in an active or passive voice? Do their inner and outer narrative universes match in ways that are healthy for them and those around them? Any changes a person makes in coaching are more likely to have a lasting and meaningful impact when their broader patterns, identity strategies and socially constructed narratives are addressed (Mattingly, 1998).

Constructing ourselves socially

By refusing his web of constructions, she also cut him off from his supporting fiction.
James Hillman

The formation of narrative coaching in my doctoral studies was influenced by a number of disciplines with critical perspectives on identity, including social constructionism. Together, they call for a new approach to coaching in which identities are seen in terms of historical, social and contextual processes not just as individual traits. The roots of social constructionism can seen in Berger and Luckmann's (1966) treatises on the sociology of knowledge and the social construction of reality and in Ken Gergen's (1973) early work which calls for the inclusion of contextual, social, political, and economic phenomena in understanding people. This echoes the work of other scholars advocating for more inclusive and collective ways to think about our identities and our stories. Examples include: Anzaldua (1987) on *borderlands identities*, Frank (2010) on *socio-narratology*, Gilligan (1982) and Sorrell and Montgomery (2001) on *feminist perspectives* on identity formation, and McLaren (1993) on *critical pedagogy*. These writers challenge us to think beyond individualistic theories and practices and to take up a contextual and co-constructed frame in coaching.

As Peter Berger (1963) writes, "identity is socially bestowed, socially sustained, and socially transformed. . . . Self and identity are not something 'given' in some psychological sense, but they are bestowed in acts of social recognition. We become that as which we are addressed" (p. 99). Our identities are social in nature even if they often feel profoundly personal, and they are constructed in nature even if they often feel profoundly real. We define ourselves to varying degrees, based on our level of individuation, in relation to the views and responses of others that are reinforced and scaffolded (Oyserman & Markus, 1993). Our stories have a real and tangible impact on our identities and our lives (and vice versa). As narrative therapists Freedman and Combs (1996) note, "Our prevailing narratives provide the vocabulary that sets our realities. Our destinies are opened or closed in terms of the stories that we construct to understand our experiences" (p. 77). Changes in and expressions of our identities can be thwarted or supported by shifts in the larger narratives in which they are embedded.

Social constructionism provides a rich foundation for understanding people's stories and helping them soften their reification of these stories as if they were synonymous with their identities. You can help people decouple what was once fused so they can imagine new ways of being in the world. One way to do so is to help them explore the subtle and often invisible ways in which their identities are shaped by their communities and culture relative to the past, present, and future (Mehl-Madrona, 2010). Be particularly curious about how their stories and the collective narratives in which they operate influence each other, the consequences of the current configuration in terms of their identities and relations with others, and the possibilities for re-narrating one or both. As Gergen & Kaye (1993) wrote, "[A] story is not simply a story. It is also a situated action in itself, a performance with illocutionary effects. It acts so as to create, sustain, or alter worlds of social relationship" (p. 253). Therefore, people are intersubjectively narrated beings who cannot be seen independent of their context.

This requires augmenting the social constructionist perspective with one that is developmental so that our approach to coaching will be more integrative in nature. As Singer (1996) noted, "Theorists who embrace a personalogical orientation . . . emphasize the individual's processes of storying and meaning making within a cultural context, whereas social constructionist theorists . . . are interested in how culture wrote the story of our lives" (p. 452). I agree with Rossiter (1999) and others in seeking a both/and approach to identities, and the term "psychosocial" (McAdams et al., 1997) is useful here as a middle ground (see Drake, 2005b). Identities, then, can be seen as moving feasts, as traveling repertory companies (Singer & Rexhaj, 2006), through which people continually calibrate their internal landscapes and external environments in ways they believe will enable them to achieve what is important to them. They do this by deconstructing, constructing and re-constructing selves based on the stories told by, around and about them.

Hermeneutics (see Heidegger, 1927/1996; Schön, 1983) also offers a useful frame for doing narrative identity work in coaching. Hernadi (1987) outlined the three classical hermeneutic elements as follows: (1) What does this text say? (2) How and why does this text say what it does? (3) What do I, the reader, think of all this? We can adapt the outline for use in narrative coaching as follows: (1) What does this story say? (2) How and why does this story say what it does? (3) What do I, the coach, hear in this? (on behalf of the coachee). In narrative coaching, we move between all three as we help coachees gain a new and deeper understanding of their experience and their expectations. We draw from hermeneutic phenomenology by "going beyond what is strictly given, reading between the lines and paying attention to what has been omitted, to the silences and the assumptions, to that which has been so taken for granted that has not been questioned" (Bergum, 1997). Social constructionism adds a fourth element to the hermeneutic process by positioning and articulating the three elements (story, narrator, and listener) as a function of the context and discourse in which they are situated (field).

The narrative coaching model (figure 12) has four phases, each of which reflects one hermeneutic element in particular:

1. *Situate* focuses on grounding the person as narrator of the story;
2. *Search* focuses on unpacking the text of the narrative material;
3. *Shift* focuses on listening to the story in new ways; and
4. *Sustain* focuses on taking new action and supporting progress.

You can help people to look at their stories from all four hermeneutic perspectives, as seen in the Narrative Diamond model (figure 18) later in the book. Even though all four are present all the time, you will often find yourself moving between them throughout a session based on what warrants the most attention at a given point in the process. In general, it is best to start by increasing a person's awareness of her current stories and the identities these reveal (*what is*) before trying to change either the stories or the person telling them (*what could be*).

If you want coachees to adopt new behaviors or attain new results, help them build an identity from which to naturally do so. The results will stick better if they are seen as a logical and natural extension of who they (and enough others) think they are. These new identities are also reinforced by the actions they choose to take over time—and the stories they (and others) tell about them as a result. As always in coaching, start where the coachee is most ready. Social constructionism played an important part of my dissertation and the development of narrative coaching. As narrative coaching has evolved, it has moved more into the background as my work has become more experiential, embodied, and integrative. For example, I have incorporated work from new fields such as design thinking[10] to help coachees experiment with and actualize new stories. In the end, narrative coaching is a psychosocial process that helps people 'come home' to themselves and 'go home' to others in new ways.

Dancing between I/Me

Every man invents a story for himself which he then often and with great cost to himself, takes to be his life.
Max Frisch

Our identities have been epigenetically shaped through our inter-actions with others since birth. They are forged in the crucible where our internal desires meet our external demands and our need for becoming meets our need for belonging. In many ways, people measure their sense of progress in life (or lack thereof) by what emerges from that crucible. There are two scenarios we see often in coaching as people seek to make changes in their life and/or work: (1) people who are living out narratives that bring worth to

---

10   The importance of design thinking in narrative coaching will be addressed in my next book on using this work at scale.

them but who have lost their connection with others in the process (becoming without belonging); and (2) people who are living out narratives others have deemed worthy but who have lost themselves in the process (belonging without becoming). I find the distinction between "*I*" and "*Me*" useful here in understanding the tensions between desires and demands and the social nature of our identities as a whole. The ability to consider the effects we have on others (and they on us) and to internalize these 'observing presences' is necessary for the formation of a mature sense of self.

Sociologist George H. Mead (1934/1967), developed the term "Generalized Other" as a composite internalized figure that represents the values and the norms of a person's community and is a necessary consequence of normal development. The distinction between *I* and *Me* was central to this process and his social philosophy. Mead goes on to describe our inner world as a "field, a sort of inner forum, in which we are both spectators and the actors. In that field each one of us confers with himself" (p. 401). This resonates strongly with how narrative coaches work with the characters in people's stories. While it is most common to think in terms of ourselves as an *I*, particularly in the West, Mead would argue that our sense of self is largely defined in terms of our sense of *Me*. It is formed, in large part, through the internalization of how others see us, respond to us and relate to us—particularly in the formative years of our life. By contrast, he saw the *I* as the individual's response to and attitude about the community within the context of the *Me*.

William James, another pioneer in this field, also wrote about this distinction in thinking about our identities. He (1892/1927) saw the *I* as the *Self-as subject, self-as-knower*, and the *Me* as *Self-as-object, self-as-known*. James (1890/1950) described the characteristics of the *I* as continuity, distinctness, volition and embodiment, and the *Me* as having material, spiritual and social characteristics. Others who came along in the field (see Kegan, 1994; Mahony, 2003) echoed this distinction in framing the *I* as the subjective self who is observing and the *Me* as the objective self who is being observed. Much of the work in coaching is helping people to reconcile the two in some new way. The I/Me distinction can be used in helping coachees recognize the multiplicity and social nature of their identities and move between telling their story as a narrator and reflecting on their story as a protagonist. In so doing, you can help them address and adapt their relationship with the cultural forces that shape their identities.

Sometimes people develop as a result of a shift in their sense of *I*; sometimes it is as a result of feedback about *Me*. Sometimes the *I* needs to shift to accommodate a new *Me*, such as when a key contributor at work is promoted to manage her team. Sometimes the *Me* needs to shift to accommodate a new *I*, such as when a person desires to be seen differently by others in her family. Problems often arise when how we see ourselves (*I*) does not match up with how we show up for others or how they see us (*Me*). Changing the *Me* is often difficult—not only because it disrupts others' patterns and habituated responses to us, but because it may also challenge their narratives about themselves and the subgroups they represent. For example, the promotion of the first woman as the head of a department may be challenging at first for both the men and women on her team—both of whom will need to adapt their narratives about themselves and what constitutes an "ideal leader."

Theodore Sarbin (Mancuso & Sarbin, 1983; Sarbin, 1986a, 1986b) translated the I/Me distinction into a narrative frame. He argues that *I* represents the self as an author, the self-as-teller; and the *Me* represents the self as an actor or figure, the self-as-tale-told. People's sense of themselves evolves over time in a dialectic manner in relation to the significant shared narratives in which they are immersed. They tell stories about themselves to retain a sense of continuity for their internally constituted *I*, even as their externally constituted *Me* evolves, in part, through the stories others tell about them. They narrate their experiences so as to accommodate, confirm, and sustain their situated identity and/or to assimilate anomalous events into their identity and restore equilibrium (Block, 1982). People can shift their identities by telling new stories, reframing old ones or stopping their investment in collective stories that no longer align with their desired identity. In saying this, it is important to acknowledge that *I* and *Me* are useful conceptual distinctions not realities unto themselves.

Still, you can surface tensions between a coachee's sense of *I* and *Me* by asking questions such as, "What did you want to do at that moment?" (*I*) followed by, "What held you back?" (*Me*). The former sheds light on his instinctive desire (for better or worse) and the latter sheds light on his concerns about how he will be perceived by others. Coaches can help people sufficiently resolve these concerns in order to act with greater authenticity, integrity and efficacy. For each coachee it will be different. For one it might be helping him to mature an impulsive *I* so he considers what others need from him (*Me*) while for another it might be helping her to mature an indecisive *Me* by considering what her *I* truly wants. Look behind coachees' actions to understand the stories that are driving them. What aspect of their identity are they defending or promoting in their stories? How do they distort their experience or sense of reality to conform to their favored identity plot lines? As a result of coaching, certain aspects of people's identities move more into the background while others are freed to move more to the foreground.

As this work has evolved, I have come to more loosely hold the distinctions between I/Me and self/other in light of my explorations of the Buddhist perspective on the illusions of mind and self. It offers a counterbalance to Western views that are often still quite Cartesian in nature. The better we are at focusing so we can move from non-self to self and defocusing so we can move from self to non-self (Graham, 2013), the better we will be able self-regulate, soothe ourselves and others, and be resilient. I think there is room for both views in taking an integrative approach to identity and development. In the end, it is about helping people grow so they are more authentically aligned with how they want to be in the world and what they want to achieve as a result. For some this will mean gaining greater access to their non-self, and for others it will mean standing more fully in their self. Either way, the net result is greater freedom, authenticity and efficacy for the coachee.

Working with the past, present and future

We make sense—or fail to make sense—of our lives by the kind of story we can—or cannot—tell about it.
Joseph Dunne

Not only can identity be framed in spatial terms in terms of how we orient ourselves relative to our inner and outer worlds, but it also can be framed in temporal terms in terms of how we orient ourselves relative to our past, present, and future. It reflects our striving to reconcile our perceptions of 'what is', 'once was' and 'what might be' (Cross & Markus, 1991) in defining and redefining ourselves. Even though the past is given the bulk of attention in conceptualizing identity and development, a clear case can be made that who we are and how we act are as much influenced by our expectations of the future as they are by our explanations of/from the past. People's stories about their lives are as much future-shaped as they are past-determined (White & Epston, 1990). What we strive for and are in the process of becoming is at least as significant a factor in our identity as what we are currently doing (Allport, 1955/1968; Goldstein, 1939; Maslow, 1954).

Stories are powerful resources for coaching because they are built around a temporal frame like our minds. People's stories about the past, the present, and the future all shape their identities over time and their experiences and actions in the moment. As such, we can see the past, the present, and the future as a reflexive loop in which each one offers information to and receives meaning in relation with the other two. This means that all three can be accessed in the present moment as a way to unpack people's narrative identity. I saw this in a recent conversation with a client:

> He commented that I often seemed to know what he would say next. I responded by saying that it felt like I was getting glimpses of the future (when he was 'retired') as it curled back into our present experience—bringing with it our shared memories of

working together in the past. All three temporal dimensions were present in that moment. As a result, he was able to see his current dilemma from all three perspectives at the same time and develop a new plan for what to do next.

Narrative coaching builds on the retrospective nature of stories by spiraling through these recursive loops such that the past, present, and future can all be available to work with in the moment. As Kearney (2002) notes, "When someone asks you who you are, you tell your story. That is, you recount your present condition in the light of past memories and future anticipations. You interpret where you are now in terms of where you have come from and where you are going" (p. 4). While much of coaching is future-focused, people often end up needing to *restory* their past as part of the process, e.g., shifting the significance and meaning of events, making new connections and associations, repositioning themselves and others (Mishler, 1999). People draw on their past, present, and future identities in telling their stories. However, the present is the only time frame for action, which means that all problems are ultimately problems of the present (Boscolo & Bertrando, 1992).

That is why narrative coaches work with people's narrative material in the present most of the time regardless of which dimension of time the coachee is addressing, e.g., recollecting a related episode from the past or imagining the future consequences of a pending decision. The key is to work with coachees in the present moment but in relation to whichever temporal dimension would most help them make progress. For example, in one of the practices we do in our Labs we use chairs to help people reconfigure the relationship between the past, present and future as a way to gain greater clarity about their situations and their choices. The configuration of chairs in the 'field' can be seen as a three-dimensional representation of their stories about the situation as they are organized in the person's mind. It reflects Saint Augustine's (400/2009) proposition that there are three times: a present of past things (memory), a present of present things (direct perception), and a present of future things (expectation). Through coaching we can help people make visible, explicit, and conscious the invisible, tacit, and unconscious ways in which their stories are narrated as a means of opening up more space for new narratives and new choices.

> **The key is to work with coachees in the present moment but in relation to whichever temporal dimension would most help them make progress.**

People flourish when the three sets of selves are aligned in service of their highest self. If their past can become more malleable through coaching, their present becomes more available and their desired future becomes more attainable. When you are coaching, ask yourself: Does the coachee believe the problem resides in the past, present or future? The solution? You can often tell by tracking people's body language (e.g., what are they talking about when they have the most energy?) and their spoken language (e.g., what verb tense do they tend to use as they tell their stories?). In working with people's stories, pay attention to how they situate themselves in time and how this configuration may need to be adjusted to free them up to accomplish what they set out to do. As people begin to open up their sense of time, it creates more breathing room in their stories and their identities to explore other configurations that may be healthier for them and more productive in their life.

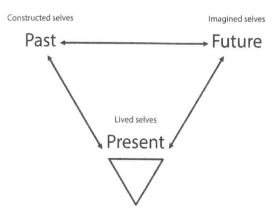

Figure 3. *A temporal view of identities*

As this diagram illustrates, identities can be seen as an evolving prism (see Stevens-Long, 2000) composed of the selves we have constructed over time (past), the selves we are living (present) and the imagined selves we seek or avoid (future). The smaller triangle at the bottom of the diagram reflects the fact that all three sets of selves are available and potentially influential in each moment. The bidirectional arrows reflect the fact that each of the three influences the other two. For example, a coachee feels unfulfilled in his current job (*lived self*) in large part because he has been unable to fulfill his dream of working as an artist (*imagined self*) as a result of having to get a job early in life to fulfill his role in the family (*constructed self*). The aim is for people to experience the constraints of their current temporal constellation and use them to explore openings for new possibilities. These openings can be found where there is: (1) a disconnect between two selves that needs to be rejoined (e.g., I don't see any value in my past self that would enable me to create the future self I want); (2) a fusion of two selves that needs to be uncoupled (e.g., my self as currently lived will automatically lead me to the imagined self I want); or (3) an absence of or damage to one of the selves that short circuits the whole self (e.g., my negatively constructed self is permanent and will always hold me back).

Identity and development can be seen as a function of what Markus & Nurius (1986) called "possible selves" that, for better or worse, beckon us from our sense of the future. They described them as those elements of the self-concept that represent what individuals could become, would like to become, and are afraid of becoming. Ibarra (1999) writes about them as "benchmarks for interpreting and judging [our] behavior . . . helping [us] to decide what behaviors to try again, reject, or modify" (p. 767). They may come as dreams, visions, plans, unlived lives, opportunities not yet imagined or experienced, new statuses, and more. Because they are not yet grounded in sufficient lived experience, they tend to be the most vulnerable and responsive to changes in the environment (Markus & Nurius, 1986). I think of them as "imagined selves" because it is less about all possible selves and more about what is relevant and important for a given person. As we shall see, imagined selves are shaped by the person's available narratives and often in ways that are significant yet tacit. As people move through narrative coaching we invite them to test out imagined selves in order to create what neurobiologist David Ingvar called new "memories of the future."[11]

This is important because people with a clear vision of themselves in a future state tend to have more accessible cues that are relevant to this future state and selectively process information that is useful in attaining it. As a coach, you can help people make decisions about which elements of these imagined selves they want to live out more fully in order to achieve more of what they want. For example, a recent Lab participant was able to temper the righteous indignation that inspired her work with a heart-felt and compassionate imagined self such that she could still approach situations clearly but with more openness and warmth. While we are free to create a variety of imagined selves, the pool of choices largely derives from valued categories and *available narratives* (Drake, 2003, 2005b) in our environments over time. Available narratives represent the vocabulary and grammar, plot lines and historical conventions, beliefs and value systems (Polkinghorne, 1988, 1991) that we inherit and internalize from our historical, cultural and situational narratives.

We narrate our identity in large part based on these unspoken, implicit cultural models of what selfhood should be, could be, and shouldn't be (Bruner, 2002). The tension at the heart of both great drama and adult development is found where the forces of continuity as represented by our constructed selves (Past), the forces of discontinuity as represented by our imagined selves (Future), and the forces of reality as represented by our lived selves (Present) converge—as seen in the figure below. For example, a coachee who has been unexpectedly laid off experiences a breach in her constructed self ("I've always worked here") and feels afraid in the moment ("I don't know what I will do next") because she has yet to access a suitable imagined self ("I don't know how to look for work anymore").

---

11   Cited in de Geus, 1997, p. 36.

You can see this in the following figure which places figure 3 in the core construct of narrative coaching based in the rites of passage. As you coach, work with the three selves in the present moment as they relate to the issue at hand and help coachees draw on available narratives that are in line with how they want to be and what they want to do.

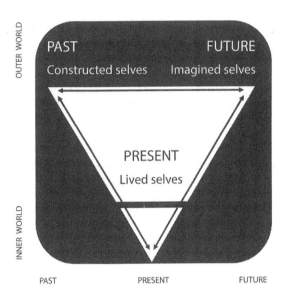

Figure 4. *Working in the moment with identities*

The difficulty for many coachees is that they often don't recognize the contours and limitations of their available narratives until they need to narrate experiences or enact selves that are contrary to them. As they recognize limitations inherent in these available narratives, they can create a sense of distance from them, see them more clearly, and surface alternative voices (Polkinghorne, 2001). The evolution of their identities can be seen as an ongoing effort to (re)claim a authentic place in their world *and* a sense of right relationship with its available narratives. Maturity can be seen as the ability to self-regulate and more consciously and fluidly choose. As with the I/Me distinction, there is an ongoing tension between our constructed and imagined selves that is often both the source of our difficulties and the doorway to our development. This can seen most vividly when people are considering major choices in relation to their lived selves. To move into right relationship may require a coachee to shift one or more of these three selves. For example, a coachee may need to prune the number of imagined selves under consideration in order to move on more decisively from his current lived self.

A major step in this process for coachees is identifying narrative data from their lives that supports an alternate view of who they are and how they can be in the world. In this process of identity re-negotiation, coachees are invited to reflect on, experience, and test new stories, and may temporarily adopt what Ibarra (1999) calls a "provisional self". Some examples from my doctoral study included: (1) "I have choices and it is important to choose (and choose well)"; (2) "I name and seek what is important to me"; (3) "I talk about what is important to me (even if it is difficult)"; (4) "I am a full partner and show up fully in relationships"; and (5) "I am a person who 'means business' in holding others accountable." The insight that coachees' constructed selves, lived selves and imagined selves can be brought together through powerful experiences in the present was instrumental in developing the pivoting process in narrative coaching. What we are often doing in sessions is helping people experiment with provisional selves as a bridge between how they saw themselves in the past and how they imagine themselves in the future.

People often seek coaching when they realize their identities no longer serve them well—and the price they pay to live them has become too high and/or they are keeping them from living out other aspects of themselves. Conflicts or gaps in people's stories in coaching often signal a parallel conflict or gap in their sense of themselves, so you can use their narrative material as a proxy and support for the changes that are underway in their identities. For example, a story about a leader's struggles with her boss becomes a conversation about a lack of passion for her current role. In the end, people can only see as far as their identities and stories will take them; they can only act as far as their identities and stories will back them. Any shifts they make in their identities will be thwarted or supported by those around them and the larger narratives they represent. Therefore, help people find receptive audiences with whom to debut their new story so they can have some early wins, learn from their initial experiences, and make any necessary adjustments. As Kierkegaard argued, it is through the process of choosing our story about who we are and how we will act that we become responsible for our identities, our states and our lives.

Chapter 3

HOW WE LEARN AND DEVELOP

Mostly we learn from reexamination of our own stories.
Roger Schank

Narrative coaching is one of the few coaching methodologies with an explicit learning and development component built into the model. It is an integrative process in which learning, development, and performance are intimately linked and simultaneously supported to create more sustainable change. It is based in a situated and social view of learning (Lave & Wenger, 1991), transformative and transpersonal learning theories (see Freire, 1970; McWhinney & Markos, 2003; Mezirow, 1991, 2000), and integrative development theory. As a result, when coachees complete the process they are better prepared and more aligned to sustain the changes they have begun. Ultimately, narrative coaching is an experiential and developmental process of awakening—to what is true, what matters and what is to be done. It asks people to keep spiraling through the question, "What is yours to learn from this story?" until they break through.

The first section in this chapter focuses on learning and highlights its transformative potential, the vital role of 'mistakes', the influence of improvisational theater and play, and Vygotsky's work on proximal development. The second section focuses on development and highlights the importance of working with dreams and projections and integrating Shadows and strengths as two unique aspects of narrative coaching. They are both based in a deep respect for the long arc of change and an appreciation for capitalizing on opportunities every day to learn and grow. The former speaks to our lifelong maturational journey to drop the socially constructed 'veils', while the latter speaks to the need for making the most of threshold moments where the learning is accelerated. Paradoxes abound: We *are* our stories and we are *not* our stories. We *upgrade* our stories and then we *let them go*. Our stories are the source of our *suffering* and the source of our *liberation*. Narrative coaching is designed to help people learn about and through their stories so they can address what matters most to them.

Facilitating transformative learning

Almost every encounter in life presents possibilities for growth. . . . But these transformations require that a person be prepared to perceive unexpected opportunities. Most of us become so rigidly fixed in the ruts carved out by genetic programming and social conditioning that we ignore the options of choosing any other course of action.
Mihaly Csikszentmihalyi

Kolb (1984) defines learning as "the process whereby knowledge is created [and retained] through the transformation of experience" (p. 38). Mezirow (2000) describes it as:

> the process of becoming critically aware of how and why our presuppositions have come to constrain the way we perceive, understand, and feel about our world; of reformulating these assumptions to permit a more inclusive, discriminating, permeable, and integrative perspective; and of making decisions or otherwise acting upon these new understandings. (p. 14)

Learning is the act of making new distinctions we otherwise wouldn't be able to make and it enables us to take actions we otherwise wouldn't be able to take. Central to the transformative learning process is the unlearning that is often required to make room for learning at a higher level (Illeris, 2004; Mezirow, 2000). In narrative coaching, we describe it as releasing or adapting old stories to make room for new ones. Otherwise, people end up like in the Zen fable with more tea being poured into an already full cup. Over the years, I have found that helping people 'empty their cup' is as important to them as adding better 'tea'. What emerges on the other side often arises with such grace once they have put down old burdens and baggage.

Transformative learning is an essential element in narrative coaching and each phase of the process is particularly well suited to support one of Mezirow's attributes as cited above:

- *Situate* is about helping coachees become more aware of their presuppositions;
- *Search* is about helping coachees reformulate their assumptions;
- *Shift* is about helping coachees develop and test new perspectives and options; and
- *Sustain* is about helping coachees make new decisions and take new actions.

Narrative coaching focuses more on awakening people's curiosity and increasing their "growth mindset" (Dweck, 2008) and far less on assessing them, which often ends up reinforcing a "fixed mindset". The result is coachees who not only learn more about themselves and their issues, but who can more readily transfer the learning and development they gain in coaching into their lives. One of the ways narrative coaches do this is by paying close attention for openings in people's stories when transformative learning becomes available at a heightened level.

For example, it is often what people learn when things don't work as they had predicted which makes the biggest difference. To make the most of these moments, you can use reflective processes to help people explore the assumptions about reality inherent in their stories and use experiential processes to help them generate new stories and new ways of being. The aim is to enhance their ability to notice what is happening in the moment: what is triggering them, what stories are they telling themselves, what is the opening for learning, and what do they want to do about it?

> For example, in working with a team leader, I invited him to pause and notice what was happening for him as a conflict emerged in the team coaching session. He was able in the moment to reflect on our earlier sessions when we discussed his pattern of stepping in to resolve differences on his team

rather than developing this capacity in them. Using the pause
and pivot techniques I had taught him, he used the occasion to
notice the tension in his body as he started to respond along the
old storyline and then shifted gears to act in new ways that were
healthier for him and his team.

Your role as a coach is to create a nonjudgmental container in
which coachees can learn from these experiences in the moment and
try new things. Sometimes being 'seen' and accepted as they are is
enough to help dissolve the issue. For those who require more, don't
allow them to settle for insights during sessions with promises that
they will act on them later. More often that we care to admit, they
don't for any number of reasons. Instead, craft experiences in the
session itself in which coachees can practice, so they can leave with
an embodied referent point. The classic 'aha' moment in coaching is
like the candle on a birthday cake; it gets most of the attention at first
but is not that significant in the end. Instead, help coachees anchor
their learning in real time and, as a result, become more open and
confident as learners. I believe this transformative approach to learning is critical in coaching because it is impossible to learn without
incurring consequences, making mistakes, and surrendering to the
process. As I tell people I am coaching in sessions and in workshops,
"It doesn't get any better than this in terms of a supportive space."

The issue for many coachees is that they are afraid of making mistakes. However, everyone is a beginner when they learn something
new; a temporary drop in performance is inevitable. Why then do
we so often criticize adults when they are attempting to learn? We
don't penalize toddlers for the hundreds of times they fall down as
they are learning to walk. Instead, we praise them for everything
they do that brings them one step closer to walking on their own.
Rather than see mistakes as failures to reach the ideal, help people
see them as events that did not turn out as they had hoped—but
upon which they can build. What coachees deem as 'failures' are
often their greatest sources for learning (see Sitkin, 1992). Therefore,
help people see that learning is not a binary choice ("I succeeded or
I failed") but a generative process ("What can I learn from what I

am doing that will bring me closer to what I want to achieve?). In her work on bouncing back, Graham (2013) invites people to reflect on mistakes in terms of "this is what happened; this is what I have learned; and this is how I can respond to life now" (p. 244). In the end, narrative coaching is a transformative learning process based in serious play.

The importance of play

Play is a useful framework for coaching because it captures people's need for structure *and* freedom, experimentation *and* consolidation, in order to learn and develop. The child development literature offers a rich resource in support of play as a social process with a social purpose that is also relevant for adults. For example:

- Bowlby's (1988) notion of a *safe haven* that provides infants with a sense of safety and a *secure base* that gives them the confidence to explore (see Ellis, 1973; Mellou, 1994) offers a frame for increasing coachees' confidence in the journey ahead;
- Winnicott's (1988) notion of the *false self* as a mask which we hide behind rather than risk exposure offers a frame you can use to help coachees' experiment with letting more of their authentic self show to others;
- Horney's (1965) notion of *divided wishes* offers a frame for exploring where coachees' feel torn or stuck, creating a better alignment with what matters most to them and freeing up more of their discretionary energy; and
- Piaget's (1954, 1962) notion of *imitation/accommodation* and *play/assimilation* offers a frame for understanding coachees' tensions between preserving safety and inclusion *and* extending self-expression and individuation.

What children experience through play has a lot in common with what adults' experience in learning new skills and making transitions—two of the most common reasons people seek coaching. Play requires both children and adults to do the following, each of which is particularly present in one of the elements in the narrative coaching process (figure 12):

- circumscribe activities within boundaries and limits in time and space (Mainemelis & Ronson, 2006)—as seen in the *Situate* phase in which the container is set for the stories to unfold and the work to be done;
- navigate the threshold between fantasy and reality (Ibarra & Petriglieri, 2010)—as seen in the *Search* phase in which significant conscious and unconscious narrative elements are explored at the edges of their stories;
- negotiate between "identities claimed" and "identities granted" (Bartel & Dutton, 2001) and inner and outer worlds—as seen in the *Shift* phase in which coachees make new choices in terms of who and how they want to be in the world;
- re-align identity and role expectations in order to be successful (Hall, 1971)—as seen in the *Sustain* phase in which coachees re-enter the world with their new story as a gift to themselves and others; and
- integrate body, spirit, and mind at a higher level yet in a non-threatening way (Erikson, 1950)—as seen in the *spiral* in which coachees integrate their progress and the cycle of growth continues.

Play helps people of all ages learn how to interact with their environment, activate more of their whole brain, experiment with new ways of seeing themselves and being seen by others, create their own knowledge of the world and shape their space in it. Incorporating a safe space for play enables both children and adults to experiment with releasing and rehearsing identities to meet their current or anticipated needs and to try out new and untested behaviors (A. Y. Kolb & Kolb, 2010). For children, play is key in forming their ego structure as they learn; whereas, for adults, play is key in suspending their ego structure in order to unlearn and learn anew. Play is both an attitude and an activity that can be used in coaching to help people to:

- experiment and make 'mistakes' with less consequence;
- have an immediate feedback loop to improve;

- ask questions that might be risky in public;
- try out new identities, approaches and stories;
- engage their whole body and self; and
- challenge the status quo; have more joy and freedom.

The literal and figurative use of play in narrative coaching offers people an opportunity to decouple their habituated associations between means and ends (Mainemelis & Ronson, 2006) through an increased emphasis on process, enjoyment, and discovery to balance the usual focus on goals, efficiency and outcomes (March, 1976). However, the notion of play and its potential for adult development is challenging because, as March also notes, the very experiences children seek out in play are the ones that social and organizational norms for adults are generally designed to avoid: disequilibrium, novelty, and surprise. Therefore, a nonjudgmental stance and a commitment to serious play is important in making it safe for people to try out new aspects of themselves, see how those new stories feel in action, and prepare for bringing them into their world. Transformative learning and development most often occurs in the fertile space between what the coachee knows and what they don't know, and between what they can easily do now and what they can't do yet.

The contributions of Lev Vygotsky

For Vygotsky (1934/1987, 1978), play was instrumental as part of the scaffolding for learning and development as social processes. He developed his theory through the study of children's development, but it has relevance for adult learning and development as well. Of particular interest is his notion of "zones of proximal development" which he (1978) defined as "the distance between the actual developmental level as determined by independent problem-solving and the level of potential development as determined through problem-solving under adult supervision or in collaboration with more capable peers" (p. 86). The actual developmental level is what the child has already accomplished and the potential developmental level is what the child is capable of—if the appropriate scaffold or support is provided. The contours of any given collaboration are defined by the space between the person's current capabilities, needs and desires, *and* the environment's demands, resources and possibilities. It is harder to learn if the gap between the two spaces is too great in either direction—leading to either boredom if the challenge is insufficient or stress if the challenge is too great.

According to Vygotsky, these zones are based in a symbiotic relationship between development and learning in which development as an individually internalized process always lags behind learning as a culturally mediated process. In part this is because it often takes longer to absorb and process what happens in coaching then we think. This is why narrative coaches engage coachees in transformative learning experiences before inviting them to reflect on these experiences as openings for their development. Without learning, there is not much hope for development (Day, Harrison, & Halpin, 2009). In order to optimally harness the potentiality in these zones as they arise in coaching, I tend to focus in depth on one thing at a time. If a coachee is building momentum toward action, I may choose to engage her in a sequence of zones so that each can build on the other. I find that an emergent yet sharp focus helps both parties in coaching make the most of opportune moments for learning and development. Also, by going deeper into fewer issues, it is much easier to track coachees' progress.

However, transformative learning and development often requires coachees to cross what feels like a chasm to them in order to reach the other side. You can use the concept of zones of proximal development in preparing people so they can make it across the threshold and start out with a solid footing on the other side. A lot of this takes the form of small steps to increase their awareness, focus and resources as they cross. Otherwise, they may end up feeling 'in over their heads' (Kegan, 1994) and their subsequent development is diminished as a result. Vygotsky's work fits well with narrative coaching because we are less interested in formal assessments which measure what he called 'fossilized' forms of learning and development (e.g., capabilities already obtained) and more interested in experiential processes through which new forms or levels of development emerge (e.g., potential for growth). We are also interested in advancing the narrative patterns and structures that enhance people's levels of learning and development in and beyond sessions (Goldhaber, 2000).

A key to learning for Vygotsky (see Chaiklin, 2003) was the role of "scaffolding" in supporting children [and adults] to stretch beyond what they know and can do, to incorporate what they do not yet know and cannot yet do. For the scaffolding to work, the task must be within the person's reach such that with effort and minimal support from others, she can move to a higher level of functioning. This scaffolding is analogous to the notion of 'broaden and build', (Frederickson, 2006) in that people are creating a more versatile and mature repertoire one step at a time.

There are four tasks typically involved in scaffolding in coaching:

1. *Situate:* Observing, modeling, and identifying the key elements of what is to be learned in order to separate from what they know.

2. *Search:* Exploring, reflecting on, and articulating new relationships between these elements as the focus for learning in order to step into the liminal unknown.

3. *Shift:* Experimenting, getting feedback and support, and extrapolating the underlying principles in order to apply their learning in the world.

4. *Sustain:* Adapting identity to incorporate new knowledge and capability, generalizing and planning for future, and integrating what has changed into their daily life.

Coaching is about helping people identify, scaffold, and leverage the learning that is just beyond their current capabilities yet within their reach and necessary for the next step forward. Having sufficient scaffolding enables coachees to step from the "known and familiar" of their problem experience into the "not yet known, but possible to know" territory of their preferred experience (Carey, Walther, & Russell, 2009). Scaffolding can take the form of deconstructing issues or aspirations into smaller chunks, asking questions that focus the attention, bringing the whole brain into the narration process to get a more complete picture, experimenting with micro-elements (e.g., body posture, gestures, key words) associated with what is being learned, and more. What this often requires is creating experiences that give coachees a taste of what is possible through modeling from you, observing others or doing it themselves with your guidance. The good news is that most of the pieces you will need to help them scaffold their learning and development are in their stories: current and desired state, preferred modality of learning, pointers to allies and resources, and related social narratives.

You can support this process by inviting coachees to engage in specific tasks and interactions in order to support the formation of new functions or the enrichment of existing functions (Vygotsky, 1934/1998). For example, with coachees whose desire is to become a more confident public speaker, you might help them deconstruct "confidence" by asking them to think of a time when they felt confident, notice what changes come over their body as they recount that story, identify a verbal or somatic anchor to recall and embody that stance, and give a presentation right then and there. Coaching provides a structured and reflective space in which people can iteratively deconstruct and reconstruct their narratives as they learn and develop. Think of your coaching sessions as transitional spaces and zones of proximal development. The scaffolding for any zone of development needs to incorporate the structural, objective 'pull' from the environment and the unique, subjective 'push' from the individual in order for what they have learned and how they have developed to stick. What they can do with you as their coach today, they can more independently and capably do on their own tomorrow (Vygotsky, 1934/1998).

Fostering development and growth

Those who grow old without learning the story that is trying to live through them don't become 'old enough' or ancient enough to serve the dream of life.
Michael Meade

One of the unique features of narrative coaching is its multi-disciplinary and developmental approach that enables people to holistically engage with their issues. It is about helping people discern what is theirs to learn in critical moments in coaching and what questions are urgent and essential to answer at this stage in their development and/or life. In looking at growth this way, I have found it helpful to draw on post-Jungians such as Ginette Paris (2007) who laments, "The idea that we 'grow,' as a child grows (or as an economy grows), has come to replace what used to be imagined as the deepening of experience and the lifelong quest for wisdom" (p. 114). A similar sentiment is found in Hillman's (1996) *acorn theory* which proposes that every person is born with a defining image that acts as a personal daimon; it not only pushes from the beginning, it also pulls toward an end.

This loss of a deeper sense of growth is regrettable even more so now as we are living longer and coming to realize with Jung (1967) that "the greatest and most important problems in life are fundamentally insoluble . . . They can never be solved, but only outgrown when confronted with a new and stronger life urge" (p. 15). Therefore, help coachees discern the life urge that is seeking to be expressed rather than dissect symptomatic 'problems' seeking to be relieved. This requires relinquishing notions of development as a linear progression or ascension, and seeing it instead as a multi-faceted ripening of what is already present. It calls for a sense of development that is deepening and connecting more than rising and separating. Bakan's (1966) classic distinction between *communion* (how and why we are in relation to others) and *agency* (how we act and express ourselves) can be useful here as a way to simply frame people's developmental aspirations (see Singer, 2005b).

When I demonstrate this work, some practitioners report that it feels slow and deceptively simple. However, they also observe that it enables people to make important shifts in brief periods of time. They also comment that these big shifts seem to happen all at once rather than through a sequence of steps. There actually have been a lot of small steps in the process to that point, but they are less noticeable because the process is layered rather than formulaic. Together, they point to the different rhythm in narrative coaching that is circling and decisive at the same time. I believe narrative coaching works well because there is something innately human about this work that puts people at ease and, in that ease, they can more fully open themselves to learn and grow. It brings together their needs for:

- Knowing where they are (location)
- Knowing what to do (force/movement)

- Having a sense of a safe haven to which they can return
- Having a sense of a secure base from which they can venture forth

- Being in communion with self and others
- Being agentic on behalf of self and others

- Retaining a sense of order, coherence and continuity
- Capitalizing on disorder, surprise and change

Many of the issues that people bring to coaching revolve around points of tension within these pairs. Their growth often emerges where there is *narrative friction* (a clash between stories) or challenges to their *narrative fictions* (a clash provoked by another story). In working with people's stories, you can help them understand where they are in relation to each set of needs, where they want to focus their attention to get more of what they want, and how to increase their capacity to attend to their own developmental rhythms. It is important to remember, though, that these are both/and propositions not either/or ones. For example, a coachee wants to fit in as the new leader of a team in order to connect with them *and* he wants opportunities to prove himself by taking the team in a new direction. The needs in both columns are essential for people to develop and grow. It is also true that development in these areas often brings people up against their defenses, especially when delving into sensitive and critical issues.

These defenses originally formed to protect their differentiating and adaptive ego (McWilliams, 1994) as an intrinsic and healthy part of development early in their life. As Gagan (1998) observed, our defenses "work on our behalf, altering reality by creatively rearranging conflicts into more manageable situations. The resulting distortions give us time to acclimate to life's contingencies until the anxiety of the threatening situation can be borne" (p. 140). People's defenses are an integral part of their psyche and identity, have played a vital role in their survival and development to date, and need to be treated with respect as part of the development process. An understanding of attachment theory (and neural resonance and dissonance, in particular) will serve you well in getting people to suspend their defenses long enough to try on new stories—and the identities and behaviors that go with them. As part of this process they will need to upgrade any counterproductive coping strategies because they generally involve denying some aspects of themselves and/or clinging to others.

When defenses are used repetitively and inflexibly in the face of threats that are perceived as otherwise unmanageable, they become a barrier to people's development and interfere with their ability to self-regulate and respond to others. In narrative coaching, we invite people to experience their defenses in action before exploring alternatives. For example, you notice the coachee uses self-effacing humor when she feels uncomfortable. You can help her notice this is occurring, observe the story she is telling herself through the defense, identify what is being held back as a result, and explore how else she could respond in those moments. What people are defending against is often the very thing they most need in order to grow. The secret is to ally with defenses rather than trying to defeat them. Their defenses and their development, and their Shadow and their gifts, are two sides of the same coin. As James Hillman (1983) observed, "Where we are most sensitive, we are most stubborn;

where we are most exposed, we expend most efforts to conceal. . . . [W]e get closest to soul when we work closely with its defenses" (p. 99). The poet Rainer Maria Rilke put it this way, "Our deepest fears are like dragons guarding our deepest treasures."

What people are defending against is often the very thing they most need in order to grow. The secret is to ally with defenses rather than trying to defeat them.

Coaching provide a safe space in which people can meet those fears head on and rediscover their lost inner treasure. In so doing, you will likely run into resistance from coachees—particularly where their narration is taking them into places that are quite new for them and/or they imagine will surface challenging emotions or insights. Be respectful of their resistances as you do so because they are likely to feel vulnerable as they traverse their developmental razor's edge. Resistance is like a closed door. One needs to open it with caution but remember it is still a door and not a wall. Do what you can to decipher the important information that is embedded in points of resistance (Cozolino, 2004) as a key to understanding their defenses and what they are defending against. Much of what we do in narrative coaching is invite people into the possibility of living in a less defended way so that more of their potential is available to them. I treasure those moments when people in our Labs or coaching sessions break through and choose to live this way. The difference is palpable and an inspiration for us all.

Like many coaches, I used to try to push past resistance from workshop participants and coaching clients so we could make more progress. However, as I developed narrative coaching and my practice over the years, I began to question the value of 'pushing', the nature of 'resistance', and the meaning of 'progress'. As a result, I have moved to a pulling strategy in trusting that coachees will find their own path, reframed resistance as self-definitional boundaries to be explored, and withdrawn my attachments to progress to make room for greater clarity and courage. Rather than waging Sisyphean battles with coachees in attempts to change them, I engage them in a process of mindful inquiry about what is true for them and what they really want. In the process, I help them imagine what would become possible if they no longer had to devote so much energy to protecting themselves, but could use it to increase their openness to experience and their fulfillment in what they do.

Growth generally involves moving toward the unknown more than the known and embracing the mystery more than analyzing the history. In doing so, you can take heart in Wendell Berry's notion that when we no longer know what to do we have come to our real work; when we no longer know which way to go we have begun our journey. This is just as true for coaches in our lives and practices as it is for coachees. It means relinquishing our need for and illusion of control. It means acknowledging that we are stepping into developmental processes with people that are already underway—and will continue on with or without us. It means not trying so hard to change others and ourselves. Instead, it calls for a deeper compassion for humanity, a deeper acceptance of reality and a deeper surrender to possibility. It is from this place, more so than from our valiant efforts, that new stories are born and new growth emerges. It is about profoundly letting go to make room for the real work to be done.

In working this way over the years, I have come to realize that facilitating development is a subtle, organic, and alchemical art. As Mary Watkins (1976) noted, in order to grow "we must be able to let things happen in the psyche. Consciousness is forever interfering, helping, correcting, and negating, and never leaving the simple growth of the psychic processes in peace" (p. 104). Much of what we do in coaching is create the space and support for the new story that is already unfolding. As such, see yourself as a midwife of a natural process more than an architect of a constructed outcome. Seize the openings in coaching when people are on the cusp of a developmental breakthrough, and work diligently to help them cross that threshold. In the end, narrative coaching is a process to help people mature as storytellers so they are more accountable for their stories, their choices and their lives. As a result, they can act in service of their deepest needs and the common good. The four-phased approach to maturing strengths that follows is an example of the provocative and powerful techniques I've developed to do this.

Understanding our Shadow

All the life potentialities that we never managed to bring to adult realization, those other portions of oneself are there; for such golden seeds do not die. If only a portion of that lost totality can be dredged up into the light of day we should experience a marvelous expansion of our powers, a vivid renewal of life.
Joseph Campbell

I've always wholeheartedly embraced coaching's call to leverage strengths rather than try to fix weaknesses because it aligns with my philosophy of learning and development. However, over time I noticed that there was little room in the coaching discourse for the critical role of the Shadow in development or a more nuanced stance on strengths. What follows is an introduction to how and why the Shadow is formed and how these hidden aspects of ourselves can be used to help people mature their strengths and enhance their development. It is based on years of facilitating Shadow workshops and learning how to transmute what seemed like lead in people's narrative material into proverbial gold. It also connects with Vygotsky's work and attachment theory in that a person's Shadow (and the archetypal energies it represents) can be seen as a potent resource in moving through zones of proximal development and developing more robust working models. Narrative coaching is designed to bring forth whole stories and whole people—both of which require working with Shadow material if they are to develop.

In the first years of our lives we instinctively strive to maintain a sufficient degree of safety, self-coherence and love as we learn to process the outer and inner experiences we encounter (Page, 1999). Infants and young children will do whatever it takes to manage the tension between who they are and who their significant others want or allow them to be—sometimes to their detriment. In the process, we all develop what Jung called a "persona" as a mask that was "designed on the one hand to make a definite impression upon others, and, on the other, to conceal the true nature of the individual" (Jung, 1972, p. 192). It expresses how we would like to be seen by our world and it reflects the coping strategies we use to maintain these views. Our persona is a psychological necessity for interacting with the world; it becomes a problem when we over-identify with it and mistake it for the totality of who we are. As with a good story, our Shadow comes into play as it rises up in opposition to our *persona* in an effort to restore equilibrium and wholeness. Without conflict, there is no story. Without conflict, there is no growth. In both cases, the Shadow plays a vital role in both the conflict and its resolution.

Robert Bly (1988) offers a wonderful analogy to describe the Shadow:

> When we were one or two years old we had what we might visualize as a 360-degree personality. Energy radiated out from all parts of our body and all parts of our psyche. A child running is a living globe of energy. . . Behind us we have an invisible bag, and that part of us our parents [and other people significant to us] don't like, we, to keep our parent's love, put in the bag. By the time we go to school our bag is quite large. . . We spend our life until we are twenty deciding what parts of ourselves to put in the bag, and we spend the rest of our lives trying to get them out again. (p. 17)

Jung saw the Shadow as composed of the parts of our personality that were repressed or suppressed for the sake of an ego ideal that was largely defined by others in those early years. It is where we bury all those qualities that don't fit our self-image, the 'inferior' part of our personality that we don't deem compatible with our chosen conscious attitude and emerging persona. Kolodzie-jski (2004) describes the Shadow as containing, "that which is feared and suppressed, that which is considered inappropriate and shunned, that which is unbearable to hold consciously and [is there-fore] denied" (p. 64). Fitzgerald, Oliver and Hoxsey (2010) conceive of it as censored feeling and cognition where our experience and/or expression is judged to not fit with accepted cultural or group norms. Our individual and collective Shadows contain *all* the elements that make us human but never made it into our conscious life, made it to consciousness but were then suppressed or repressed, or that hang around the fringes between the two worlds.

Our Shadow is a natural part of our early development, but it generally becomes an issue for us later in life as it demands more attention and equal time. Jung believed it does so as part of a primal quest from birth to balance opposing images, feelings, and points of view. The Shadow comes into being because our psyche (particularly the unconscious) is constantly striving towards a greater wholeness and a dynamic homeostasis. It is compelled, if you will, to keep bringing into our lives any elements that remain unintegrated—no matter how uncomfortable it may seem at the time. Van Eenwyk (1997) put it this way:

> If the ego cannot, or will not, embrace the complexity of tensions of opposites, preferring instead to embrace sim-plistic views of itself and reality, then individuation stalls until the ego can be shaken from its one-sided perspec-tive. Thus the unconscious . . . confronts the ego with the unrecognized dimensions of its existence, often in the form of dream images and daytime life experiences that are deeply symbolic. (p. 163)

The Shadow is compensatory to the conscious self, always thrust-ing itself onto consciousness, and it is a source of tremendous untapped potential. Our unwillingness to face our Shadow often leads us to make unwise choices and generates conflicts in our lives, relationships, and organizations. The more we repress a part of our-selves, the more the repressed part will return into our lives; the brighter the light, the darker the shadow. The unconscious does not make the distinctions our conscious *ego* does in order to stay within the confines of our self-definition. It does not make distinctions between good and bad; it just is. The developmental progress people make in coaching often unravels in time if its Shadow elements are not addressed. In summary:

The Shadow is
- a natural by-product of the development of our ego,
- where we bury qualities that don't fit our internalized self-image,
- a strategy to retain sufficient safety and love,
- most easily seen in our projections onto others,
- an untapped reservoir of vital energies and potentialities,
- an invitation to keep dying to be reborn, and
- a guide for our unique path to maturation.

In working with Shadow material, help people acknowledge the heavy 'bag' they have dragged around and reduce any associated shame or blame—as both impede their growth. In so doing, invite them to look at how it has shaped them, what they have gained and lost as a result, how they might lighten the load, and what this would make possible that is important to them. Shadow work helps people reclaim more of their personal vitality and energy as well as more of their diversity and richness as a human. This is especially important during periods of transition, and it is important to remember that working with the Shadow often requires people to let go of the very things they have worked hardest to achieve. They come to realize that their efforts to compartmentalize aspects of themselves have failed— and will ultimately always fail—and that the continued repression of any aspect of themselves will lead to an overall loss in their life. They may have to release some cherished images of themselves and/or some of the compromises they have made along the way in order to develop a greater wholeness, vitality and maturity on the other side.

Working with our Shadow can be summarized as follows:

The Shadow is formed

(1) People are born with a whole self → (2) Develop attachment patterns as needed → (3) Form an Ego and a Shadow → (4) Store the untapped energy → (5) Protect the associated wounds through narrative defenses → (6) Project the Shadow onto others → (7) Restrict their identity and develop habituated responses

The Shadow is reintegrated

(7) People access their identity through openings in their stories → (6) Reclaim their projections → (5) Enhance their working model → (4) Release trapped archetypal energy → (3) Integrate their Shadow → (2) Express themselves more fully → (1) Become more whole again

Projections and Dreams

In part, the idea for narrative coaching was born in an epiphany I had while attending a Jungian workshop on group dreaming. The following question came to me while watching a demonstration: "What if the stories we tell during the day have the same function as the dreams we have at night?" The answer was instantly and unequivocally a resounding "Yes," and in that moment everything fell into place. I realized that stories and dreams are both vehicles for our unconscious to sort through issues related to our identity and development. This support's van Eenwyk's (1997) view that, "the unconscious . . . confronts the ego with the unrecognized dimensions of its existence, often in the form of dream images and daytime life experiences that are deeply symbolic" (p. 163). This insight became the nucleus for my dissertation and what was to become narrative coaching. Three aspects of Shadow work played an important role in answering the "What if . . . ?" question above: (1) the 'field' as the primary space and resource for change, (2) the function of the unconscious in narration, and (3) the projective nature of our stories.

"What if the stories we tell during the day have the same function as the dreams we have at night?"

Before I share more about how it all came together, let me back up a few steps. I had already identified rites of passage as the framework for change best suited for a narrative approach to coaching because it addressed both the personal and social dimensions of development and change. I brought together earlier studies of hermeneutics and liberation theology with my doctoral work in narrative structure, critical approaches to identity, and transformative learning and adult development. The result was a new way to help people develop themselves, find their authentic voice and resolve issues that were important to them through using their own stories. In particular, it involved looking at people's stories through the lens of the characters—particularly the way in which the narrator, the characters, and the story were triangulated. I quickly came to see that openings for change in a person were often signaled by changes in his narration. Therefore, I began to track the connections between people's internal and external stories. The initial models evolved to become the Narrative Coaching model (figure 17) and the Narrative Diamond framework for listening (figure 18) as the two cornerstones of this work.

Given that there are both conscious and unconscious elements in our stories, particularly in a context like coaching, it is fair to assume that many of the latter are projections. I came to recognize that many of these projections were channeled through other characters in the stories, just as they are in dreams and in everyday life. Therefore, it made sense to think in terms of a projective space in coaching and the need to identify what gets projected onto which elements in the stories and for what purpose. Page (1999) describes projection as the psyche's capacity to "maintain the distorted self-image that results from splitting off aspects of personality and rendering them seemingly invisible, which acts as a psychological and emotional pressure valve" (p. 17). For example, a coachee's anxiety and desire to set a clearer course in his own career gets projected onto a story about a micro-managing boss. As a narrative coach, I invite people to recover these split-off elements through working with the characters in their stories (and sometimes their dreams as well) and the projected Shadow elements they often represent. From there, they will have a much richer palette to choose from in crafting a new narrative.

People's conflicts with others—in their stories and in their life—are often a reflection of conflicts they have within themselves. As such, many of the issues they ascribe to and project onto others are better seen as characters in their own inner drama. Their individuation and maturation will, in large part, depend on their willingness to withdraw and reintegrate these projections and take full accountability for their stories and their lives. I know from personal experience that this is some of the most challenging yet most vital work we will ever do. In narrative coaching we immerse people in powerful experiences that bring people's projections into the conversational field so the dynamics are more visible and they can be addressed in real time not in abstract terms. For example:

> A recent coachee felt frustrated with the group with whom he was working because he perceived they were in denial about their lack of progress. The turning point in the conversation was when I asked him to say out loud some of the messages he had given them while imagining that they were sitting in front of him. I then asked him to sit in a chair where he had imagined the group sitting and notice his experience *as one of them* receiving this message from their leader. I asked him what he was feeling while he was looking up front at where he had been standing.
>
> I then invited him to return to the front and talk with me about what story he had been telling himself and how the group seemed to him now. In the end he realized that he had projected his own frustrations as the leader of this important project onto the group and excluded himself in how he talked about it in order to avoid his disappointment in himself. By putting himself

back into the story he was able to take back his projections and
move into dialogue with the team to find a new path forward.

This illustrates how symptoms that appear in coachees' relationships, dreams, bodies, etc. (Hollis, 2013) often provide openings to
work in projective spaces and increase people's awakening. As Jung
noted, whatever we deny within, we will seek in the outer world, and
what we do not face within our psyche we will be forced to confront in the outer world. This reinforces Wallin's (2007) insight: "If
a person cannot or will not articulate his own dissociated or dis-
avowed experience he will inevitably evoke it in others, enact it with
others, or embody it" (p. 4). These projective processes are a natural
part of our development. They enable us to separate from more challenging aspects of ourselves until such time as we are ready to take
them back as parts of ourselves. Narrative coaching offers people a
space and a process in which people can begin to take back the work
that only they can do. For example, a coachee takes back his projections onto a narcissistic team member in order to access more of the
selfish aspects of himself—which he can then use to stand up more
often for what he wants.

Our psyches also use dreams to bypass our need for control so
we can retrieve the exiled aspects of ourselves that were left behind
so we can become more whole. Dreams present us with aspects of
our personal and collective unconscious that are not consistent with
our waking, conscious identity but are seeking resolution (see Boa,
1988; Johnson, 1986; Jung, 1964, 1969). As Jung (1970) suggested, "In
each of us there is another who we do not know. He speaks to us in
dreams and tells us how differently he sees us from the way we see
ourselves" (p. 76) and, in so doing, compensates for places where our
stories about ourselves are one-sided. Dreams often contain familiar images, places, and people to aid in our comprehension of this
largely unconscious process and reflect aspects of ourselves as the
dreamer. Johnson (1986) compared a dream to a screen on which the
unconscious projects its inner drama. Breakthroughs in narrative
coaching often occur when people step into their drama—whether
from within a story or the material from a dream—so they can

experience and experiment with less familiar parts of themselves and ways of being.

This brings us back to the insight that helped catalyze the formation of narrative coaching: we can learn a lot about the projective nature of our stories from our understanding of dreams. This notion was echoed by psychotherapist Thomas Moore (2000) who wrote, "[I]t is helpful to approach the narrative as we would a dream; that is, as a composition containing both conscious and unconscious material" (p. 9). In bringing together stories and dreams as projective activities, I kept coming back to the question, "What if the characters in the stories we tell represent parts of ourselves projected onto the 'other' as a means to work through our own development or identity issues?" (and vice versa). If so, would not the changes people are going through somehow be evident in the changes as seen in the characters and relationships in the stories they choose to tell? Narrative coaching is based in the fundamental belief that this is indeed the case, and it offers practices to operationalize this process in working with people and their stories. Let us turn now to one of these developmental practices that is unique to narrative coaching.

"What if the characters in the stories we tell represent parts of ourselves projected onto the 'other' as a means to work through our own development or identity issues?" (and vice versa).

Integrating shadows and strengths

I believe that what we do not digest is laid out somewhere else, into others, the political world, the dreams, the body's symptoms, and becomes literal and outer (and called historical) because it is too hard for us, too opaque, to break open and gain insight.
James Hillman

Narrative coaching blends the appreciative stance of positive psychology and the deconstructive stance of narrative therapy to offer an integrative approach to working with strengths that I believe is more aligned with how people develop. It conceives of people's defenses as a reflection of their lifelong strategies to avoid feeling overwhelmed, alone and/or powerless. These strategies often compensate for and protect those aspects of a person's humanity that sit in Shadow—e.g., using humor to deflect and move away from conflict rather than engaging the archetypal warrior energy in herself to step toward conflict to resolve it. These strategies often served us well enough when we were young, but tend to become important thresholds for development later in life. Coaching involves helping people release their defenses, update their strategies and narratives, and temper key strengths in order to achieve their current aspirations. The more we can leverage people's intrinsically motivated strengths, the more likely they are to sustain the gains they make in coaching. Therefore, it is more productive to tweak one of these strengths than it is to try to adapt extrinsically motivated strengths. Either is definitely preferable over trying to turn a weakness into a strength.

People have evolved their strengths for a variety of reasons, many of which have served them well just as they are. However, strengths are often double-edged swords in that they can cut in our favor or to our detriment. I can think of no better way to make this point than to share what actor Peter Coyote (2014) wrote after the death by suicide of his friend, the actor and comedian Robin Williams:

> Robin's gift could be likened to the fastest thoroughbred racehorse on earth. It had unbeatable endurance, nimbleness, and a huge heart. . . . Sometimes Robin would ride it like a kayaker tearing down whitewater, skimming on the edge of control. We would marvel at his courage, his daring, and his brilliance. But at other times, the horse went where he wanted, and Robin could only hang on for dear life. In the final analysis, what failed Robin was his greatest gift—his imagination.

While we treasure those like Robin who live on the edge, we wish for them and all of us the space to develop further. When people over-use one of their strengths it often leads to an over-reliance on it that is reinforced by others. This creates a feedback loop that often keeps them from deeper gifts and opportunities to grow. One of the first steps in coaching someone around their strength using a narrative approach is to determine its nature. The key is to identify if the strength is more intrinsically motivated (*innate* or *acquired*) or extrinsically motivated (*normative* or *compensatory*). *Innate* refers to strengths like physical or cognitive attributes we were born with. *Acquired* refers to strengths we have developed in order to achieve something that mattered to us. For example, I don't have much *innate* strength as a musician, but I have developed an *acquired* strength as a discerning listener to music because it brings me satisfaction.

Normative refers to strengths related to our gender, nationality, birth order, family or work culture, etc. that we have developed because they are expected of us. *Compensatory* refers to strengths we have developed to deal with perceived shortcomings in other areas, either in ourselves or in the systems in which we operate. For example, I developed a *normative* strength in bridging between the thinking world and the feeling world as the oldest son often called upon to bridge between an engineer (father) and a teacher (mother). I developed a related *compensatory* strength around remaining calm in challenging situations, though I see now how often I've historically used it on behalf of others rather asserting my needs or growing my capacity to stay present to strong emotions. The secret for working with extrinsically motivated strengths is to help the person tap into an underlying intrinsic motivation that can serve as a more sustainable and valued driver for change. The better you are in discerning which type of strength a person wants to address, the more effective you will be in working with it.

Developing a more nuanced view of strengths enables you to better understand what is motivating and resourcing people and how best to approach their development as a coachee. While every strength has its counterpart in Shadow (such as the aggressor to a conciliatory style), it is important to move beyond polarizations and getting stuck in those dualities if we want to support people's development. Thus, strengths and their Shadow are better seen as complementary to one another, two aspects of the same whole. Without its Shadow side, strengths can easily remain one-dimensional and over-used—and therefore less productive. Without being grounded in a currently active strength, Shadows often appear in our lives in ways that are not convenient for us or others. In coaching, help people discover their Shadow and their defenses since it is difficult for them to see either one on their own. For example:

> In coaching someone with a strength in *love of learning*, the coachee came to see how often she over-prepared for meetings (her defense) to avoid her anxiety about being caught off-guard and having to think on her feet (her Shadow).
>
> Conversely, in coaching someone with a strength in *improvisation*, this coachee came to see that he kept rewriting his business plan (his defense) to avoid his anxiety about confronting two key associates who had not delivered on their commitments (his Shadow).

When people are reactively caught up with a strength, they tend to either habitually use it (and, as a result, bypass their defense and the Shadow behind it) or they habitually activate their defense (and bypass their true strength and its Shadow) to ease their anxiety. Either way, they are stuck in a tension between the two and tend not to see any other choices in terms of the stories they can tell and/or the behaviors they can exhibit. Talking about 'weaknesses' is not useful here from a narrative perspective because they are better seen as over- or mis-applied strengths. By not optimally using their strengths, people often miss out on the opportunity to learn more about themselves and increase their range, repertoire and results. To get at this hidden 'gold', people need to soften their defenses and temper the strength using its Shadow. Some of the questions I use include: What are you avoiding by engaging in this defense? What are you afraid might happen if you didn't engage in this defense? What might become possible if you didn't engage it? What would you do then?

I use the following process in coaching—starting with #1 at the bottom—to help people mature a strength using its Shadow. The process is based in the core narrative coaching technique of creating simple yet powerful pivots (see figure 14) with coachees as a guide for their daily choices. The four steps reflect the developmental phases coachees go through as they work on maturing their strengths. Stories are useful here because they provide access to unconscious elements of their stories and glimpses of their Shadow that can be used in the process.

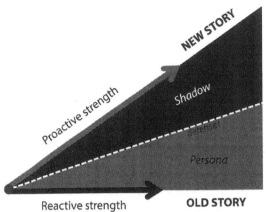

4. **Generative phase of development**
Integrating your Shadow to mature your strength and embody new story

3. **Transformative phase of development**
Experiencing and understanding your Shadow as a resource for your growth and new story

2. **Inquisitive phase of development**
Experiencing and understanding the defenses you use to protect your persona and old story

1. **Reactive phase of development**
Experiencing and understanding the strength you use to perpetuate your persona and old story

Figure 5. *The strength maturation process*

- In the *Situate* phase, people are often in the *Reactive phase* in their use of this strength in line with the old story. Help them to clearly and nonjudgmentally see their habituated response, persona (mask) and underlying narrative.
- In the *Search* phase, people are often in the *Inquisitive phase* as they start to question the old story. Invite them to explore their defenses, their value(s) at risk, and what keeps them from fulfilling their desire.
- In the *Shift* phase, people are often in the *Transformative* phase as they start to imagine a new story. Guide them to engage their defenses to get at the Shadow elements they will need in order to mature their strength and form a new story.
- In the *Sustain* phase, people are often in the *Generative* phase as they hone their new story. Help them integrate their Shadow into their strength so that it matures and experiment with using it more proactively.

Here is an example of this process at work:

1. Cynthia[12], a participant in a recent narrative coaching program, realized she has a strength in compassion but often used sarcasm as a defense when she was feeling unappreciated in the wake of showing concern for others. Her coach Jennifer*, a peer in the program, invited her to share and unpack a couple of recent occurrences as is the norm in dealing with someone in the **Reactive** stage. The aim was to help Cynthia develop a deeper understanding of her current pattern and the stories that went with it.

2. Jennifer helped Cynthia move into the **Inquisitive stage** by inviting her to experience and explore what triggers the defense, what internal or external stories arise in those moments, and what needs to shift to minimize the use of the defense and maximize the efficacy of the strength. Cynthia realized that her defense masked a fear that others would not meet her needs—a fear that had been held in place by a narrative that it was better to not acknowledge that she even had needs. With her coach's help she saw that she often felt caught between caring for others (strength) and judging others (defense) and, therefore, needed to address her defenses if she wanted to grow in this area.

3. Through working with her peer coach, Cynthia moved into the **Transformative stage** where she began to explore her Shadow side and how that might contain some clues that would help her. Together they did some archetypal exercises to help Cynthia identify what energy was missing for her that, if she had access to more of it, would enable her to relax her defense and achieve more of what she wanted (including truer intimacy with people). What emerged were two aspects of her Shadow she wanted to address: being more compassionate with herself and being more direct in asking for what she wanted. Jennifer led her in some exercises in

---

12 The names and identifying information have been altered to preserve anonymity in all the cases in this book.

which she could experiment with how she was now versus how she could be in relation to these two aspects.

4. As the final step, Jennifer led Cynthia in the process described below so she could start to integrate these Shadow elements into her identity and life. To support her in sustaining this growth, they addressed how her internal and external stories would have to shift to better support her progress. As a result of this **Generative stage**, Cynthia reduced her use of sarcasm, tempered her strength so it was more well-rounded, and slowly replaced the old story with a new one in which she was more transparent about what she needed and what she was willing to offer others. As a result, her strength in compassion could be used more consciously and less compulsively, and her stories about herself and others changed accordingly.

The four-step process we go through to mature a strength:
1. Reactive: One of my strengths is . . . However, I get defensive when . . .
2. Inquisitive: Because I . . .This shows up most often as . . .
3. Transformative: I would grow by . . . (incorporating this aspect of my Shadow)
4. Generative: Therefore, I will mature my strength by . . .

Example of how I used the template with a coachee:
1. Reactive: One of my strengths is: *doing whatever it takes to complete a task or project.* However, I get defensive when: *I feel others are holding me back.*
2. Inquisitive: because I *am afraid of not being 'good enough' and letting others down.* This shows up most often as: *impatience and stubbornness.*
3. Transformative: I would grow by: *being more vulnerable.*
4. Generative: Therefore, I will mature my strength by: *managing expectations of myself and from others at the start of any project and throttling back when it is better for our long-term success.*

Coaching is not about fixing anything. Start where people are right now; work with what they have; and build up and out from there. Help them integrate more of their Shadow and its archetypal energies as a source of untapped potential so they can mature their strengths and step into more of their full humanity. You can think of this narrative process as the fire in which steel is tempered to make a sword. It is a process of individuation as a person sharpens their strength and makes it more their own. As Jung described it, this process of individuation is "as much a separation from one's cultural conditioning as it is a unification with the deeper aspects of one's psyche" (Paris, 2011, p. 63). People's most potent strengths and biggest developmental opportunities are both concealed precisely where their weak points seem to be (Carotenuto, 1979). It is also true that many of the behaviors they depend on most to maintain their identities and lives may also be the very things that are holding them back. Most simply, it is about helping people tap more of the energy that has been in them all along.

Coaching is not about fixing anything.

It takes enormous energy to maintain our Shadow aspects. We must be constantly on guard, making certain that nothing sneaks out, making sure that no one can see these hidden aspects of ourselves. Through narrative coaching, people can free up the psychic energy they currently spend on vigilantly keeping watch so they have much more energy for intimacy, creativity, heartfelt compassion, and their own growth (Brehony, 1996). Both contemporary neuroscience research and Eastern spiritual traditions support this quest for a more holistic approach to suffering and freedom. As a developmental approach, narrative coaching is designed to help people: experiment as needed, fail well, and learn from their mistakes; take advantage of zones of proximal learning and development; engage their Shadow so their strengths mature; and create the scaffolding and social systems they need to flourish and bring their new story to life.

II. NARRATIVE PROCESSES

Chapter 4

HOW WE MAKE SENSE AND MEANING

*Our stories go deep, into the archetypal realm, into the genetic code, the
tribal history, the family of origin both known and repressed, as well as
the mythologies we live out on a daily basis.*
James Hollis

Stories have been integral to human communities since the dawn of
time as a primary means of preserving, transmitting and, at times,
imposing or transforming culture. What we believe, to whom we
belong, how we behave and who we become are profoundly shaped
by our stories and the larger narratives in which we live. We use
stories to remember and organize our past, communicate and negotiate our present, and envision and act into our future. They mirror
how our minds develop and operate, and it is through them that we
make sense and meaning of our lives. We listen carefully to people's stories in coaching to gain access to the idiosyncratic narrative
processes by which each person perceives, frames and acts on her
experiences. As we saw in the last chapter, stories support our needs
for order *and* disorder, stability *and* disruption, continuity *and* discontinuity, and coherence *and* change. The creative tension between
the narrative forces in each pair is at the heart of both our struggles
and our growth.

**What we believe, to whom we belong, how we behave
and who we become are profoundly shaped by our stories
and the larger narratives in which we live.**

Barbara Czarniawska (2004) identified three fields that fed into
what became narrative studies and are, therefore, key to understanding narrative coaching: literary theory, humanities, and psychology.

Each of these reflect one of the three pillars of narrative coaching: (1) *narrative psychologies* for supporting people's development and performance as narrators; (2) *narrative structure* for hearing and reconfiguring the material that is narrated; and (3) *narrative practices* for helping coachees bring new stories to life (Drake, 2008b, 2009c). Together, they provide a good working knowledge of how (and why) people tell stories, how to listen to their stories, and how to help them transform their stories. The narrative coaching model integrates them into a unified process of change you can use to deepen your coaching capabilities. Our focus in this chapter is on stories themselves so you can work with them as deeply as you work with your coachees.

Stories are useful in coaching because they
- engage the whole person → improves their attention in and retention from sessions;
- can be accessed at many levels → increases the number of anchors for their change;
- offer new perspectives → improves their potential for mindful empathy and connection;
- catch the edge 'in-between' → enriches their imagination and possibilities;
- mirror the mind's time/space orientation → increases their positional repertoire;
- contain event sequences and problem-solving steps → improves their planning;
- enable us to self-regulate → increases their resilience and resourcefulness;
- make sense and meaning from experience → guides their reconfiguration; and
- clarify, express and advocate for values → increases the impact of their pivots.

In this chapter I will look at the key functions stories serve, provide a simple four-phase structure for stories based in the literature, and talk about how to use each phase in working with people's stories in coaching. I will also explore the importance of narrative structure in narrative coaching. As my colleague Reinhard Stelter has written about on a number of occasions (see Stelter, 2007, 2013; Drake & Stelter, 2014), narrative coaching has a stronger philosophical foundation than most other approaches because of its focus on the building blocks of human experience and development at individual and collective levels. There are strong parallels between the four elements of narrative structure and function, the four phases in narrative coaching, and the four phases of transition and development for the person being coached which will be explored throughout the book. I will start by defining some of the key terms.

Key terms

Pekka Tammi (2005) identified three ways to conceptualize narrative in general: (1) as discourse; (2) as speech act; and (3) as cognitive schema. You can see this in narrative coaching with our interest in (1) the language people use in their stories, (2) the way in which they tell their stories in the context of coaching, and (3) what the story reveals about how they see themselves and the world. It is related to our curiosity about the connections between the cognitive, discursive, and dispositional aspects of coachees' narratives (Gergen & Gergen, 2006) as reflected in their stories. It is why we pay attention not only to each of the three conceptualizations, but also to how they are in relation with one another. For example: What is the coachee leaving out of the story she is telling you as her coach? What discrepancies do you notice between how she seems to view herself and the words she uses in her stories? As we look at these three conceptualizations, it is important to distinguish between "narrative" and "story" as the terms are most commonly used in narrative coaching—even as we acknowledge that the word "story" has to stretch across a wide variety of uses in everyday interactions.

I predominantly use *narrative* to refer to broader patterns and *story* for specific instances, such that stories (for example, about my boss) can be seen as an expression of a larger narrative (about authority figures). A narrative is a socially- and contextually-constructed communication *structure* marked by temporality and causality, plot and purpose, that enables meaning- and sense-making for those involved. A story is an episodic *form* of communication within oneself or with others that has both conscious and unconscious elements. It has certain culturally-defined properties and serves descriptive and/or interactive purposes. Much of what we hear in coaching are actually story fragments—what narrative scholar David Boje (2001) calls "antenarratives"—which coachees use as they are forming a more complete story or set of stories about their situation. The stories they share provide the access and material you need to help them bring about change and growth in their lives. In calling this work "narrative coaching"—as opposed to "story coaching"—I established the field as distinct from but on par with narrative therapy as a recognized practice modality.

Mattingly (1998) describes a story as a "rhetorical structure which is meant to persuade, to provide a perspective on what happened as part of telling what happened" (p. 26). However, I have found great value in the notion of *invitational rhetoric* because it provides a healthy balance for the over-emphasis on *persuasive rhetoric* in our culture. It is not about dissuading people of their current narration, but rather about helping them to accept it for what it is, assess its consequences and explore what else might be possible. Invitational rhetoric (Foss & Foss, 2003) is characterized by five assumptions which align beautifully with narrative coaching:

> (1) the purpose of communicating is to gain understanding; (2) the speaker and the audience are equal; (3) different perspectives constitute valuable resources; (4) change happens when people choose to change themselves; and (5) all participants are willing to be changed by the interaction. (pp. 9–10)

To make the most of stories that emerge within an invitational stance, it helps to have a good understanding of the functions and structure of people's stories.

Understanding the functions of stories

Leaving home isn't really completed until we create a new center.
James Hollis

Narrative coaches are keenly interested in the stories that people tell about their lives because "there is an intimate connection between the ways in which people construe themselves and the way in which they are likely to behave" (Novitz, 1997, p. 146). Hanninen (2004) describes this movement between our inner narrative, told stories and lived stories as "narrative circulation." Our role as coaches is to notice where the flow is blocked and impinging on the results the coachee is seeking. This notion of circulation echoes findings from social psychologists who posit that our expectations, explanations and behaviors all strongly affect one another (Sherman, et al., 1981). Our actions, therefore, can be understood as enacted narratives (MacIntyre, (1981). Stories are about someone trying to do something, what happens to them and others as a result, and what sense and meaning they make of it. In this sense we can think about the function of stories at three levels: our *intention* (conscious or otherwise) for sharing this story this way in this moment; our *impact* (intended or unintended) of telling this story on ourselves and others; and our *interpretation* (spoken or unspoken) of the impact and our efforts.

Coaching often involves helping people to reconcile the gaps or tensions between two or more stories. Although both coaches and coachees may be tempted to perfectly align these stories in working together, it is important to remember that it is the gap or tension between them that most often provides the catalyst for growth (Pearce & Pearce, 2001). It comes when coachees' usual stories prove to be incomplete and/or ineffective and they must face the resulting discrepancy between their verbalized concepts of themselves, their felt awareness of themselves (Fritz S. Perls et al., 1994/1951) and/or their impact on others. Therefore, invite coachees to step into the discomfort of these gaps or tensions in search of deeper truths about themselves, their lives and their stories. In so doing, you will likely encounter two of the key functions of their stories: to distance themselves from uncomfortable pieces of their underlying narrative until they were ready to deal with them, and to give them clues about where to find the doorway to their growth (McLeod, 2006).

Understanding the core functions of narratives will help you to better understand what coachees are consciously or unconsciously trying to accomplish with their stories. You can often get a sense for this by noticing what role they are implicitly or explicitly asking you to take up as they tell them and/or what emotions or responses they are evoking in you as they do. Sometimes I will take up that role to provide the resonance they need to embark on the journey (e.g., "I care for you") or provide a sense of dissonance by showing them a new way it can be played (e.g., "I will show you I care without having to rescue you"). Sometimes I will not take up a role, but instead invite them to search inside themselves for that character and capability (e.g., "Yes, I've been in that place myself, and I'm more interested right now on what you can draw from in your own experience"). Which stance you take depends on what seems most useful for the coachee's development.

Stories, and the larger narratives they represent, incorporate five primary elements (K. J. Gergen, 1994), underlined below—each of which serves a vital function (Drake, 2003, 2007). I have paired (and italicized) each of Konstantin Stanislavsky's (1936/1989) essential questions for actors with one of the five functions. They are written from the perspective of a coachee as a character seeking to more fully understand his stories and his place in them. In training actors, Stanislavsky believed that characters are always coming from somewhere toward the stage and heading somewhere when they leave. I operate from the same belief in that while I focus mostly on stories that are 'on the stage' in a coaching session or workshop, I am always curious about the backstory and the epilogue. Where did the coachee come from and where are they headed next? You can use these five functions in listening to coachees' stories and discerning where to focus their attention as they seek to make changes.

Five functions of stories

Stable identities
What are your circumstances (physical and non-physical)?
Stories help people orient themselves in their environment, shape how they interact with others, and address the question: To whom do I belong?

Ordered events
Who are you as a character?
Stories help people orient themselves in time, bring together the past, present and future in a meaningful way, and address the questions: Who have I been? Who am I? Who am I becoming?

Valued endpoints
What do you want? What are you seeking?
Stories help people orient themselves relative to their values, inspire them to move toward what brings them meaning and fulfillment, and address the question: How do I decide what is right? What is important?

Demarcation signs
What are the obstacles (physical and non-physical) in your way?
Stories help people orient themselves in the midst of disruptions to the status quo, notice and step into the openings for growth they provide, and address the question: Where do I stand?

Causal linkages
Given the above, what would you do and why?
Stories help people emplot themselves and others within larger narratives in ways that make sense and provide meaning, understand power and motivation, and address the questions: Why are things the way they are? Why do I do what I do?

The following story illustrates one of these functions (valued end-points) as it played out in a coaching conversation.

> One of my early questions of Tom* was, "How did you come to be a lawyer?" In answering, he shared several stories about Bruce*, a lawyer who had been a mentor for him and the other kids in his neighborhood. As a result of Bruce's influence, Tom had carried into adulthood a strong value for justice and fairness and he eventually chose a career in law himself. As he and I moved from these stories to the present day—and stories of Tom's work in coaching other lawyers and developing new modes of mediation—there emerged a moment when it seemed important for the two sets of stories to meet.
>
> I said to Tom, "I bet Bruce would be really proud of you right now." In the profound pause that ensued, Tom was able to recognize for the first time a central narrative thread that ran through his life and to be witnessed in that recognition.

Understanding the five functions will help both you and your coachees better understand what they are trying to accomplish with their stories and to listen to them in new ways. The same is true for understanding how their stories are structured.

Understanding the structure of stories

The way we describe our lives and understand them is ultimately and inextricably connected to the way we live them.
Mandy Aftel

The importance of understanding how stories are structured can be seen in Ted Sarbin's (1986a) notion of the "narratory principle" according to which "human beings think, perceive, imagine, interact and make moral choices according to narrative structures" (p. 9), and in David Carr's (1986) argument that narrative is a "primary way of organizing and giving coherence to our experience" (p. 65). The stories we hear in coaching are often profoundly, albeit unconsciously, shaped by narrative structures formed early in life through a wide array of internal and external influences. They are also embedded in a complex network of narratives that tend to either reinforce or challenge these structures. You can think of the structure of people's stories as a skeleton upon which the details are hung. These skeletons set the tone and direction for the way in which people narrate their experiences and live their lives. Over time we reinforce our own constructed reality by finding the events that fit the skeleton convenient for us to believe (Schank, 1990). We also tend to overlook (or reframe) events that are inconvenient truths for us. Both are addressed in narrative coaching as we track the subtleties of the story material, their skeletons and larger narrative patterns.

According to renowned screenwriter Robert McKee (1997), the energy of the protagonist's desire forms the Spine of a story as its primary unifying force. He and others describe how stories can be seen in terms of a three-act structure that reflects our efforts to: (1) respond to inciting incidents that throw our life out of balance or equilibrium; (2) identify the object of our desire that we believe will restore the balance; and (3) overcome a series of barriers in pursuit of that object until there is a resolution (see also Burke, 1969; Czarniawska, 1998, 2004; Ricoeur, 1984; Todorov, 1971/1977; Vogler, 1998; H. White, 1981). The Spine reflects the clash between the *epistemic stance* (what occurs) and the *deontic stance* (what the protagonist values and/or believes should occur) (Bruner & Luciarello, 1989). Interestingly, protagonists often discover in the end that what they first sought was only a proxy for what they truly desired and what they sought outside themselves was within them all along. All the more reason to be patient and let the stories unfold . . .

Interestingly, protagonists often discover in the end that what they first sought was only a proxy for what they truly desired and what they sought outside themselves was within them all along.

It is not uncommon in books and movies for the story to end when the original narrative arc has been resolved. There is often a sense at the end where the character is heading next. To pursue it much further would be anticlimactic and require the beginning of a whole new arc. Coaching is different in that where the characters (coachees) head next is of the utmost importance to us. This is why I included a fourth act (see figure 6) as I developed the narrative coaching model. It accounts for the character's need to sustain and integrate the results from the first three acts. I also added the spiral to acknowledge the fact that narration is an ongoing and iterative process. The respective phase in the narrative coaching process is listed for each quadrant so you can begin to see the connections between the structure of a story and the structure of this process. The next section looks at these four acts in more detail and features a case story to illustrate the model in action.

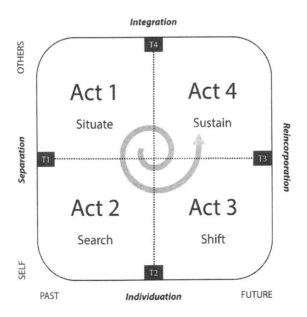

Figure 6. *The four acts of narrative coaching*

Working with stories in coaching

We dance round in a ring and suppose,
But the secret sits in the middle and knows.
Robert Frost

Jerome Bruner (1986, 1990) suggested that our stories are defined by a *landscape of action* which answers the epistemic question of what happened (e.g., the scene and setting; what the protagonist and other actors do in a given situation; and the sequential unfolding of the event) and a *landscape of consciousness* which addresses the deontic question of what it means (e.g., emotions, beliefs and intentions; what the protagonist believes and feels about the situation; and the internal responses of the protagonist and others) (Ochs & Capps, 1996). By integrating the material from these two landscapes, people can construct a full narrative account of their experiences. As coaches, we are curious about how the two landscapes affect each other and how they shape coachees' "storyworlds" (McLeod, 2004). There have been a number of attempts to identify the elements and structure of a well-formed narrative as well (see Burke, 1969; Czarniawska, 1998, 2004; Ricoeur, 1984; Todorov, 1971/1977; Vogler, 1998; H. White, 1981). They have occurred in fields such as historiography (see Mink, 1969), linguistics (see Labov, 1982; Mandler, 1984), literary theory (see Frye, 1957; Scholes & Kellogg, 1966), and semiotics (see Propp, 1968; Rimmon-Kenan, 1983).

In developing the narrative coaching model and process, I drew in particular on Burke's (1969) work on dramatism as the search for a person's motive as the driver of their narratives. His Pentad offered five questions you can use in unpacking stories, their structure and their motive: "what was done (act), when and where it was done (scene), who did it (agent), how he did it (agency), and why (purpose)" (Burke, 1969, p. xv). I (2008b) added the coda (Bruner, 2002) as a sixth element to address the action orientation in coaching and the reincorporation phase in coachees' development. Other key sources for the initial frameworks included: Stein and Glenn's (1979) grammatical structure for stories, Ollerenshaw and Creswell's (2002) problem-solution narrative structure approach, McKee's (1997, 2004) story elements in screenwriting and Campbell's (1968, 1973) mythological narratives. Let's look at each of the four acts in a story in more detail in leading up to the narrative coaching model itself.

Act 1: Situate

Situate incorporates the *setting* (Stein and Glenn, 1979; Ollerenshaw and Creswell, 2002), the *scene* (Burke, 1969), in which there is a protagonist (Stein & Glenn, 1979), and an *agent* (Burke, 1969) about whom we care. A story's setting is "four-dimensional: period, duration, location, level of conflict" (McKee, 1997, p. 68). Other elements and characters are also introduced, often foreshadowing events to come. What turns a routine sequence of events into a story and sets it in motion is often an inciting incident, a disruption in the status quo, which upsets the balance of forces in his life. This reversal in circumstances—what Aristotle saw as a *peripeteia*—forces him to conceive of what will put it back into balance (the object of desire). The story describes the protagonist's efforts to come to terms with the breach and its consequences (Bruner, 1986, 2002; Riessman, 1993) and get the situation back to what he perceives as 'normal' (Bruner 2002). The conflict that emerges is the engine of a narrative. It is often in these gaps—where the objective realities of the world do not conform to the subjective assumptions and expectations of the character (McKee, 2004; Ochs & Capps, 1996)—which serve as the catalyst to embark on a search (Ibarra & Linebeck, 2005).

Act 2: Search

Search involves an *act* (Burke, 1969), including the protagonist's internal *reaction* or *response* (Stein and Glenn), as she attempts to deal with the situation created by the *initiating event* (Stein and Glenn). It involves a search to determine what she believes will restore the lost equilibrium and put her life back into balance if it is achieved; and it defines the spine of the story. Along the way, she will often be challenged to release old attachments for the sake of making progress with the search. As McKee's (1997) noted, "The more powerful and complex the forces of antagonism opposing the character, the more completely realized the character and story must become" (p. 317). Trials and tribulations, encounters with individual and collective shadows, the sense of being 'in-between', and the appearance of allies and guides are common here. This is important in coaching as we gauge how deeply to work with coachees on a given issue. Once people become clear about their prevailing "attitude" (an element Burke later added to his Pentad to tie the other five together) and what is truly at stake for them, they can move on to explore how to make the necessary shift(s).

Act 3: Shift

Shift involves what Burke (1969) referred to as the *purpose*, and it reflects the actions taken by the protagonist to deal with the search (Stein and Glenn; Ollerenshaw and Creswell). It is about what happens to the protagonist (e.g., his sense of self, mental models, expectations, narrative strategies) as a result of his journey to this point. People often become aware of deeper, often unconscious, desires in this phase and find themselves being led in new directions as a result. It is often found where people must face the greatest challenge, answer the most essential question, or make the hardest choice. This obstacle is often the very thing they have feared the most, and yet more often than not it ends up being the doorway to their greatest gift. It is at these junctures in the story that we get to see their true character and if they can convert what they have been through into growth (Yanno, 2006). It is important to remember, however, that the 'gift' may or may not be the one they were originally seeking (McKee 1997, 2004). This phase is about identifying what is being asked of the person, and inviting him to explore and experiment with how to put it into action. Once this becomes clear, they can move into the final phase to enact what has been discovered and developed.

Act 4: Sustain

Sustain involves a sense of *agency* (Burke, 1969) in responding to the consequences of the protagonist's actions and the often climactic process by which she reaches a resolution. This phase is marked by the person's return to the outer world bearing the gifts of her journey, during which she will receive support from some and further challenge from others. This phase is crucial because it is far easier for people to accomplish and sustain their new stories if they have or can create a supportive collective context (Rappaport, 1995). To be successful, the person will need sufficient scaffolding to support her emerging new narratives. The good news is that a major source of this scaffolding can be found in the raw material in people's own stories (Drake, 2003, 2005; Gergen & Gergen, 2006). Providing the necessary scaffolding enables coachees to experience and practice what it would be like to live with their new story and to develop themselves such that it becomes part of who they are. And the spiral comes full circle and begins again . . .

The Spiral

The spiral reflects the moral of the story (Stein and Glenn)—what Bruner (2002) called the "coda." It serves as a platform for new awareness and new action, and it has benefits for both the characters and the audience. In coaching, the spiral is a reminder to not worry too much about which story a coachee chooses to tell in a session because most any story offers a door into the presenting issue. Openly receive whatever is presented and invite it into the field, trusting that everything you need is there to move forward. The spiral is also a reminder to maintain a dual focus on the stories *and* the larger narratives they reflect, the issue at hand *and* the pattern it reflects. Lastly, the spiral is a reminder to patiently circle the tree even as you are prepared to step into openings for growth at any point in the process. The deeper the change a person is seeking in coaching, the more often he may need to spiral through the issue in order to get to its core and develop new patterns. The following case story offers a look at how the four elements of narrative structure and the four phases of the narrative coaching process were used in a single session.

Case story

Act 1: Situate: I worked with a medium sized service organization that was experiencing turbulence in the wake of the sudden departure of the CEO. Nancy* was a senior manager in her late 50s who was increasingly being called on to step up and advocate for the management team and the staff in the midst of this unexpected leadership vacuum. She was resisting these pleas even though she was not clear why she was doing so. The purpose for our session was to help her decide what she wanted to do about the current situation.

> Nancy's first story was about coaching a young staff member who felt stuck in not knowing what to do about a client's difficult legal situation. What struck me about this story was her mentoring of her new staff member about how to "get out of the middle." It echoed the sense of feeling stuck that she herself faced as she was caught between those who wanted her to step in and her own uncertainty about what was hers to do.

Act 2: Search: At one level, Nancy seemed to be quite willing to let things drift along as they had always been. However, parallel stories emerged about how she had responded at earlier times in her life when she faced big changes, e.g., stepping into new roles when she divorced and more recently as her children moved away from home. This began to open the conversation to larger themes at play in her life and to what was calling her now.

> Nancy spoke about her young adult children as establishing their own lives and continuing to evolve a new relationship with their mother. She saw herself at a turning point with them. The poignancy of this phase in her life also came across through a

story about her return to her alma mater to take some classes and soon finding herself talking with young women who "didn't know the history of what went on here."

She said that she wanted to be able to build relationships at work on her own terms before the "huge stereotype of older women gets in the way." She expresses her ambivalence about this transition, "because I'm older than everyone, there's an expectation about knowing things in a way that I don't think of myself as knowing things . . . . But I see myself as somebody at the table, like everybody else at the table, and you're just tossing out ideas. . . . You know that feeling of just being peers . . . and now that's not true. Now that's not true." This was said with a sense of sadness and loss, as often is the case in this phase as people confront that which is ebbing away in order to prepare for what is to come next.

Act 3: Shift: Her "object of desire" emerged through an inquiry about role models that yielded stories about the pioneering women in her family of origin. She saw herself as entering a time in her life and her career that called for redefinition, but she wasn't sure what that looked like. She described herself as "betwixt and between," and "not quite sure what it meant to be 58". She became aware that her lingering uncertainty reflected the fact that she was being asked to choose a new place for herself at work at the same time she was seeking a new place in her own life. We returned to the stories of the elder women who somehow seemed important for her at this juncture.

She remarked at one point, "I have great role models going into old, old age. We have a very strong Irish woman connection through the generations in my family and a strong ongoing community in our family, particularly through my aunts." She regaled me with some of the powerful tales they told her over the years.

I asked her near the end, "If you were to take these older women as your council of elders, how would that change what you did at work?" She responded that she had taken them in as her council and they were with her all the time as wise voices even when they were not nearby. She then went back into a story she had mentioned before, but this time she told it in more detail. In so doing, she was able to break through to the heart of her dilemma about what role to play at this critical time of change in her life and in her organization.

"There was a ritual in my family, and I don't even know if it was conscious, but the women in the family would get together and the tea would come out. They would sit around the table and they would drink tea. That was always the first question when I came in the door, 'Would you have a cup of tea? Can I fix you a cup of tea, darling'?

And you knew that you had been accepted, that you had passed from childhood into a new status as a young woman, when you were invited to the table for tea. It was a huge honor for my daughter when it was her turn, though she didn't really appreciate it until she was older. That's one of the family rites."

[Long pause…] **"It is my turn to serve tea, isn't it?"**

And with that insight, tears came to her eyes. She realized that while she was not "just one of the gang" anymore as the most senior member of the management team, she still was free to make her own choice. In recognizing that "it's my turn now to be an elder," she realized that all of her life she had been the youngest (the last of 36 cousins, for example).

"I am truly a youngest child and only know in an academic sense what an oldest does—and I am an oldest now."

She realized that the challenge at work was emblematic of a much larger transformation in her life. From this new narrative about herself she could begin to explore what being an oldest would look like for her.

Act 4: Sustain: After the session, she decided not to take on the role as interim leader, but to use her experience to help her peers on the management team move through the crisis. While our formal work was done, I stayed in touch as part of a larger project. She remained content that she had made the right choice and seemed to have found a new vitality for work.

As the curtain comes down on the final act for this chapter, I hope it has given you a clear sense of how stories help us make sense and meaning. By introducing the four acts of a story, the groundwork has been laid for the basic structure that underpins the narrative formulation model, the change/transition model and narrative coaching model itself. We looked at the differences between narratives and stories and why both are so important in coaching. You will be more adept at listening to people' stories if you have a strong sense of how narratives and stories are structured and what functions they serve. It enhances your ability to (1) track the arc of people's stories *and* notice the often subtle, yet significant, openings for change; (2) notice what is present in their stories in greater detail *and* what is absent yet yearning to be heard; and (3) connect more deeply with the person brave enough to bring their stories into the room *and* attend more closely to the unfolding of the stories themselves. What are they each trying to say?

Chapter 5

HOW WE CREATE STORIES

Part of what separates a story from a mere chronicle is the presence of a plot. Emplotment is the process by which we connect events and experiences in such a way that they make sense and provide meaning (Hermans & Kempen, 1993; Polkinghorne, 1988). While some well-plotted stories are linked to self-defining memories and have strong neural ties, stories are not stored in our minds as if they are folders in a filing cabinet. They are assembled and expressed to suit our needs in the moment. As such, there is not a singular true story, but rather, a constellation of situated retellings. Narrative coaches are interested in the nuances of a particular telling and the broader constellation of which it is a part. This applies to both the coachees' narration (the stories they tell us) and the coach's formulation (the stories we tell ourselves about their narration, what we think it means and what should be done as a result). In both cases, how people act is closely linked to the stories they choose to tell. Coaching is most effective when there is an alignment between narration and formulation, though this may include both resonance and dissonance in support of the change process.

As such, there is not a singular true story, but rather, a constellation of situated retellings.

The aim in coaching is to help people discover frames which yield healthier emplotment strategies and better results—not so much to do "story repair" (Crossley, 2002). In so doing, both coaches and coachees can ask themselves questions such as: How is your frame serving you? Not serving you? What are you afraid will happen if you let that frame go? What other frames would open up important new perspectives for you? In our Labs, we invite coaches to notice their formulation patterns, deconstruct their implicit assumptions and experiment with a more collaborative narrative process driven by the shared experience more than their professional discourse. The first half of this chapter looks at narration through the lenses of emplotment and authoring. The second half looks at formulation from a narrative perspective and offers a framework and a case story on how to use it. The chapter ends with a look at the Three Windows you can use to increase your mastery in this area.

Understanding narration

As we've seen, people use stories to situate themselves in time and space, and coaching can help them re-situate themselves in service of new realities or aspirations. Their narration can be seen through two lenses in coaching: *emplotment*, the way they organize their stories (structure), and *authoring*, how and why they tell them (function). Charon (2006) writes about this distinction in terms of the "autobiographical gap" between the narrator-who-speaks (authoring) and the protagonist-who-acts (emplotment). It can be quite fruitful for coachees to explore this gap between their roles as *subjective author* and *objective actor* in order to "re-story" an experience or sense of themselves they no longer find sufficient or satisfying (Kenyon & Randall, 1997). This requires people to first loosen the grip of an existing narrative as it is emplotted and authored to make more space—and then to rearrange, replace and/or reframe certain aspects to form a new one.

However, it is important to do so from a place of respect for coachees' current patterns because as Mattingly (1998) points out, "emplotments which disregard [their current] narrative sense-making are unlikely to succeed" (p. 74). One of your best gifts to coachees is to reflect back to them what you are hearing and observing in terms of their narration (voiced or not) and its consequences. This is important because their explanations, expectations, and enactments all strongly affect one another (S. J. Sherman, Skov, Hervitz, & Stock, 1981) and their overall ability to author their lives. For example, "I see the world like this and therefore expect this to happen, which is why I must do this". Development can be seen as a progressive alignment of peoples' explanatory narratives, anticipatory narratives and participatory narratives along a matured plotline. Helping coachees become aware of and address the reinforcing causal loops in their narration is critical to their success in coaching.

Plots reflect the way that people organize the elements of their stories in time (to provide coherence) and space (to provide direction), and the criteria they use to decide which events and interpretations will be included in the story (to further its purpose) (Polkinghorne, 1995). Plots link these elements together by sequencing and situating events in an unfolding movement culminating in a conclusion (Mishler, 2000). In forging a plot, narrators build a "theory of events" (Foucault, 1965), which then guides and justifies their subsequent actions. People selectively recall past behaviors to make them consistent with their current attitudes. "This can be an issue for people when their past behavior is seen as irrevocable, leaving them with a sense that they cannot undo what has been done" (Ross & Conway, 1986, p. 129). When that is the case, these persistent emplotment patterns tend to become attractors such that similar events are drawn into the same frame and may eventually become self-fulfilling prophecies.

Narration can also be seen as "authoring" in referring to the person who is telling the story and the purpose for which it is being told. Therefore, pay attention to how the coachee's narration is affecting her, you and the conversation. Some of the specific things to look for include: Does the coachee (1) tell his story in the first or third person; (2) portray himself as an active author or a more passive actor; (3) take accountability for his actions in the story and his choices in how he tells it; and/or (4) empathize with other positions in his story and reflect on his own? It is important to note here, as Michael White (2007) did, that this gap is accentuated by the fact that much of what goes into people's narration is "absent but implicit". This notion is based on Derrida's idea that how we make sense and meaning of things depends on the distinctions we make between what is presented to us (privileged meaning) and what is left out (subjugated meaning). For example, a coachee realizes that the posture, voice and frame he is using to describe his situation are more a reflection of his familial and cultural heritage than his actual experience in the moment.

In working with their narration, many coachees start to realize that the development of their lives and the development of their plots as narrated are often two distinct unfoldings (Hillman, 1975a), and their growth often comes at points where there are significant gaps between the two. In my experience, they need to be accountable as both author of and actor before they can close these gaps and form a new story about themselves that is more mature, intelligible, and purposeful (Strupp & Binder, 1984). It is about becoming increasingly able to critique the plots and genres (e.g., tragedy, comedy, drama) by which they narrate their experiences and live their lives, individuate in relation to the larger narratives in which they operate, and experiment with new plots in support of their growth (Hillman, 1975b; Randall, 1995). This is why we are keen to understand coachees as authors, particularly in terms of what coachees are trying to accomplish within themselves and with others by narrating their story as they do.

Narrative coaching is about inviting people to take more experiential freedom *and* more existential accountability for their narration and subsequent action. This is true for coaches and their formulation as well. Interestingly, there is often a strong parallel between the two types of stories in coaching sessions as each is formed in part by the stories of the other. For example, their stories might coalesce around a frame of the coachee as a "victim" in a mutually reinforcing loop. Conversely, the coachee might come to a place where she releases that frame for herself and rebuffs the coach's efforts to continue down that path. As coaches, our aim is not for people to simply replace one story with another, but to invite them to "participate in the continuous process of creating and transforming meaning" (K. J. Gergen, 1994, p. 245). We can help them become more adept and accountable in doing so by mindfully attending to our own formulation.

Understanding formulation

Beware of the stories you tell yourself—for you will surely be lived by them.
adapted from William Shakespeare

Formulation can be seen as our explanatory accounts of what is happening in coaching, what we should say and do (and why), and what we believe will happen as a result. Formulation tradition-ally referred to the stories that professionals such as therapists and doctors formed as *experts at a distance*. However, we will look instead at formulation as *expertise in relationship* as seen from a narrative and coaching perspective. I will focus on how coaches formulate, even as I acknowledge that the formulations in coaching sessions are also influenced by the stories coachees tell themselves about being coached, the stories the two of them co-create in and across sessions, and the stories of key stakeholders about the whole process. Formu-lation needs to be done systemically because the stories both parties bring to coaching are inseparable from the context in which they are performed, lived, and held inside and outside of the session (Boje, 1998; Rossiter, 1999). Formulation is ultimately a shared and symbi-otic framework of understanding that has major implications for the trajectory and efficacy of coaching.

The coachee and the coach are in a co-constructive process in the moment and across the engagement in which their two narra-tive worlds temporarily coalesce (McMahon & Patton, 2006). This requires coaches to be critically aware of their own systems of influ-ence and how these play out in the coaching process and to develop the discipline to continuously monitor their internal and external narration. I find Casement's (1991) question helpful in this regard as a reminder of the collaborative nature of formulation: "Who is putting what into the . . . space, at this moment, and why?" (p. 27). We use the image of a bird circling a tree in narrative coaching to reflect the recursive nature of formulation (and narration), and the value of checking in on where we have arrived in the conversation and why. As Kierkegaard observed, our life is lived forward—encounter by encounter—but our sense of ourselves and what we are doing and saying is constructed in retrospect. It is only when we tell a story that we "retrace forward what we have already traced backward" (Ricouer, 1984, p. 87).

Before introducing the narrative formulation framework, let's look at the more traditional approach as a point of comparison. Louis Cozolino (2004) offers a useful synopsis of the traditional approach that provides a good jumping off point for this discussion. He identified four tools to guide therapeutic practice that I find germane to coaching as well—theoretical orientation, case conceptualization, treatment plan, and case notes—each of which shapes the one that follows. The case conceptualization includes: "(1) a description of presenting problems, symptoms, and possible diagnoses; (2) a theory or theories accounting for how and why the problems have arisen and evolved over time; and (3) a general description of how problems are addressed and cured" (p. 35). This classic approach to formulation is useful to a point as a way of structuring one's thinking as a coach, but it focuses too much on the need for the coach to understand as the basis for progress. I would suggest that a more complete model would also account for the emergent and eclectic nature of our formulations, the connections to forces outside the coaching conversations that shape/are shaped by the process, and the fact that coachees are formulating both personally and collaboratively with the coach.

This calls for moving beyond the traditional notions of formulation as the detached prognosis of the expert upon which decisions are made about how best to proceed. To be clear, it is about expanding and repositioning the role of expertise, not banishing it from the conversation. A narrative approach to formulation de-emphasizes the coach's analysis and assessment as the primary sources for formulation to make more space for the coachee's experience and for guidance from the narrative material as it emerges. Formulation is always a 'work in progress.' A first step in making more conscious and attuned choices in your formulation as a coach is to recognize your reactions and actions in sessions—and reflect on the stories on which they are based. Where are your comfort zones? What are your habits? Your blindspots? How do you tend to participate in the stories coachees tell you? What we are aiming for in our formulation is to provide enough structure and direction for the coaching conversation without overly imposing our own frames or needs.

Narrative formulation incorporates the same three elements as the case conceptualization method, but does so with more equity and fluidity. Most importantly, it shifts the emphasis from the coach and the professional discourse to the coachee and the coaching dialogue. As a result, it helps practitioners address four of the limitations with traditional notions of formulation and their tendency to: (1) privilege professional expertise; (2) overemphasize the past; (3) simplify causality; and (4) take a mechanistic view. It does so by offering an approach to formulation that (1) draws on multiple sources of expertise; (2) incorporates the past, present, and future; (3) presumes various streams of causality; and (4) takes a holistic view. Formulation is a dynamic and mutual process of discovering what seems true and workable in coaching conversations as a platform for change. It is embedded *in* rather than detached *from* their experience in sessions; progress is not exclusively dependent on diagnosis; and it is drawn from and requires multiple sources.

Formulation is a dynamic and mutual process of discovering what seems true and workable in coaching conversations as a platform for change.

Let us look at a brief case synopsis with this view of formulation in mind. Before you read the following description of a brief encounter with a potential coachee, imagine for a minute that it is *your* phone that is ringing. How would you feel? What comes up for you? What would you most likely say and do? Why?

> Robert*, a quiet middle-aged man, calls your office saying that he may be interested in working with you as a coach. He has tried for six months to get a new job but, even with his credentials, he

has yet to find one. Being out of work has created friction with his wife and he has noticed a lack of energy lately. However, he is also adamant that he doesn't need to "see a shrink" because he knows that all he needs is to find a new job. In speaking with him, you get a sense that he may be somewhat depressed.

You ponder whether to take him on as a coachee or refer him to someone else. As you ponder, the formulation process has already begun. You and Robert are each forming an initial story about the other and already deciding, albeit largely unconsciously, whether or not to work together.

However, at this point, what do you or Robert really understand about why he can't find work, what he truly needs, and how best to serve him? What stories did you already make up about him? About how you would coach him? How were these influenced by your background, training, approach, and/or life experience? Is his a deep personal issue—for which a psychotherapist may be called for? Did his wife stop having sex with him when he lost his job because in her eyes his masculinity and status dropped—and a couples' counselor would be useful? Is his skill set no longer marketable in his geographic area—and he needs a recruiter to help him relocate? Does he need broader help on vision setting and goal attainment from a life coach? Is he having an existential midlife crisis for which a spiritual director would be appropriate? And this is for just one of the facets of the presenting story; it does not address the possibilities related to what is perceived as depression, for example. Even with this small anecdote we can see some of the issues related to formulation and a reminder to not rush in with our interpretations as coaches.

I use the following formulation model in teaching this work to professionals around the world. It is based in the same four-phase structure as the coaching model to reflect the need for your formulation to stay in sync with the coachee's developmental journey. It requires close attention to both people's internal and external narration as well as its impact on the session and the outcomes for the coachee. The focus is on what is actually happening in the coaching conversation rather than your beliefs about where it should be going and why. Page (1999) provides a wonderful description of the spirit of this approach:

> The path is one of mindfulness more than a master plan, seeking clarity more than certainty. Formulation is less about providing expert judgment and more about increasing the collective ability among coaches and coachees to notice what is going on, the stories they are telling themselves and others about it, and the possibility for new options at both the narrative and behavioral levels. (p. 58)

Using a narrative approach to formulation

Narrative formulation is as much a call to continuous self-reflection and self-regulation as it is a construct for the content of your professional narration. Your efficacy as a coach is affected by your ability to do both as you make sense of what is happening in sessions and respond accordingly. Most coachees appreciate having a clear frame for their sessions as it offers them a sense of safety and a structure to guide them as they tell their stories. At the same time, these frames can limit the emergent storytelling possibilities in ways that are detrimental to coachees if they are adhered to rigidly. In part, this is why I focus on the relational field rather than a linear process and on patterns as well as particulars in people's stories. I believe that:

> Many of our challenges in formulation are a result of the tension between remaining stable and compliant within the professional, commercial, and regulatory demands of the systems in which we and our coachees operate *and* being flexible and responsive in light of the evolving demands of the [conversations,] contexts and cultures in which we and our coachees operate. (Corrie, Drake, & Lane, 2010, p. 323)

We are wired as humans to recognize patterns as guides for our listening, e.g., this is a grief story, a bad boss story, a victim story. However, these cognitive shortcuts may or may not match the intent of the narrator. This is why formulation is an ongoing process of course correction—a dance of leading and following—in which you are encouraged to be deeply focused *and* profoundly open. Hold your formulations lightly as people's stories begin because you can seldom be sure where they are headed. Otherwise, it is too easy to either get trapped in a storyline that precludes the path the coachee actually wanted to take with their story in the coaching session or lock in prematurely or rigidly to a particular formulation. Notice your formulative patterns in sessions and reflect on them over time so you can stay fresh and make conscious choices as often as possible. For example, do you tend to seek a resolution for every issue coachees bring to coaching out of your own desire for closure—when sometimes what they most need is your warm and courageous witnessing?

To develop greater awareness and discipline in your formulations, regularly ask yourself questions such as:

- "What story am I in?" (Mattingly, 1998, p. 72). "What role(s) am I playing and how are these affecting the coachee's narrations, reactions and actions in the session? What assumptions do I unconsciously make as a listener that may constrain people's storytelling? What do I miss or disallow as a result?"
- "In what ways do I steer their storytelling into my preferred frames and language in an attempt to reduce my own anxiety, stay within my loyalties and cater to my strengths? What is the repertoire of life stories I can allow, or allow myself to hear, and consider plausible? What are the acceptable shapes of a life that I, by virtue of my profession, my theoretical allegiances, and my conscious and unconscious aesthetic preferences, find myself promoting?" (Phillips, 1994, p. 70).
- "To what extent should my formulations remain within the confines of the 'received view' of what is acceptable, and to what extent should they challenge prevailing ideas about legitimate explanations? When should I deviate from contextually bound, socially sanctioned interpretations, and if so, where is the margin of that boundary?" (Corrie et al., 2010, p. 325).

- "What factors in the session inhibit certain selves and certain versions of a life story and activate others?" (M. Gergen & Davis, 2005, p. 243). "What are the narrative constraints from the environment and how should they be addressed? What are my constraints as a professional and how should they be addressed? What are the constraints of 'coaching' as the construct for our work together?"

Any formulations you make as you coach will inevitably privilege some questions and trajectories more than others. The key is to develop yourself using the *Three Windows* at the end of this chapter so you can be more present, agile and masterful in using knowledge and evidence in your formulation. Be conscious as you coach and reflect on your choices such that your formulation stays attuned to what is *actually* happening and what is called for next. One way you can become more aware of any unhelpful formulation habits is to observe what happens in moments of silence in sessions and in gaps in coachees' narration. It is in those moments when we are most tempted to intervene in the storyline in accordance with our preferred tales about what should happen. Another pattern to watch out for is smoothing out the rough edges of coachees' stories so as to make the formulation process more manageable for everyone involved. It is similar to the difference between the way we see ourselves in the mirror (smoothed by our brain) and the way we often look in candid photos.

Narrative medicine practitioners (see Charon; 2006; Kleinman, 1988) have wrestled with these tensions between professional discourse and personal experience in their formulation, articulated the narrative differences between providers and consumers of health care, and advocated for a shared approach. As Haidet and Paterniti (2003) noted:

> The physician's perspective may exclude crucial patient-oriented data necessary to achieve therapeutic effectiveness.
> The patient's perspective may miss critical biomedical facts needed for accurate diagnosis. Physicians need a

method of fostering efficient sharing of critical biomedical and patient-specific information necessary for both [the] biomedical management of disease and [the] therapeutic healing of illness. (p. 1135)

There is a lot we can learn from their research and practice. Narrative coaching takes a similar approach based in a strong belief that formulation is a co-constructed process in which there is continuous interpretation, translation, negotiation, and calibration in both directions. Since most of it is nearly instantaneous and tacit, it is helpful from time to time throughout your coaching sessions to verbalize what you think is going on to make sure that you and the coachee are still on the same page.

There are no 'right' or 'perfect' formulations. Every formulation captures some portion of the reality of what is happening and yields results of some sort. What seems most productive is when the coachee and coach are working in tandem around a shared narrative about what is happening and where they should head. Sometimes we invite a coachee into a new formulation to make the most of a 'teachable moment'; while at other times the coachee leads the way by reframing or refocusing the conversation in a direction that fits better for her. Formulation is an ongoing process during and between sessions that creates a sense of shared direction and markers along the way. It is analogous to the 'ducks' that hikers make out of stacked stones to indicate a route through the wilderness when there is no formal trail. In your coaching, balance the need for a coherent formulation that supports safety and security with the need for an emergent formulation that fosters experimentation and adaptation.

In your coaching, balance the need for a coherent formulation that supports safety and security with the need for an emergent formulation that fosters experimentation and adaptation.

The four phases in narrative formulation are intertwined in a flow not as independent objects. The key question is, "To what degree are the stories you are telling yourself about the situation leading to actions that are yielding valued, positive results for your coachees?" The secret is to not get too far ahead with your formulation by assuming you know where the coachee or her stories are headed *or* how they could or should get there. You can use the narrative formulation framework below to help guide you in the process and gather the knowledge and evidence you will need along the way. You can use this framework before, during, and after a coaching session to create, reflect on, and adapt your formulations—and identify key opportunities for your development. For example, you might notice that your solution orientation sometimes leads you to look for and move toward resolution or action before the issue is sufficiently understood or the coachee is ready. You can also use it in comparing notes with coachees about what is happening or has happened in their session.

Reflecting on your narrative formulation
1. Situate: What story am I telling myself about this Person and her situation?
2. Search: What story am I telling myself about the Purpose of this conversation?
3. Shift: What story am I telling myself about what needs to Pivot or change?
4. Sustain: What story am I telling myself about her Progress on the desired outcome?

Case story

1. Situate: What story am I telling myself about this Person and her situation?

Sally* was a middle-aged female manager and a long-time supervisor in a program serving low-income families. She had volunteered to be coached in front of the group during an internal coaching skills workshop I was running. Her presenting issue was that she wanted help buying a car after months of no resolution but lots of trips to dealer showrooms.

My reflections: Is my formulation supporting a useful and respectful frame for the conversation?

This seemed like an important personal decision for her. I avoided the temptation to move into problem-solving mode (which assumed she needed my help in making this decision) or focus on the decision itself (that we were there to talk about cars). Instead, I engaged her at the Person level to start our conversation. I encouraged her to be her own expert about herself and a full participant in our formulation of the Situation. As we proceeded, her growing clarity about herself and her stories reinforced each other.

2. Search: What story am I telling myself about the Purpose of this conversation?

After a few questions, I had a clear sense that she did not need help researching what car to buy (she had narrowed it down to two), how to negotiate with the sales people (she was quite strong here), or if/how to make a large purchase (she had saved the money). Acting on a sense of what was not being said about why we were here, I asked her what kind of car she wanted to buy. She responded, "a BMW or Chevrolet." I responded that she was considering two very different cars.

My reflections: Is my formulation enabling us to explore in places that seem important and generative?

My sense was that deciding which car to buy was not the real story here or the path that would lead to a sense of resolution for her. As a result, I began to formulate a different story that drew on the past (her history), the present (a values crunch), and the future (her desire). I used my experience in working with dualities in narratives to invite her to talk about her two choices—and the stories that went with them—as part of the Search to figure out what was really at stake for her.

3. Shift: What story am I telling myself about what needs to Pivot or change?

I soon discovered that her husband wanted her to buy the Chevy because it was practical and it was what they were used to in their lives. However, she let it slip that she secretly wanted the BMW. In unpacking this story, I learned that her kids were now off on their own and she had driven the same station wagon for a long time to haul them around. She became aware that for the first time in her marriage she wanted to buy something just for herself. She had worked hard for a long time and saved the money for the car.

I invited her to unpack the associations she had with the two options. I was able to use my knowledge of her organization and profession in exploring her dilemma and what would help her break through to a decision. The Chevrolet was consistent with the story of her life thus far. I sensed that this decision was ultimately about a turning point in her life, not just a car.

Moving deeper, I asked her why she didn't just buy the BMW. I received some fumbling responses at first. So, I invited her to close her eyes, take a few deep breaths, and the visualize driving the BMW to work. Tears formed in her eyes as she talked about pulling up to visit one of her low-income client families.

She couldn't see herself getting out of the car, so I asked her to close her eyes again and just imagine sitting there for a moment in the gravel driveway in front of their home. In the precious silence that followed, I invited her to consider the possibility that once she could see herself driving up in the BMW and getting out to see this family, she would buy that car.

My reflections: Is my formulation aligning to the new possibilities that are emerging for the coachee?

She got to a place where she could begin seeing herself as someone who could buy a BMW *and* stay within her values. I used my awareness of the values issues at play to help her Shift her frame by rising above the literal choice of cars to make her decision at another level. Paradoxically, this made it easier for her to decide what car to buy (and why). A big part of this came through inviting her to viscerally experience her desired choice in order to identify and address the key obstacle for her. As a result, she began to see herself as someone who could care for herself as well as she cared for others.

4. Sustain: What story am I telling myself about her Progress on the desired outcome?

A few months after our program she wrote to let me what she had decided. As I suspected, she bought the BMW. She still drove her old station wagon from time to time, but otherwise proudly enjoyed her new car. In the end, it was not about the possession, but the freedom she experienced in putting herself first—for what seemed like the first time in her life. She had worked hard to make that moment possible.

> *My reflections: Is my formulation equipping the coachee to take it from here?*
>
> My knowledge of the cultural and class complexities at play was useful in helping her find a sense of peace with her decision. If coachees are to Sustain the changes and choices that emerge in coaching, they need to take the 'baton' when they are done because it is their race to run. She used the guided visualization in our session as a reminder about what this decision meant to her as she moved forward.

Improving your formulation

In narrative coaching, we look beyond the traditional bias for specialized professional knowledge to make room for other forms of knowledge that are essential for a conscious and comprehensive approach to formulation. These include research guidance, practice experience, client experience, local context knowledge, and professional knowledge in working with people (Rycroft-Malone et al., 2004). It is not about searching for the 'correct' diagnosis or the perfect formulation, but rather about engaging in a mutual and mindful process with coachees aligned around what to do next and why. This requires you to track the formulation as it unfolds, both in each moment and across the conversation, in terms of how well it is serving the coachee and her process. It echoes Lane and Corrie's (2006) observation that coaching is a "radically unpredictable, almost iterative process in which the next step is informed, in large part, by the conditions immediately preceding it" (p. 155).

In a recent piece I wrote on coaching supervision (Drake, 2014c), I outlined three frameworks that can be used to assess and guide our professional development in relation to formulation. There are defined as "windows" because they are descriptive frames to look through as you coach not prescriptive steps to follow. They can be used to assess your work in sessions and your overall mastery as a guide for your professional development. You can use the four gateways in the *Artistry Window* (Figure 7) to increase your awareness of what is happening in and around you as the coach so you can be more present and open (Drake, 2011a). You can use the four functions in the *Identity Window* (Figure 8) to assess and adapt the roles you play so you can better meet your coachees' needs (Drake, 2011d). You can use the four domains of knowledge (and their related approaches to evidence) in the *Mastery Window* (Figure 9) to determine where to invest in developing yourself as a professional (Drake, 2011e). Taken together, these three windows (AIM) provide a way to improve your formulation through developing who you are, how you are, and what you say and do.

The Artistry Window

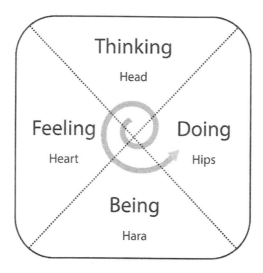

Figure 7. *The Artistry Window: Four gateways to embodied knowledge*

I developed this framework to teach coaches how to be more aware of and access their somatic experience in discerning what is going on in sessions and how to respond. The body is an often overlooked but very important source of evidence about what is happening and how we are formulating as we coach. The bottom line is that the more you develop your somatic acuity the better you will formulate. You can use the four gateways to help yourself and your coachees become more grounded in the truth of your respective stories and more aware of your own somatic knowledge. They are found in a number of ancient modalities such as chakras and they represent access points for the literal and symbolic energy in the body. They can be used to notice where it is flowing and where it is blocked, where it is aligned and where it is not. I focus on four of them in my work and find them very useful as checkpoints in my formulation:

- The *Thinking* gateway (the head) connects us to our mind; it supports our ability to theorize about what is happening as we work and what it means.
- The *Feeling* gateway (the heart) connects us to our values and emotions; it supports our ability to humanize our work so we can connect with ourselves and others.
- The *Being* gateway (the hara) connects us to our gut instincts, grounded knowing, and drive; it supports our ability to prioritize our work and get to the crux of matters.
- The *Doing* gateway (the hips) connects us to the lower half of our body and calls to action; it supports our ability to actualize what we know in a fluid and effective manner.

The spiral from the narrative coaching model is here as a reminder to continually move through the gateways as you coach so that you remain current with what is unfolding. In our programs we teach people how to use their hands as a conduit for sensing what each part of the body has to say about the issue they are contemplating for themselves or hearing while coaching others. For example, a coach notices a tightness in her belly (hara); pauses and realizes that she feels disconnected from the coachee (heart) even though the content of the conversation is making sense (head); she acknowledges that she is avoiding the harder issue which is the action to be taken (hips). You can also invite the coachee to do the same in order to get a truer and fuller sense of his experience and history about it.

The more fully you can access your body as you formulate, the more it opens up possibilities for coachees to do the same through dyadic regulation. This is important because narrative formulation is less about figuring things out and more about paying attention to what is already present. This is important because most coachees will not be able to travel farther in sessions than their coach is willing to go.

The Identity Window

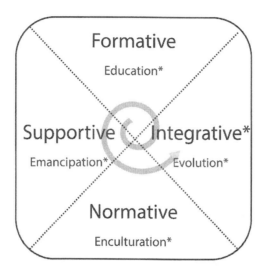

Figure 8. *The Identity Window: Four functions of coaches*[13]

In my research on how practitioners become masterful in their craft, I noticed that most of the classic models (e.g., in supervision) only identified three functions. I determined there was a need for an integrative function to account for the contextual and action orientation in coaching (Drake, 2014c) and the need of coaches to continually evolve. Having this additional function gives you a wider palette to draw from as you develop yourself and your formulative capabilities. Each of the functions (*Formative*, for example) is expressed through

---

13 The asterisks indicate a fourth function and the primary outcome for coachees of each of the functions that were added to the literature by the author.

a primary role you can play in coaching (*Education*, for example) and, together, they inform what you focus on as you formulate. You can use the framework to determine which function and role is being called for by the person and the process. For example, if a coachee wants to learn more about how to modulate her energy in meetings you could use the *supportive* function to help her release unrealistic expectations of herself, the *formative* function to help her learn new skills, the *normative* function to help her become more astute about the politics of meetings, and/or the *integrative* function to help her better understand and enact what is expected of people at her level in the organization.

We can use the four functions to assess and support our own development as coaches as well:

- The *Formative* function relates to our *education* in the core knowledge and skills of coaching so we can be *instrumentally competent* in our formulation.
- The *Supportive* function relates to our *emancipation* as we mature (e.g., self-awareness, self-regulation, individuation) so we can be *relationally competent* in our formulation.
- The *Normative* function relates to our *enculturation* as ethical members and stewards of the field of coaching so we can be *professionally competent* in our formulation.
- The *Integrative* function relates to our *evolution* as practitioners who can weave it all together so we can be more *systemically competent* in our formulation.

For example, in coaching someone who is seeking a new job you can use the Identity Window to assess how well you are formulating and to what degree he is getting what he needs:

- Do you have a good working knowledge of coaching and career searches that will support his *education* in this area? *(Formative function)*
- Do you have the ability to be with and hold the space for someone who is in distress until he finds his own *emancipation*? *(Supportive function)*
- Do you have the ability and integrity to recognize when the person needs expertise outside of yours in order to further his *enculturation*? *(Normative function)*

- Do you have the wisdom to help the person address the issue at the right level in order for him to take the next step in his *evolution*? *(Integrative function)*

The Mastery Window

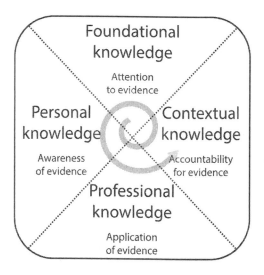

Figure 9. *The Mastery Window:*
Four domains of knowledge and evidence

The third window was actually the one I developed first (Drake, 2009a, 2011d, 2011e) and relates to the types of knowledge and evidence we draw on when formulating. As you can imagine, there is a strong connection between our functions as a coach and the knowledge we need. I am using the word "knowledge" here in the fullest sense of the word to reflect the fact that there are many ways of knowing and many types of knowledge. This framework rebalances the epistemological bases for coaching by highlighting the two domains of knowledge (personal and contextual) that are often less privileged in commercial, professional and academic circles. The four types of knowledge parallel other four quadrant frameworks for professional practice, such as the four levels in the *Goals for Driver Education* matrix (cited in Passmore & Mortimer, 2011) basic vehicle control (*foundational* knowledge), driver characteristics (*personal* knowledge), skills in traffic situations (*professional* knowledge), and trip-related considerations (*contextual* knowledge). Evidence is seen here as a dynamic process that "informs the decisions made in [coaching], emerges from what is generated in the conversation, gleans meaning from the results, and feeds back into the conversation and the broader evidentiary base" (Drake, 2011e, p. 163).

The four domains of knowledge and evidence can be described as follows:

- *Foundational knowledge* pertains to the *principles* of coaching. It is about having a sufficiently comprehensive base in the relevant theory and research about how people learn, develop and perform. You can ask yourself as you coach, "What do my actions reveal about my interpretation and understanding of what is going on, and what else do I need to know?" in order to be more *attentive to evidence* as you formulate. The greater your foundational knowledge, the richer and more nuanced your understanding of what is happening for coachees will be.

- *Personal knowledge* pertains to the *person* doing the coaching. It is about having the maturity and wisdom to be aware of yourself as well as your assumptions and actions as you formulate. You can ask yourself as you coach, "What seems true in this moment, and how is it that I know?" in order to be more *aware of evidence* (internal and external) as you formulate. The greater your personal knowledge, the more you can differentiate yourself from your coachees, hold space for them, and proactively self-regulate.

- *Professional knowledge* pertains to the *practices* used in coaching. It is about having a pragmatic, ethical, and grounded approach so you can be effective across a range of situations. You can ask yourself as you coach, "How will I enhance what I know to meet the needs in the moment and what role will I take in doing so?" in order to be more diligent in *applying evidence* as you formulate. The greater your professional knowledge, the more you can appropriately apply what you know, engage in challenging issues, and adapt your approach as needed.

- *Contextual knowledge* pertains to the *power* to bring about change through coaching. It is about being culturally and strategically astute in helping coachees enact new stories when they return 'home'. You can ask yourself as you coach, "How will I use evidence to adapt my approach and what difference would it make if I did?" in order to be more *accountable to evidence* as you formulate. The greater your contextual knowledge, the more you can address the systemic complexities related to people's issues and help them create sustainable outcomes.

You can use the Mastery Window to recognize the strengths and limitations of your development in each domain of knowledge (and its related evidence) and to increase your range and repertoire in order to work more effectively. This is important because multiple sources of knowledge and streams of evidence are increasingly necessary to address the complexity of coachees' needs; no one type of data can give you a complete picture of what is going on or needs to be done. You can look at a coaching conversation through this window and ask yourself, "What knowledge and evidence can we activate in this situation that will foster progress for this person?" As coaches, we base our implicit and explicit formulations about coachees and coaching conversations on the experience we bring, the knowledge we consult, the evidence we tap, and the meaning we make of it all. Your ability to masterfully apply relevant knowledge and evidence from all four domains affects whether or not people achieve optimal learning, development, and results through coaching.

For example, if we return to the story of Robert who was looking for a new job we might eventually discover that his depressive experiences are largely a signal that he is no longer motivated by his career and that, rather than trying to reinvigorate it, he needs to let it go to discover what is calling him now. This insight would yield a very different formulation and trajectory for the work in coaching than if he had come to other conclusions. Therefore, it is important to discern what coachees are trying to accomplish with their stories and for whom, and determine how you can best respond to help them meet their needs. What do they ultimately believe will put their life back into balance if it is achieved? Is that true? If so, what needs to shift for them to make this possible? If not, what is the deeper truth? Narrative formulation is a collaborative process that reflects the stories coaches and coachees tell themselves about what is happening in a coaching session, what they think that means, and what they should therefore do.

As a coach, it is a dance between using what you know so you can coach with confidence and moving toward the unknown so you stay attuned to what is emerging. Sometimes this means inviting coachees to explore their stories and use the material in them and sometimes it means inviting them to move outside their stories to explore the larger narratives or other possibilities. It all depends on which would most benefit the coachee where she is right now in the broader arc of her development and progress. In the end, it is about their journey not our jargon. Either way, learn to be comfortable with silence and listen into the gaps for what is not being said rather than rushing their narration or your formulation. The reward for doing so is often the discovery of the real agenda for change that will only surface when the 'field' and the person is ready. In the end, it is about being fully present to yourself, your coachees and the narratives in play as well as formulating with a duty of care (Spence, Cavanagh, & Grant, 2006) for people and their stories.

In the end, it is about their journey not our jargon.

III. NARRATIVE PRACTICES

Chapter 6

HOW WE CHANGE AND TRANSITION

In performance training, first we learn to flow with whatever comes. Then we learn to use whatever comes to our advantage. Finally, we learn to be completely self-sufficient and create our own earthquakes, so our mental process feeds itself explosive inspiration without the need for outside stimulus.
Josh Waitzkin

People come to coaching because they want to change something in themselves, their life and/or their work. Sometimes they think they know what they want, but often they are surprised by what emerges as important to them in the course of coaching. One thing that is certain is that it will inevitably involve change and transition. A transition is an internal process related to, but neither synonymous nor necessarily concurrent with, change as an external event. Either of them can be the trigger for the other, and it is often our stories about them that matter most in terms of how we fare. For example, the same change can happen to a group of people (e.g., their team is disbanded), but they may have very different experiences of the transition and responses to the change. In this chapter we will look at change and transitions as a rite of passage and the role of liminality as an undervalued yet essential resource for transformation. Narrative coaching is a semi-structured process in which you can use people's own stories to help them move through transitions and bring about desired changes.

Narrative coaching is about surrendering and slowing down in order to succeed and move ahead, and not trying so hard to change in order to actually change. You can also see this in David Grove's work in which he found that "the less he attempted to change the client's model of the world, the more they experienced their own core patterns, and organic, lasting changes naturally emerged from 'the system'" (Tompkins & Lawley, 1997, p. 1). This is why I encourage both coachees and participants to focus on their presence in the here and now, to allow themselves to consciously circle the tree with intention but without an agenda. At first this may not seem like it is enough. However, in due course people come to realize they can make more progress by focusing on one shift or decision at a time. It focuses their energy and enables them to self-regulate more readily so they can learn and notice more opportunities for practice. Narrative coaching works well because it mirrors the phases that people go through as they change and transition. It is a parallel process in which the experience itself is often as healing as the content.

Narrative coaching is about surrendering and slowing down in order to succeed and move ahead, and not trying so hard to change in order to actually change.

Understanding rites of passage

Those who do not regularly shed their psychological skin in order to become new again become old before their time. Death–rebirth rituals allow us to reemerge in the present, free to perceive without the veil of personal history that may dull your perceptions and keep you from detecting the road ahead.
Mikela & Philip Tarlow

The roots of the approach to change and transition in narrative coaching can be found in van Gennep's (1960) work on rites of passage, Turner's (1969) work on applying this model more broadly, and Campbell's (1973) work on the hero's journey. Arthur van Gennep studied a number of communal ceremonies accompanying people's "life crises" (e.g., birth, initiation, marriage, death) and he came to call them *rites de passage*. One of the primary functions of a rite of passage as a cultural practice was to guide people through important and/or cyclical transitions in their personal or communal lives using ritualized processes and resources. He distinguished three phases these practices had in common: separation, transition (from a French word meaning, "margin"), and incorporation. The three phases involved both external changes (e.g., state, role, status, etc.) and internal transitions (e.g., identity, orientation, attitude, etc.) in ways that were both complementary (ensuring continuity) and contrary (enabling challenge).

Early on Van Gennep (1960) used territorial and spatial terms in developing his framework; it is from this perspective that the view of passages as crossing thresholds took hold. The thresholds in the model below (separation, transition and reincorporation) represent the movement from the outer world to the inner world and back as well as the shifts in the inner world as people leave behind one role or status and prepare to take on a new one. The term "liminal" is used to describe the transition phase as "betwixt and between," and it comes from the Latin "limins" in referring to the threshold or boundary between two separate places. It is important to acknowledge the role of portals as signs one is approaching a boundary and the fact that they are generally only found at points of passage (van Gennep, 1960). I have placed the elements of his framework in the following graphic along with Eliade's (1959) distinction between profane and sacred spaces.

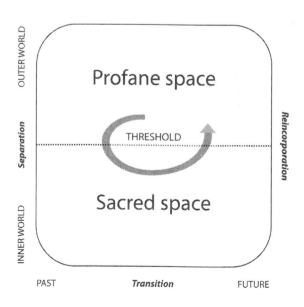

Figure 10. *Classic rites of passage model*

Zadra (1984) offers a clear description of what happens in a rite of initiation or passage:

> In this first phase, which is one of separation, symbolic behaviour demarcates the sacred from the profane and indicates the detachment of the ritual subjects from their previous social statuses. During the next phase of transition or limen, the ritual subjects pass through a period and area of ambiguity with reference to the social structure, in which few of the features of the preceding and subsequent profane statuses or cultural sates are present. The symbolic phenomena and actions of the final phase of re-aggregation or re-incorporation represent the return of the subjects to newly defined positions in society. (p. 84)

Victor Turner (1960) later recognized that these rites and practices were not confined to culturally-defined life crises but could also be used to describe any significant change from one state to another. Turner (1969) also observed that decisions to perform a rite or ritual were often connected with a crisis in the social life of a village and served as a container for the structural and anti-structural energies that were stirred up. Rites of passage provide the means to manage the paradoxical requirements of individual and social development: structure and anti-structure, elevation and subversion, transition and continuity. However, they only have power as long as they are vital and imbued with a current mythology as a coherent system of narratives that is shared and meaningful within the system (Petriglieri & Petriglieri, 2010). This is why it is important to place people's aspirations and stories in a broader narrative context if they are to bring about change. For some people it entails a deeper connection with a broader narrative (e.g., accessing an archetype, reclaiming part of their heritage) while for others it entails a looser connection (e.g., individuating beyond stereotype, redefining their relationship with heritage).

Rituals of passage are symbolic of the larger rhythms of nature (Gluckman, 1962); they make visible the natural pattern of dying, chaos, and renewal that operates everywhere in the universe. Van Gennep (1960) saw this regenerative flow as a law of life in which the energy in a system runs down and must be renewed at intervals.

One of the challenges many of us face in moving through change and transitions now is that we have lost touch with these natural cycles. Another issue is that these ceremonies were designed to "enable the individual to pass from one defined position to another which is equally well defined" (van Gennep, 1960, p. 3). However, we are often coaching people now who are seeking to make passages into positions that are not yet defined. Narrative coaching is designed to re-create rites of initiation and passage that "interrupt a person's life and arrest their vision, . . . stop their habitual ways of seeing life and open the psyche to a greater view of the world and their place in it" (Meade, 2006, p. 147). It also brings in new elements such as design thinking to re-conceptualize change in important new ways.

Moving through the phases

All changes, even the most longed for, have their melancholy; for what we leave behind is part of ourselves; we must die to one life before we can enter another.
Anatole France

I saw a need to make some finer distinctions about rites of passage if I wanted to get the most from it as a framework for coaching. In particular, there was a need for a vertical axis in the diagram to acknowledge: (1) the movement through time between the past and the future; (2) the changing needs as one moved through the liminal phase; (3) the transitions were not just in the liminal dimension but were occurring in each phase, albeit in different ways; (4) the thresholds between each of the four phases, each with its own role in the passage; (5) the sacred spaces are not an absolute but are brought into play in relation to a particular situation (ven Gennep, 1960); and (6) we return 'home' a different person on a different mission than when we began. The result is the figure below. It provides an enhanced perspective on the rites of passage framework, a useful way to map where people are in terms of their transitions and the skeleton for the narrative coaching model. Each of the four Ts (e.g., T1) indicates a threshold between two phases.

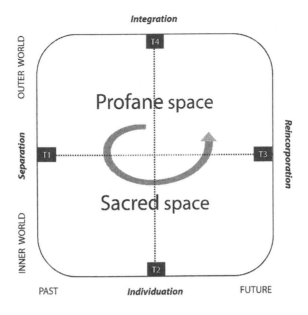

Figure 11. *Enhanced rites of passage framework*

A rite of passage is now seen as a movement through four phases:
- a *separation* from the outer world to embark on a journey into the inner world to undergo a transformation in one's identity and narrative,
- an *individuation* as one overcomes obstacles to transit the inner world in search of what will bring restoration and maturation,
- a *reincorporation* as one leaves the inner world to return the outer world with what has been gained through exploration and experimentation, and
- an *integration* of the transformation into a new identity and narrative in the outer world, often with subsequent changes relating to the environment.

You can see the need for these added distinctions in the work by more contemporary writers on transitions, such as William Bridges (2001) who identified four types of natural endings that often accompany such a journey: disengagement; disidentification; disenchantment; and disorientation. For example, in the midst of change people may *disengage* from the world as they knew it, *disidentify* with who they were/thought they were, become *disenchanted* until they break through the spell or veil, and feel *disoriented* until they can settle into their new story. A successful passage includes a surrender or loss of an old narrative identity, an in-between time that is neither here nor there, and the formation and integration of a new narrative identity. As Turner (1979) noted, "the first phase detaches the ritual subjects from their old places in society; the last installs them, inwardly transformed and outwardly changed in a new place in society" (p. 149). Rites are important because they provide a safe yet challenging structure for the energy that is in motion so people can successfully complete their passage. Stories that are located and shared in ritual actions often take on special therapeutic powers (Mattingly, 1998).

As we will explore later in the chapter, thresholds represent powerful developmental moments because they provide opportunities for people to release *from* what no longer serves them and release *into* what becomes possible now in terms of how they see themselves, tell their stories, and live their lives. Thresholds 1 and 3 in the model are important for people's development in relation to the world, with a focus at T1 on their internally-focused deconstruction and a focus at T3 on their externally-focused reconstruction. Thresholds 2 and 4 are important for people's development in relation to themselves, with a focus at T2 on their internal authenticity and a focus at T4 on their external accountability. T1 is often a release of who others think we are (in order to separate); T2 is often a release of who we think we are (in order to individuate); T3 is often a release of how we think we need to be (in order to reincorporate); and T4 is often a release of what we think we are supposed to do (in order to integrate).

Your role is to support coachees to stay open yet conscious, firm yet fluid, throughout the ordeal; and to foster the courage they will need to complete their passage. This is critical in order to keep them on the path, especially when it gets hard, e.g., in the betwixt and between places where powerful forces are afoot. It is in these liminal places where people often come into closest contact with a truer sense of themselves, their most potent questions, and their deeper hopes and fears. Their discoveries there often precipitate the biggest shifts for people because they ripple out through many aspects of their lives. It helps to have strong cultural and spiritual awareness, physical and emotional resilience, and personal and relational maturity to guide people through these fiery yet precious spaces. To work this way requires a sense of sacred leadership (R. L. Moore, 1987) if the sessions are to serve as a crucible for big shifts in people's narratives, identities, and lives.

Your role is to support coachees to stay open yet conscious, firm yet fluid, throughout the ordeal; and to foster the courage they will need to complete their passage.

As I started using this framework in my coaching, I found myself working more freely and effectively. I was less constrained by many of the traditional notions of what coaching was 'supposed to be'. I started

- actively using the whole space in sessions rather than staying seated;
- seeing time as malleable rather than seeing the past as fixed, for example;
- flowing between external change issues and internal transition needs with ease;
- being fully present more often rather than thinking about what to do next; and
- moving in and out of their stories as needed rather than asking sequential questions.

It represented a profound shift from seeing myself as an expert who guided people through a set process to seeing myself as an artist who worked masterfully with the narrative material at hand. To understand how you can make the same shift, let's look more closely at what people go through in a rite of passage as a way to understand their journey and how to coach them.

Separation

Transitions, just like stories, begin because something has changed. Separation marks the departure from one's current situation (with its identities, roles, status, narratives, etc.) with an intent to seek out a new one. These points of separation can be chosen intentionally (e.g., a marriage or a new job), emerge disruptively (e.g., a break-up or a layoff) or happen biologically (e.g., a coming of age or a retirement). Traditionally in this first phase, initiates would be ritually separated from the social group that had defined their cultural role and identity; taken to a special, and usually secluded, place (Turner, 1967); and the loss would be literally and symbolically marked. The purpose of this phase was to accentuate, sometimes quite starkly, the boundary between the two worlds such that it was undeniably clear there was no return. Unfortunately, many people these days lack sufficient support structures for this phase or clarity about what is next. To paraphrase Tennessee Williams, for many of us the Separation phase is still a time for departure even when there's not yet a certain place to go.

This first threshold marks the departure from the profane space as the person knew it and the entry into the unknown of the sacred space. This space is collectively sacred relative to those in the person's profane world and personally sacred relative to the profane aspects of the person. Preparation for this crossing often includes the dissolution of old stories and senses of oneself—often through a ritual wounding or engaging with existing wounds. As Michael Meade (2006) has written, "Initiation leaves certain wounds and scars that mark a person specifically as who they are and where in life they have been. . . . Ultimately, the wound that makes him limp a bit is his passport for crossing between the daily world and the otherworld" (p. 305). We can see the connection between our wounds and our healing in the fact that the word "blessing" comes from *blesure*, a French word that means "wound." The doorway to what we seek is often in places we might otherwise avoid. "We each seek a blessing exactly where a wound waits; we each become wounded exactly where we seek to be blessed" (p. 60).

A key role for coaches is to help people increase their window of tolerance so they can *be* with their anxiety long enough to imagine there is blessing in the wound. In the process, the coachee begins to let go of the "attitudes to which he clings for safety, of the perspectives which these attitudes give him on the world, and of the familiar labels for what he sees in the world" (Schachtel, 1959, p. 195). Critical questions for coachees at this juncture: What is it time to let go of? What in me is dying or must die to make room for what wants to be born? What am I leaving behind? When people separate from their familiar patterns of self-organization and their tidy distinctions, such as "I am this, not that" come apart, they are often left wondering who they are and what they are 'really' like. The ties of meaning that once linked them with everyday life—and to which they were accustomed—are now stretched or even severed (Deegan & Hill, 1991). The Separation phase is often marked by breakdowns and a sense of regression as people step back to reconsider their identities and their lives.

Carotenuto (1985) poignantly describes this threshold:

> Anyone who undertakes [this journey], even or especially if he has been driven to his knees by suffering and necessity and initially unaware of what awaits him, chooses the path of deep awareness, which in itself is already a heroic act . . . A withdrawal of energy from the outside world is also necessary, and for this a certain price must always be paid. (p. 45)

As with all thresholds, this work brings coachees into contact with internal and external forces that are often greater than they expect. In moving beyond the comfort zone of their familiar narratives they encounter elements of their personal and collective Shadows, their own divided wishes and countervailing narratives around them.

However, it is through this proverbial fire that the true nature of the transition crystallizes and this clarity sets the direction for the quest. Your role as a coach is to strengthen the working relationship and the quality of the 'field' so the person feels safe enough to embark on a journey into the unknown. They will be able to attend to the essential inner work ahead once they can quiet the grasping of their ego. This threshold is about helping people develop greater trust in themselves, the process, and the allies they will meet along the way—and, ultimately, to take more existential responsibility for their own choices (Raff, 2000).

The more they surrender, the more unflinchingly yet compassionately they will be able to see the reality that is before them. The less willing they are to surrender, the less they will see or grow—and the more they will continue to suffer. As the knights discovered in their search for the Holy Grail, each coachee must enter the 'forest' at a point where it is darkest for her and with the recognition that there is ultimately no map. Even if there was, they are only useful "if a) you are able to locate your position, and b) if you have a sense of your destination" (Paris, 2011, p. 63)—neither of which is the case as people start on their journey. This is why, as the great myths have shown, people will go astray if they attempt to follow someone else's path. As James Hollis (2004) once said, "Their individuation task has already been accomplished. Our duty is to risk living our lives as fully as they have risked living their truths" (p. 61).

In understanding the role of suffering in Separation it is important to remember Jung's view that our psyche is by nature continuously moving towards wholeness. For example, when our psyche calls out for a change, it often takes away something we truly value to force us to go in search of fuller consciousness. Therefore, 'sit' with people as they begin their descent rather than rushing to make it all go away. As Paris (2007) observes:

> Moments of great suffering usually signal that the old self needs to die, and because it is painful, we are tempted to look for quick solutions, buying into the common illusion that every psychological 'problem' calls for a positive

'solution.' Yet, this well-intentioned approach increases the suffering because it ignores one of the great paradoxes of psychological wisdom: the activation of the death principle has more power than anything else in the psyche. The destructive impulse can be crucial if we are to get rid of what oppresses us. (p. xii)

Once people move through these 'deaths' in the process of Separation, they find themselves in the liminal phase—and the search begins to restore what they have lost and awaken to what they most desire.

Liminality

The Grail King Speaks
Oh Speaker,
There is no place to hide,
And you will go directly
Toward what you most fear

Van Gennep saw the middle phase as the transition between the profane and sacred worlds (and back again), and he portrayed it as both a process and a state of its own. It is the ultimate 'both/and'— "an extended and ambiguous state of 'in-between-ness, a back and forth process between states" (McNamara, Roberts, Basit, & Brown, 2002). Carson (1997) described the liminal state as a "place of sacred time and space, set apart and separated, the locus of revelation" (p.11). It can be seen as a container that holds the primal energies people encounter in this phase (Ramsay, 1997) and offers them a new perspective on lives and stories once taken for granted. It must be strong enough to hold all that is stirred up without getting blown away or over-inflated and discerning enough so that the purification process is deep and real. Other characteristics include: a profound sense of ambiguity, confusion and uncertainty; a loss of power, status and/or role; a loss of normal relations but a gain of temporary *communitas*; a designation as 'contaminated' yet connected to divine energy; a subversive challenge that also provides continuity; an encounter with death and a dark night of the soul; and a feeling of depression and despair.

Liminality is paradoxical in that it is defined in contrast to the clearly defined states on other side and yet is marked by a fundamental lack of clarity in itself. A person in this space knows that everything is different now, but they typically cannot say why at first. This is why it is critical for people to stay in this space long enough to discern what the passage is truly all about. It is an ambiguous period in which their hold on a particular reality loosens and "the past is momentarily negated, suspended, or abrogated, and the future has not yet begun, an instant of pure potentiality when everything, as it were, trembles in the balance" (Turner, 1982, p. 44). The structures of their former identity are dissolved and new structures are constellated (B. C. Alexander, 1991; J. O. Stein & Stein, 1987; Turner, 1967), often with instructions from ritual elders (Moore, 1987) who ensure there is sufficient structure and guidance for people as they pass through these uncharted territories.

Moving into, through, and out of the in-between spaces exposes and scrutinizes the basic building blocks of a culture (e.g., its norms, values, axioms, traditions) in ways that are not generally available through people's everyday experience (Turner, 1969). As a result, liminality creates a frame within which people can experiment with the familiar categories of culture by isolating these elements and recombining them in new ways (Turner, 1967, 1974, 1982). Sometimes these experiments are built into the social processes in order to maintain some boundaries around them (like with court jesters of old), and at other times they emerge on the margins of the society and its rituals. It is a place where expectations are challenged, unspeakable subjects discussed, and new roles tested. In the process, people are not only attaining a new status, role, or identity in relation to their social systems, but there is also a change of being itself, an ontological passage (Carson 1997).

This echoes Vygotsky's work on zones of proximal development in that people generally cannot go directly from an old state or story to a new one, but require an intermediary step that is neither old nor new (T. Barrett, Cashman, & Moore, 2011). As he pointed out, this requires carefully stewarded boundaries, a sense of containment to manage people's vulnerabilities in this in-between phase, and access to scaffolding to support their learning and development. This is critical because in this phase people can become a stranger to themselves, feel empty and drained, lose their sense of certainty and solidity (Ashton, 2007), question what they know and who they are, feel afraid and outcast, and feel anxious as their ego resists the requisite surrender (Miller & Miller, 1994). People in liminal space are "both weak because they are outside the group and the profane space, and they are also strong because they are in the sacred space relative to the group" (van Gennep, 1960, p. 3). People in this in-between space require both social structures and guidance from designated others who can traverse the unknown with them and on their behalf.

It is challenging work to persevere as a *liminar* (Turner & Turner, 1978), a *liminal self* (Deegan & Hill, 1991), in large part because people's ego generally experiences a sense of loss as they move through the liminal phase. Old habituations dissolve and possibilities for a new direction resolve into focus—as with the acorn that gives up its life to become a mighty oak or the phoenix that rises from its own ashes. Finding our way to a new attitude, a new story, necessitates an acceptance of and surrender to the descent, the depressive state that often accompanies it, the release of what must be left behind, and the work that must be done (Tarrant, 1998). When this occurs, a person's pretenses and compromises fade away as she is confronted with stark truths that have become more visible and accessible during this period. As a result, she can challenge old narratives to make more room for new stories, and she can release energy that was once trapped and channel it in new directions. She can then bring more of herself to her life, particularly aspects that had previously been put aside or under-developed but would now come in quite handy.

Many people describe moving through liminal spaces as like trying to pilot a rudderless ship through a thick fog. In part, this is due to the temporary lack of referent points in their inner and outer world. The good news is that if a person is able to endure this disorienting lack of referent points he begins to find and hone his own internal compass. There is a delicate balance in this for coaches as there is for parents who realize they cannot protect their child from everything and, even if they could, much of the resilience and confidence the child will need for the rest of his life is born from these challenges. Therefore, focus on holding a safe space for coachees to do *their own* work. Help them recognize the literal and symbolic resources that often appear in this phase, often in forms they would not normally recognize or expect. These often turn out to be essential for breaking through this phase and on to the next (Shenk, 2005). It may take awhile for the fog to lift and they may feel lost at seas or crashed on the rocks at times. However, in the process, you can help people develop a better feel for the boat, the seas and themselves so they can find their bearings and move forward again.

Given the loss of rites of passage for many of us in our postmodern cultures, coaching can play an important role in helping people do their liminal work as the individuating bridge between separation and reincorporation. However, one of our challenges as coaches is to deal with the commercial and professional pressures to quickly move the process toward goals and, in so doing, short-circuit real growth for coachees and those around them. Growth requires this descent, this voyage of discovery, this shedding of old skins so that the new story and the renewed person can emerge. While the liminal process can be intensified and focused to enrich people's awakening, there are no shortcuts. Instead, it requires the courage of coaches and coachees to immerse themselves in this unknown and sacred space. We can take comfort in the fact that at the *nadir*—the darkest point at the proverbial, and often, literal bottom—the person is also closest to the divine, the light. It is the place where the veils are removed so people come face to face with the part(s) of themselves most in need of surrender and, in so doing, they begin to glimpse what is waiting to be born on the other side.

While the liminal process can be intensified and focused to enrich people's awakening, there are no shortcuts.

By walking with coachees on the liminal portions of their journey, you can help them make sense of and find value in this phase as an "occasion of fruitful darkness . . . and the ground of renewal" (Halifax, 1993, p. 19). This passage often requires people to

- go as deeply into the darkness as is called for, and deal with whatever must be faced in the chasms of their fear and self-doubt (Hollis, 2004);
- name the pain and truth they find there, and emerge on the other side with greater permission to name their reality from their own point of view (Feinstein & Krippner, 1988); and
- stop struggling to escape the emptiness and darkness which is theirs in the end (Miller & Miller, 1994), and rest in it until a resolution emerges (Tarrant, 1998).

Your role as a coach is to help them navigate these depths where "obscure resistances are overcome, and long lost, forgotten powers are revivified, to be made available for the transfiguration of the world" (Campbell, 1973, p. 29). It is from here that the person prepares to return to the world, transformed by the process.

Reincorporation

We would rather be ruined than changed.
We would rather die in our dread
Than climb the cross of the present
And let our illusions die.
W.H. Auden

The reincorporation phase is an important one as the person rejoins the profane world—but does so as a changed person. In more traditional settings, the return would often be as stark as the separation to emphasize the significance and unidirectional nature of the transition. While in many ways it is the culmination of one journey, it is also the beginning of another as the person takes on a new identity. That is why it was a time of both celebration and further initiation in traditional settings. There was a need to keep people focused on the tasks at hand and sufficiently supported as they entered the new role as a novice. Then, as it is now, this was rarely as easy as it first seemed because there were many facets of their life that needed to be adjusted to align with their new identity. What they had gained often seemed clear and compelling to the people who had come through the process, but that was not always the case for those around them. While rites of passage have evolutionary value to the community as a whole, not everyone will embrace the new person with their new narrative. Therefore, people need to carefully choose their re-entry points back into the world and prepare themselves for those who may be challenged by their return.

This is significant because people need others around them to support the new narrative if it is to take hold. For example, a new manager who wants to move away from micromanaging when her anxiety goes up will need others to step up and play a bigger role in order to get the work done. When I am coaching someone in this situation I will often ask the team members what they will change in themselves to support their leader's success. It reflects the need for the community to receive the new person as they are becoming *not* as they were. In addition, many of the coachee's gains will be lost if he does not pay sufficient attention to embedding the shifts he has made in his everyday life. Many people experience a sense of deflation after the 'high' of the liminal phase and need to be reminded to address the demands and details that await them as they reincorporate. This is why, as we shall see in the next two chapters, the final phase in narrative coaching is so critical.

At this point in the process, people tend to get much clearer about what they truly want and their intrinsic motivation tends to increase. This generally culminates in identifying and claiming their gift ("boon") and accelerating their development to be able to carry it forward. It represents the key lesson, insight or offer that grew out of the fires of their liminal experience. It is a time when people start getting ready to bring it back to their world and, in so doing, bring their journey full circle. The irony is that at the end of their great search, often to far away lands, they discover that the gift was right in front of them or inside them all along. Regardless of where the gift is found, bringing it back to the person's world can be tricky in a number of ways, including: (1) getting caught up in the thrill of the epiphany and, as a result, not reconnecting with reality; (2) feeling bored or impatient and, as a result, forgoing the hard work to bring it to life; (3) rushing to take action and, as a result, losing sight of the true nature of the gift; (4) ineffectually communicating the new reality to others who have not been on their journey and, as a result, failing to attain their support; and (5) underestimating the power of narratives that will challenge them and, as a result, failing to adequately prepare.

Traditionally, rites of passage were seen as occurring in relation to singular events (e.g., entering manhood/womanhood, marriage, death). However, we can extend Turner's sense of rites to any transition by looking at it developmentally. Each of the three phases (separation, transition, and reincorporation) can be seen as a milestone that signals an opportunity for a significant shift in a person's development. In this case, reincorporation is both the completion of one cycle and the start of another—albeit at a higher developmental level. I have experienced this in my own life when I have sufficiently resolved an issue—only to discover that in addition to enriching my life it also reveals the next layer to be addressed. And so, the bird circles the tree once more . . . though hopefully with greater wisdom and ease. In the end, whatever comes through the reincorporation phase needs to be integrated into the person's identity and life if it is to be sustained. Therefore, I focus on fewer things in coaching sessions to keep the person's reincorporation process manageable, and I use simple, binary pivots to help people nudge themselves toward their new narrative.

Crossing thresholds

A mode of entrance is crucial. A door. A window. A chink in the otherwise unbroken surface of what we consider real and proper.
Thomas Moore

Turner (1986) noted that "the word 'threshold' derives from a Germanic word which means to 'thrash' or 'thresh', a place where grain is beaten from its husk, where what has been hidden is thus manifested"

(p. 92). Eliade (1959) described the threshold as "the limit, the boundary, the frontier that distinguishes and opposes two worlds—and at the same time the paradoxical place where these worlds communicate" (p. 24). A threshold is a noticeable crossing between one phase and the next as part of a broader transition and change process. Thresholds can be found wherever there is an in-between zone where passage from one sphere or way of being to another is made possible. Thresholds both divide and bring together significant 'regions' such as: inside and outside, sacred and profane, psyche and matter, self and other, conscious and unconscious. Thresholds can be seen both spatially as a doorway, a *place* of transition; and temporally as a movement, a *process* of transition.

Thresholds can be seen both spatially as a doorway, a *place* of transition; and temporally as a movement, a *process* of transition.

While thresholds get the most attention, I would reiterate that there are other aspects of a doorway which make the crossing both recognizable and possible. Buck (2004) uses the entrance to Carl Jung's Kusnacht home in Switzerland to talk about one of the other aspects:

'Called or not called, the gods will be present.' Everyone who walked down the path saw this enigmatic message [on the lintel] as they approached. . . . The lintel is the weight-discharging horizontal piece above the door and directly over the threshold. . . . In partnership with the grounded threshold, the lintel above creates the opening between two places. This doubling reinforces the entrance as a power place; it is both the potent symbol and powerful vehicle of passage from one world to another and must be crossed with care" (p. 4).

Thresholds are a powerful place of communication between the opposing worlds that lie on either side of them—for example the sacred, metaphysical world of soul and psyche can be found on the other side of the profane world of history, human affairs and events (Eliade, 1987). As a place, they mark the boundary between two opposing regions; as a process, they hold together the tensions inherent in the duality. Thresholds provide a stable center that mediates between and holds the tension of the opposites; they are "a place of possibilities where both sides have the potential to be seen and where energy has the opportunity to flow in either direction" (Buck, 2004, p. 3). They provide an opening and a beginning to a state or action; and they offer a third space with a changing combination of attributes of the two bordering spaces (Muller, 2001) at the edge, the frontier, where they intersect. Paying attention in these spaces demands commitment and endurance; "simply to keep oneself there, in open and honest relationship, requires a fitness of soul" (Kaplan, 2002, p. 67). Otherwise, the person attempting to cross is often defeated and turned back—and the necessary communication and transition between the worlds is thwarted.

Thresholds are also a process in time. It is often the case, however, that while the distinction between before and after is often experienced as pointed and stark, the complete transit is often extended and blurry. Crossing thresholds often marks a point in time that serves as a new referent point going forward in terms of the person's plotline and identity. We can see this at points in our own life where the counter from the last major event gets reset to zero in the wake of the next big event in that relationship or context. Moving across thresholds requires strength of character to contend with the polarizing energies of the opposites and deal with the ambiguities in the unknown on the other side. For those on the journey, it is imperative to not take these passages lightly. They are not for the ill-prepared or faint-hearted as they can often challenge our core constructs about ourselves, others and life itself. This is why the guardians at thresholds are so important; they ensure the person is prepared for dealing with the powerful forces in play and the other side.

It has been my experience in coaching over the years that there is something palpably different when a person approaches a threshold.

Many times it is a subtle energetic or somatic shift that comes over the person that can only be described as an *urgent calm*. It feels urgent because there is a readiness to make a big move and big issues are often at stake, and it feels calm because there is a clarity and a certainty about what is to be done (and why). Thresholds are both the culmination of a longer process and a very distinct moment in time. Common examples I see in my coaching are decisions to end relationships, change jobs or careers, or stand up for something the person deeply cares about. Timothy Carson (1997) offers an insight that helps us see why the notion of thresholds fits so well with coaching, "Rather than merely attempting to return a person to a past state of equilibrium, their approach is oriented toward the future. . . . Liminal categories construe crisis in terms of progress rather than regression" (pp. 89–90).

In the classic rites of passage model (see figure 10), the threshold was crossed twice—once as a person left the world to embark on a journey through the 'lower' world and once to return from liminality into the 'upper' world. In more contemporary contexts like narrative coaching, people cross the horizontal axis of space twice and the vertical axis of time twice. Each of these represents a critical point in people's process where they often need to make important developmental breakthroughs and decisions in order to move through to the next phase of their transition. Each one involves moving from the known to the unknown as they move through their metamorphosis. Crossing a threshold enables people to develop a new vantage point from which to see the world and a new starting point from which to discover what is next. To move through the passage, coachees need a safe container, a robust yet experiential process, and a guide to accompany them.

In more contemporary contexts like narrative coaching, people cross the horizontal axis of space twice and the vertical axis of time twice.

Markers

Markers and guardians are two aspects of working with thresholds in coaching that warrant additional attention. Markers are often found at the boundaries in stories, at points where the narrator is on the edge of entering new territory in their narration. They mark the point where the person is approaching a new aspect of her identity (Strauss, 1997) as a result of gaps that have been revealed; e.g., between life as lived and life as desired or between identity as self-constructed and identity as other-constructed. Think of them like the porch lights that you leave on so a visitor can find your house on a dark night. You can often notice their presence through the sudden shift in the rhythm or energy of a coachee's narration. I generally pause the conversation when I notice markers that feel significant because they are often indicators that a threshold is nearby. They act as stewards of thresholds—reflecting the person's desire for and fear of the changes they represent.

For example, laughter in participants' stories was one of the markers I tracked in my doctoral research. I had noticed there was a certain type of laughter that would often occur when the participant was about to surface a potential story, a new sense of herself. Many of these points seemed to be associated with a positive, desirable aspect of self; it was almost as if they found it difficult to openly admit their wishes. There often seemed to be a higher level of truth telling in those openings as people moved away from their usual story and hinted at a new awareness or imagined self. Their laughter also served as a socially acceptable rehearsal of sort. It was a way to downplay what was to come in case it was not well received, and to try out a new identity to see how it fits before showing it to others. Markers not only indicate shifts in the narration and thresholds for development, but they also signal spaces where people can try out parts of themselves so they can live more fully. Your role as a coach is to be a compassionate *and* fierce guardian of these gates where markers appear.

Guardians

At the threshold of each hour
To open the gates in the underworld
One must know the names.

Once people are at a threshold it is incumbent upon them to know what it will take to cross it. Their crossing may involve a single bold act or a series of major moves, though either way there is almost always a moment of reckoning when it all becomes very real. This requires the person to address the forces at the doorway— 'threshold guardians' as Joseph Campbell (1973) called them. They are symbolically and literally there to remind people to not take thresholds lightly, to fully appreciate what is truly at stake and to challenge them to be ready. These guardians are often either close allies or people deemed as enemies because, paradoxically, each is especially well equipped to point out the truth of the situation and what is called for. Psychologically, these guardians can often be seen as projections of the fears and aspects of our Shadows that are critical for the crossing of this threshold. Terms such as 'good' and 'bad' are not relevant here because every guardian serves the same purpose: to lift the veil that has kept the person from seeing what was there all along and help him cross the threshold of his truth.

Every guardian essentially asks the same questions, "What do you need to confront to gain access to what you are seeking?" "What projections do you need to withdraw so you can bring that energy into yourself to support your growth?" Guardians can play many roles in the process, such as helping her to see the situation more clearly, providing her with aid, or testing her to make sure she is ready. Not only are guardians protecting us, they are also protecting the thresholds themselves. Their task is maintain those places where sacred and profane meet, to keep the boundaries in good repair, and the center fresh and strong. Their power is both focused in the moment *and* tentative over time. When we do threshold work in our

Labs, I often act as guardian to support the person seeking to cross and the integrity of the threshold itself. As part of my role I often challenge people to sink deeper into the truth of that moment. In so doing, they discover the real name that will unlock the potential of that threshold and enable them to cross it.

Guardians matter-of-factly stand at the doorway because they recognize the potency and power that reside at the threshold. That is why they challenge people to be prepared and to face the threshold with both fierceness and surrender. Guardians play an important role here because, "When some part of us dies, there must be a time of mourning, a period of withdrawal and introspection, a period of allowing the tears to fall. Tears connect us to our hearts, our real values, our own inner Home" (Woodman, 1987). Guardians are stewards of these vital crossings and of the deep grief and deep joy that often are found there. They are also important in getting people to pay attention to the social structures (e.g., team, family, community) they will encounter on the other side so they can enter with their eyes wide open. Narrative coaching facilitates change at a transpersonal level, brings together transitions and development in the same process through a rite of passage, and helps people heal old stories and bring new ones to life.

Chapter 7

HOW NARRATIVE COACHING MODEL WORKS

Aborigine trackers are the best in the world, able to follow a man even years after he has walked through a dry desert terrain. An anthropologist asked one of these expert trackers how he did it. The tracker responded, "Oh, it's easy. We walk with him." He does not look for clues; he enters the time and space where the journey occurred. He knows how to walk in the same world as the event he seeks.
Mikela & Philip Tarlow

In this chapter we will explore the narrative coaching model, its trialogic and hermeneutic foundations, two key practices from narrative therapy (externalization and unique outcomes) that are used differently in this context, and four of the key narrative reconfiguration tools. Of particular note are two of the unique features of narrative coaching: the emphasis on third spaces and the de-emphasis of goals. A fuller version of the narrative coaching model (figure 16) is offered in the next chapter as we look at how it is used in coaching. While narrative coaching has deep roots in psychology, it draws on other disciplines to offer an integrative approach that enables you to work with people's stories at multiple levels simultaneously. The model can be used not only to help people resolve specific issues in their life and work, but also to help them develop themselves as more mature storytellers. Marshall Edelson (1993) has a wonderful description of this progression:

> As [the person] becomes able to identify what evokes his telling or enacting a story on each of many occasions, he increasingly understands its value to him—the purpose it serves. Typically, he begins by viewing himself as passive victim. He attributes causation to the external situation.

Eventually, he comes to see that what he has attributed to external reality stems from what he carries in his own mind, and what he does, through imagination or action, to make external reality conform to it. (p. 298)

If people are to bring about and sustain change through coaching, they will need to reconfigure key elements in the related narratives. However, the stories they consciously know, or believe they know, are seldom the whole story that is actually unfolding within them (Rennie, 1994). Therefore, a critical role in narrative coaching is to draw people's attention to what their psyche is trying to bring forth through their stories. It is almost as if it is leaving a trail of breadcrumbs, hoping they will notice and follow it. In the same vein, you can help people notice the ways in which the narratives they are living clash with the stories they are telling and/or the narrative they want to be living. By working with their stories in coaching, people have the opportunity to surface and address their largely unconscious narration processes. This is important because, as Ricoeur (1992) noted, our destiny is profoundly shaped by our stories—and our stories are profoundly shaped by the larger narratives about our destiny.

Sometimes a change in a person's life calls for a new narrative and sometimes a new narrative calls for changes to be made in his life. Sometimes an increased level of awareness leads him to take new actions and sometimes the new actions he takes increase his level of awareness. I tend to start with the one in each pair with which the coachee is most familiar and then invite him to scaffold from there to the other. For example, with a reflective person I might start with accessing her awareness and then shift to inviting her to spontaneously take actions in the direction of her aspiration. The fundamental questions come down to: (1) What has been your story about your issue up to this point? (2) How is that working for you? (3) Do you want to continue or change your story? (4) If you want to change it, what pieces can you bring forward to help you? (5) What are you hoping the new story will do for you? (Singer, 2001; Yalom, 2000). The narrative coaching model is quite useful in this regard because its flow reflects both the process by which people narrate their identity and experience *and* the process by which they develop themselves and learn new behaviors.

In developing the academic foundations for narrative coaching, I was especially drawn to (1) Freire's (1970) critiques of the traditional 'banking methods' of education and the over-privileging of the dominant narratives at the expense of personal narratives; (2) Jung's (1969) insights into the collective and unconscious influences on the self and the search for a means to connect the two worlds; (3) Clandinin & Connelly's (2000) use of Dewey to create a set of spatial-temporal terms that form a three-dimensional narrative inquiry space (personal and social interaction, temporal continuity and situations as place); (4) Tillich's (1965) notion of a third area where one can stand for a time without being enclosed in something tightly bounded—a concept that was later explored in depth by Schwartz-Salant (1998) as an imaginal vessel in psychoanalysis; and (5) Oldenburg's (1989) work on "the great good place" where he talks about the important role of a third place outside home and work. What these all have in common is the addition of a third space to what are traditionally seen as dualisms and dialogues in order to open up new and more generative possibilities.

Coaching in third spaces

For he that is freed from the pairs
Is easily freed from conflict
Bhagavad Gita

Narrative coaching began to take shape as I started teaching coaching skills in organizations and laying the groundwork for my dissertation. I had come to realize that in the public domain, storytelling is often seen as a monologic process that focuses on the oratory, dramatic, and/or persuasive skills of the storyteller. In the fields of communication studies, narrative analysis and related fields, storytelling is often described as a dialogic process that focuses on the exchange between a teller and a listener(s). However, through my research I came to see that tapping the full hermeneutic potential of narrative work required a "third space" beyond the narrator and her story (the first and second spaces respectively), with the listener being moved off to the side to form a diamond (see figure 18). As a result, the listener is seen as the steward of the field and as part of the co-narration process—not just as a receiver of what the other person has to say. The formation of a trialogic frame reflected a shift in thinking about stories as commodities transmitted from one person to another, to thinking about stories as co-created in a narrative field that lies between, yet beyond, the participants. The focus moves back and forth between nurturing this field and attending to what emerges there.

In the course of my doctoral research, I identified the three spaces in this trialogue as the *declarative space* of the narrator, the *narrative space* of the story itself, and the *projective space* of the narrative elements. I (Drake, 2008b) later described the three spaces in terms of 'once, twice, and thrice upon a time' to extend the classic opening frame for fairy tales and highlight the need for multiple perspectives on the same story. Using a trialogic approach enabled me to move between these spaces in coaching as I worked with stories in real time. Focusing on the narrative elements in the field proved to be powerful as it exponentially increased the places from which transformation could emerge. For example, an opening for awakening or change could emerge from a deep exploration of a single element (e.g., a metaphor) used to describe the situation, a change in the relationship between two elements (e.g., when the person saw her situation from the other person's perspective), or from a third space beyond the two elements (e.g., when a new option or a better solution unexpectedly arises from the gestalt). As Mishler (1999) pointed out, "Given the interconnectedness of its parts, which are variable in form and strength, a change in one part of the field is consequential for all other parts" (pp. 121–122).

> Focusing on the narrative elements in the field proved to be powerful as it exponentially increased the places from which transformation could emerge.

Third spaces are based in the recognition that two terms are seldom sufficient to describe the situations people bring to coaching and, therefore, it is often necessary to introduce a third term to find a resolution (Evanoff, 2000; Lefebvre, 1980; Schwartz-Salant, 1998). This is because our psyches are self-regulating systems that largely evolve through the integration of unconscious material into the pairings that we use to define ourselves ("I am this, not that"). Many of the stories that people bring to coaching reflect an unconscious search to resolve an inner conflict resulting from what they perceive is a pair of opposites. Their stories can be seen as an attempt to get unstuck from an oscillation between the two poles or a fixation on one. Their attempts to resolve the conflict by choosing one of the two opposing positions may temporarily relieve their internal unrest, but they don't reveal the deeper truth or provide a strong enough platform for real change.

Jung repeatedly argued that the tension of opposites must be held until their meaning, the unknown "third", appears. However, since it is difficult to do that through direct introspection we project this conflict onto other people in our life and in our stories. In this sense, projection can be seen in the ways in which characters in people's stories are made to carry certain emotions, positions, characteristics, etc. on their behalf. This conflict can also be projected onto the coaching relationship as seen in Ogden's (1999) notion of the "analytic third." Projection provides a temporary outlet valve for our psyche but, in the end, development only occurs when we take back the projection and own it as a part of ourselves. We would be forever stuck in our current state of consciousness if what Jung called our transcendent function did not continually create symbols, such as the characters in our stories, to help us grow beyond our either/or thinking to the next level. They are valuable as surrogates for the same reason that coachees learn new things about themselves through looking at their stories as the protagonist instead of as the narrator.

By allowing each opposite in a pair to exist in equal dignity and worth (Jung, 1970, p. 304), the contents of the unconscious can join with the ego to create a third position and a new state of consciousness can come into being (Raff, 2000). It is about bringing one and one together to equal three, as we saw with Shadows and strengths. For example, I can be passionate *and* decisive in stepping up as a *compelling* change leader. You can help coachees to better understand the nature of their issues if you see them as projective spaces in which to explore the characters (including the coachee) and how they inform and relate to each other. This is consistent with narrative researchers such as Riessman (2002) who wanted to know, "How does she place herself in relation to the audience, and vice versa? How does she locate characters in relation to one another and in relation to herself?" (p. 701). The aim is to help people identify, reclaim, and integrate the projected material—and the potential it represents—so they can resolve the issue within themselves. Development occurs in third spaces through integrating the split-off energies of these potential stories and the imagined selves that go with them.

Your role as a coach is to bring out these energies and attributes from the characters in question so they become more available for the coachee to use for his own development. For example, a coachee's story about an angry boss could yield insights for him about a need to embody more of his own power in asking for what he needs. To do so often requires confronting an imagined self he has avoided for fear that he would become like his boss (with memories of his raging father blended in as well). By de-stigmatizing and de-polarizing the issue, more space opens up for a third way through which he can change, his relationship with his boss can change and his underlying narratives can change. *Crucible* and *crux* are two etymologically related words that capture the essence of how this happens. A crucible is a vessel used to contain high-temperature chemical reactions. The coaching relationship, the field, and the coach must all be strong enough to contain what are often strong emotional or developmental experiences brought forth in the process. Narrative coaching offers a crucible in which people can bear the opposites at the core of their issue long enough to find a third way, a path with heart (Meade, 2006), which enables them to get to the *crux* of the matter and resolve it.

These third spaces are projective because they tend to capture elements outside of the conscious awareness of the person telling his story and the usual frame for how the story is told. Working in this projective third space is powerful because it allows people to stay in relationship with the other characters in their stories while they access their inner experience. This is important not only to help them deepen their inquiry in the coaching session, but also to start building the scaffolding they will need to put their new insights into action. People will be more able to sustain the changes they begin in coaching if they can experience these changes through working with the characters in their stories as a practice ground. You do not need to dig into their past or gather numerous details since their unconscious tends to bring enough of what is needed into their stories and the conversation. Instead, imagine yourself off to the side of the conversation with the narrative landscape spread out in front of you such that you can see the three spaces (narrator, story and characters). You can always re-establish a relationship with a coachee in his first space as needed—e.g., to reassure him, draw his attention to a truth in the moment or invite him to step into it.

The secret is to notice which elements of people's stories are being re-experienced in the session and why (Casement, 1991) and to see where they take you. Whenever possible, I use the entire area where I am coaching or teaching to give people the room they need to experience the differences between the first, second, and third spaces. I do so because I want people to live and breathe their stories rather than try to hold it all in their head. I want them to work with a deep sense of serious play so they can move between experimentation and examination in any given moment. The aim is to bring the elements in their stories alive and out in the open so they can be observed and experienced. It allows people to be *in* but not *of* their stories. They can then see them with fresh eyes, explore their elements with more courage, and discover new ways of moving forward. It is the fastest way I know to get people in touch with the deeper change that is being called for. When I look around the room in our Labs it is not uncommon to see laughter and tears side by side.

Understanding the narrative coaching model

Let me fall . . . for I will be caught by who I am becoming.
Cirque de Soleil, "Quidam"

In the beginning I found kindred spirits in Kenyon and Randall's (1997) work on "restorying, as it too was based in both narrative structure and narrative psychology. They shared my appreciation of: (1) the actual words people use in narrating their experience, (2) the genres and points of view they habitually use, (3) the importance of finding their authentic voice amid the cacophony in and around them, (4) the interpretations they and others rush to make, (5) the need at times to change their narrative environments if they are to flourish, and (6) the untapped value of the material that they have overlooked or left untold. I opted to speak of narrative coaching as a "reconfiguration" process rather than as a "restorying" or "reauthoring" process because I wanted a more integrative term. Change happens when people make shifts in who and how they are as *author* of their stories, as *actor* in their stories, and as *agent* in the narratives around them. Narrative coaching facilitates transformative learning and development through the reconfiguration of the elements in people's stories to align more fully with their aspirations.

> Change happens when people make shifts in who and how they are as *author* of their stories, as *actor* in their stories, and *agent* in the narratives around them.

The narrative coaching model depicts people's movement between their inner worlds (e.g., identities, beliefs, attitudes) and their outer worlds (e.g., states, roles, statuses), between their past worlds and their future worlds, and between their constructed selves and their imagined selves. The basic model (Figure 12) aligns the four acts of narrative structure, the four phases of development and the four phases of transition in an integrative process in which change is occurring at multiple levels. The beauty of this approach is that coaching is experienced as a natural process rather than as a mechanical intervention. It shifts the emphasis from coaches and their methodologies to the coachee and their stories in the field. This human-centered approach to coaching moves beyond modernist assumptions, linear development models, extroverted goal orientation, and lingering biases toward behaviorism to create a more holistic approach to development. As a result, the changes people experience in coaching can more readily be applied and integrated when they return to their life and/or work.

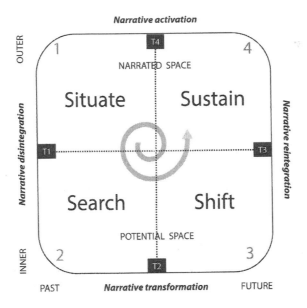

Figure 12. *Basic narrative coaching model*

This figure offers the basic outlines of the narrative coaching model. It is built on the enhanced rites of passage framework (figure 11) and adds narrative and coaching components. The details of the model will be fleshed out in the next chapter, but here are the key additions for now:

- The spatial-temporal coordinates for the four quadrants remain the same, but the upper half is now the "narrated space" and the lower half is now the "potential space" to reflect the shift from an anthropological frame to a coaching frame.

- The 4 S's are now used to indicate the four phases of narrative coaching. The process begins in the upper left quadrant and spirals counter-clockwise. The spiral runs in this direction to reflect the disruptive nature of transitions and change that require us to move in a different direction than the status quo.

- What was labeled "Transition" in the liminal phase is now "Individuation" to reflect the fact that the entire process is really a series of transitions and maturation is the aim in this phase. Also, "Integration" has been added as its counterpart at T4 to reflect the need for people to embed the new story in their life and environment.

- The path of narrative reconfiguration is depicted around the outside: (1) the quest begins with the disintegration of the current narrative in light of internal transitions and/or external changes, it is then (2) transformed through liminal experiences, (3) reintegrated in a new configuration that reflects both what has been discovered and what is now desired, and (4) activated as part of a new identity.

Taken together, the model reflects the phases that people go through as they reconfigure elements in their stories to create a new narrative. Reconfigurations generally come sooner and have more impact when coachees frame them in language and images from their own stories and in terms of aspirations they are seeking not problems they are solving. It is a process that is both expansive in holding space in the field and laser-focused when it comes time to zero in on openings for change. If the process is only expansive, changes dissipate into the wind because they are ungrounded; if the process is too laser-focused, they often wither under the glare because they are unsupported. Reconfigured stories are like new shoots in the garden in that they need care and time to grow. As such, let any new stories that emerge breathe until they settle and feel rooted. In the end:

- some stories will lose their relevance and/or influence;
- some stories will take on new relevance and influence;
- some stories will come more to the foreground and are "thickened" (Geertz, 1978); and
- some experiences will be "de-narrated" and allowed to drop back into the sea of life.

Reconfiguring stories for a change

There is only one problem, ever: your uninvestigated story in the moment.
Byron Katie

Early on in developing narrative coaching I moved away from the term "re-authoring" (White, 1995, 2004, 2005; White & Epston, 1990) that was made famous by the early narrative therapists. I appreciated the phrase for bringing attention to the need to foster greater agency and autonomy in people in the midst of dominant social and professional discourses. However, I came to the conclusion that the word—like "re-storying"—was not fully representative of what I saw happening in narrative coaching. I agree that focusing on how people narrate themselves and their experience is key if they are to bring about change in their life. However, I found it limiting to (1) focus solely on the author or the story when it comes to bringing about change as it is a systemic and hermeneutic process, (2) assume that change and development emerge primarily in opposition to dominant narratives, and (3) minimize the existential and developmental need for accountability for one's narrative choices.

Narrative coaching helps people shift narrative patterns through reconfiguring elements in representative stories in order to attain what they are seeking. It starts with helping them be mindfully present as a foundation for taking multiple perspectives on what they are seeking to shift as noted below. It also helps them develop themselves and remain agile in terms of how they resolve their issue. Reconfiguration can be seen in terms of the following shifts in people, each of which relates well to one of the phases of the narrative coaching model:

- A shift in their agency and accountability as the author of their stories (Situate)
- A shift in their role as an actor in their stories of self and significant others (Search)
- A shift in how the elements in their stories are organized and for what purpose (Shift)
- A shift in the impact their stories have on themself and others (Sustain)

For example: A coachee who starts with a story about being the victim of an unfair partner:

- *Situate:* I notice that my language is mostly in the passive voice, as if all this is just happening to me. I wonder why I am telling it this way. I think I have a belief that I have to take whatever is given to me—and make the best out of it somehow.
- *Search:* This often leaves me feeling like I am trying to catch up . . . and a bit resentful. However, the story feels incomplete, like there is so much more . . . I wonder what would happen if I changed my story into the active voice. *[He re-tells the story from this place . . .]*
- *Shift:* It was hard to stay in that voice at the point in the story when something was asked of me. *[He practices with the coach and moves through his fear to feel a new sense of power . . .]* I need to be clear about what I need in order to be at my best and what I am willing to offer so I can respond differently in those moments. *[He creates a pivot for himself . . .]*
- *Sustain:* I notice my voice is quite shaky as I ask for what I want in this new way. But it feels good too. It helped me to plant

my feet firmly on the ground and pause to give myself time
to think. It feels like you are taking me more seriously now.
*[He makes commitments about whom to try it with first when he
leaves.]*

You can help coachees release or reconfigure narratives that no
longer serve them—not because they are inaccurate but because
they are less functional in current circumstances. Like a masseuse
who presses into a muscle to release its tightness, you can do the
same by entering into coachees' stories to help them release their
narrative tension. In so doing, you can help people see that their
personal stories are developed in a social context—with its preferred
discourse, histories, and expectations—and serve social as well as
personal functions (Rappaport, 1993). Think in terms of situated
identities (Ochs & Capps, 1996) and Gergen and Gergen's (2006)
request for "an account of human change in which all that we have
understood as distinctly psychological can be understood in terms of
relational action" (p. 119). This requires coaches to work with people
in terms of:

- *time* (reconfiguring the relationship between the past, present
  and future),
- *space* (reconfiguring the relationship between outer and profane,
  inner and sacred, and in-between and liminal),
- *identity* (reconfiguring the relationship between the constructed, lived and imagined selves), and
- *action* (reconfiguring the relationships between characters in
  their stories and with the narratives in which they reside).

Reconfiguration can also be seen as a rebalancing between what
we see as given, what we see as possible, and what we see as desired
(see Bruner, 2002; Maddi, 1988). The need for it is often triggered
when people recognize that what once provided them with a sense of
protection has now become constrictive or at times even destructive.
What was once the mask they wore, the artifice of their persona, has
now become a self-imposed prison (Hollis, 2013). As we shall see
in the next chapter, narrative coaching is a process through which
people can learn to live more fully by putting down their masks

in relating to others, openly encountering more of their whole self, nonjudgmentally experiencing reality as it is, and reconfiguring their narratives and stories accordingly. The aim, as Boyd (2009) observed, is to support transformative narrative work that "helps us not to override the given, but to be less restricted by it, to cope with it more flexibly and on something more like our own terms" (p. 50). Before I share how this is done, let's look at three familiar tools and how they are re-conceptualized in narrative coaching.

Externalization

Externalization and *unique outcomes* are two well-known concepts from narrative therapy. They have a place in narrative coaching, and they are conceived of and used differently in some important ways. Externalization is a process in which a quality or problem that is seen to be subjective and internal to a person is objectified and moved outside the person. Fox (2003) offers a couple of examples of how this would be done in narrative therapy: "I am weak'" becomes "you get overwhelmed by a feeling of weakness"; or "she is anorexic" may become "a fear of food has taken control of her life." By casting the problem as outside of the person it becomes easier for her to see and enter into a relationship with the problem and revise it (White, 1989). Otherwise, she can only attack the problem by attacking herself. Externalization can be helpful when a person first engages an issue, particularly if it is stigmatized and/or she would benefit from a sharper distinction between her own experience and others' narratives. The narrative therapy community has done great work in this regard.

There are three differences in how externalization is used in narrative coaching. Firstly, we would agree that externalization interrupts the habitual formation and performance of our stories by allowing us to stand back from them and separate our identities, stories and performances from each other. In narrative therapy, the person and the therapist would then assume a united stance *against* the problem (Brimhall, Gardner, & Henline, 2003, p. 406) which is outside the system, whereas in narrative coaching the coachee and the coach would assume a united stance *with* the problem which is part of the system. Secondly, while externalization in narrative therapy thankfully reduces the experience of blame it can also reduce the level of accountability and what Mahony (2003) saw as the person's existential responsibilities. Narrative coaches think in terms of third spaces in which people gain some temporary distance from their issues and stories without replacing one binary frame with another. The aim is to soften the fused "narrative grip" while acknowledging that whatever they are dealing with is part of the same system.

Thirdly, I sometimes find the way the externalization language is used in narrative therapy to be awkward and overly problematized. For example, to translate the phrase, "I am weak" (Fox, 2003) as uttered by a client into "you get overwhelmed by a feeling of weakness" seems awkward, passive and presumptive. "I am weak" does not have to be a summative statement of a person's identity that needs to be amended. Instead, it may be a truthful description of his current state or an opening for an exploration of that phrase. In a narrative coaching session, this phrase might be reframed in more natural terms by the coachee, for example: "I am feeling weak" or "When you say that, I notice myself feeling weaker," or "I frequently position myself as weak in my stories about my team." We would explore the current and potential positions of "weakness" as a character in her stories to see how this aspect of herself (and potentially larger narratives) could be reconfigured to generate new options. In this way, the person is no longer conflated with his stories yet still retains a sense of accountability for them.

Narrative coaching is about helping people recognize that what they once saw as a natural and inevitable reflection of their world, is actually a construction; and their suffering stems from an adherence to that construction—particularly when it contrasts with reality (Fulton & Siegel, 2005). So, ask yourself as you move through your coaching sessions, "Where is this person right now and what does she need in terms of her stories about reality in order to move forward?" To support their growth, you can help people make distinctions between their stories and the larger narratives and between their identities and their issues. The focus is less on determining the reasons why things are the way they are and more on defining the results the person wants to attain. Be willing to move between internalization and externalization, depending on which would best serve the developmental needs of the coachee. Sometimes this means matching where they are right now (e.g., letting the painful story element they have externalized stay there until they are ready to address it) and sometimes it means challenging where they are (e.g., inviting them to consider the role they have played in creating the situation they have experienced as painful).

This requires coachees to stay actively connected to and engaged with whatever has been externalized as they work with it. By keeping it within the field, they can more freely move in and out of relationship with it until such time as they can reclaim it and internalize it at a higher level. This is why there is so much emphasis in narrative coaching on attention to the field and holding space there. Elements in people's stories and larger narratives as well as aspects of themselves can be temporarily suspended in the field as part of a reconfiguration process. People can then separate what has been projected from the other person (Fraser & Solovey, 2007), externalize it into neutral territory to see it more clearly, and take more responsibility for their narrative construction as they internalize it as their own. I find this blended approach is also useful for coaches because it lessens our need to 'make something happen' by keeping the focus on coachees' accountability for their own stories.

We can work openly with the narrative material because we trust that a more desirable reconfiguration is already present. Sometimes it is discovered by inviting the coachee to "circle upwards" through externalization to more astutely observe her story from above, while at other times it is discovered by inviting the coachee to "circle downwards" through internalization to experience her story from within. Externalization can be quite useful when there is a need for greater awareness and acceptance, and internalization can be quite useful when there is a need for greater accountability and action. Either way, it calls for a deep curiosity as you help people explore new ways of relating to their stories. Narrative therapy tends to focus more on deconstructing the external and dominant narrative as a requirement for liberation from others; narrative coaching tends to focus more on deconstructing the internal and embodied narrative as an opening for a fuller expression of ourselves. These are both important processes; the secret is to move between them to meet the unfolding needs of the coachee and the process.

We can work openly with the narrative material because we trust that a more desirable reconfiguration is already present.

Unique outcomes

The second resource from narrative therapy that is useful in recon-figuration is that of "unique outcomes." Following Erving Goffman (1959), Michael White referred to the contradictions to the dominant narratives within people's stories as "unique outcomes" (White, 1988; White & Epston, 1990) and saw these "sparkling moments" as the gateway to alternative territories to be explored in terms of ways of being in the world (White, 1992). Other narrative therapists have described them as "unique experiences" (Bird, 2000) in referring to newly noticed behaviors or as "exceptions" (de Shazer, 1988; Hewson, 1991) to establish them as behaviors that are consistent with the person's unwritten history. In general, narrative therapists use questions to elicit, clarify, and enhance descriptions of times in the past when the 'problem' was not influential in clients' lives (Chang & Phillips, 1993). One of the values of eliciting alternative stories that reflect these exceptions is that "other sympathetic and previously neglected aspects of the person's experience can be expressed and circulated" (White & Epston, 1990, p. 17).

With his Story Spine framework, Kenn Adams (1991) illustrates how "exceptions" are central to what makes something a story in the first place: (1) Once upon a time . . . (2) Every day . . . (3) *Until one day* . . . (4) Because of that . . . (5) Because of that . . . (6) Because of that . . . (7) Until finally . . . (8) And ever since then . . . The need to formulate a story arises on that "one day" as a way to explain how it was different, how it came to be different and what it means. When I am coaching, I look for moments when these types of experiences are recounted or emerge in sessions. I typically pause there because the moment is often quite rich, and it needs to be handled carefully lest the spell break. I am curious about what breached the common-place and set the protagonist and the story in motion. What were they expecting instead? What triggered the change in course? What feelings and assumptions do they have about it? Through exploring these questions and others like them, you can begin to get a sense for the elements that need to be reconfigured.

In narrative coaching, the notion of "exceptions" resonates because we frame these outcomes in terms of a person's past behaviors more than in contrast to dominant narratives. They are framed in terms of what people are 'standing for' more than as 'acting against'. We also shy away from making normative evaluations of identities, stories, or actions as 'positive' or 'negative', 'good' or 'bad', as these judg-ments tend to shut down learning and perpetuate a dualistic way of thinking. Instead, we focus on increasing people's candid aware-ness of their stories (what *is*), the impact and consequences of those stories, and what they want to be different (what *if*). This is based in the narrative coaching principle that everything you need is right in front of you. We invite people to externalize when they need to sep-arate what was once fused in order to better articulate the dilemma. We invite them to internalize when they are ready to reconfigure the elements at stake and attain a resolution that brings healing and strength (Raff, 2000).

Goals

People have used goals as a resource for achieving great things—from losing weight to meeting sales numbers to putting a man on the moon. There is a great deal of research suggesting that goal theory can be useful in understanding how people achieve their desired outcomes (see Grant, 2012). They are well suited for tracking readily measurable tasks (funds raised, time in a race, score on a test) and as markers for novices and benchmarks for experts. However, I have also observed that goals are often counterproductive—in large part because of the way they are used. I find that in many organizations they end up increasing people's (1) over-emphasis on the end state, often at the expense of other considerations (e.g., ethics and unintended consequences); (2) orientation toward short-term pressures and measures; (3) fatigue with goalposts that keep moving, are not aligned and interfere with healthy lives; and (4) sense of overwhelm and feeling disconnected from themselves (see Ordóñez, Schweitzer, Galinsky, & Bazerman, 2009). A narrative approach to coaching pays far less attention to goals yet still provides supportive internal and external structures people can use in pursuing their aspirations.

Austin and Vancouver (1996) succinctly describe goals as "*internal*[14] representations of desired states or outcomes" (p. 388). However, in real life, goals are almost exclusively discussed in terms of the *external* manifestations of desired states or outcomes and there is often a disconnect between the two. Goals are often formed along the lines of, "I am here and I want to be there." While this is useful as a focusing construct, it assumes that people (1) actually know where they are now, (2) are certain that "there" is where they want to be, and (3) can know the linear path they need to get there. Unfortunately, this is often not the case. Working toward distant goals often leads people to act as if they can just jump across the chasm without understanding their current reality (inner or outer), doing the essential developmental work or investing in what it takes to 'stick the landing'. This seldom works because people often go into it with the same mindset and approach as they had in the past. To bring about change, coachees need to start from a new position that can only be found as they move into Shift. As they look 'up' at Sustain with a fresh perspective, they will see themselves, their issue and their resolution in new ways.

Another issue is that goals are often depicted mechanistically as described in this critique by David Clutterbuck & Susan David (2013):

---

14   Italics added.

"You decide what you want to achieve, gather the necessary resources and motivation, and take appropriate action. With apt, positive feedback you continue until the goal is achieved" (p. 31). However, having taught coaching skills to thousands of people inside and outside organizations over the past 20 years I find that they quite often have the opposite experience. They (1) seldom know what they truly want when they start (let alone why); (2) seldom have all the resources they need; (3) waver in their motivation, particularly since it is often extrinsic in nature at first; (4) don't know what actions will lead to success; (5) rarely get apt, positive feedback; (6) feel challenged by too many, often competing, goals (that keep changing); and (7) have a hard time shaking the feeling that their pursuit of goals is keeping them on the same treadmill. In the end, the pursuit of goals is seldom as simple and linear as it is often portrayed.

We have also been taught to believe that the best way to achieve our goals is to carefully reason about them and consciously strive to reach them. However, "many desirable states—happiness, attractiveness, spontaneity—are best pursued indirectly, and conscious thought and effortful striving can actually interfere with their attainment" (Slingerland, 2014, p. 18). When people focus too much on the external actions related to a goal they often lose touch with themselves and what is true for them and about their situation (see Gallwey, 1981/2009; 2001, 2009). As such, they lose track of their higher-order, values-based goals that are linked to their desires and, instead, chase after lower-order goals that are often linked to other's demands. When people focus too much on the internal representation of a goal they often become disconnected from their environment. Narrative coaching is designed to keep people connected with themselves, their environment and their desired outcome as they move forward in coaching. In so doing, they can be more adaptive and have better scaffolding to support their success.

This is particularly important when the truly desired outcome is uncertain in the beginning or their aspirations don't lend themselves well to a goal-oriented approach. As Kay (2010) noted, "Breaking down well-defined and prioritized objectives into specific states and actions that can be monitored and measured is not how people tend to find fulfillment in their lives, create great art, establish great societies, or build great businesses" (p. 71). In addition, the traditional view of goals does not account for the complexity and contingencies that are pervasive in modern life or help people authentically and effectively align their inner and outer worlds. As Ordóñez, Schweitzer, Galinsky, & Bazerman (2009) argued:

> The simplest things to measure are not necessarily the most important factors in achieving the overall purpose, and focusing on short-term performance may impede learning and lasting personal growth. . . Setting and pursuing specific goals may cause people to ignore important dimensions of performance that are not specified by the goal-setting system . . . [N]arrow goals can promote myopic, short-term behavior that harms the organization [or the person] in the long run. (p. 8)

At a more basic level, the challenge with goals in real life is that people often set them for things they might not otherwise do and/or do not want to do (e.g., I will go to the gym three times a week regardless) or in terms of what they are not going to do (I will not have dessert this week). These are both noble intentions, but they often fail because will power alone is seldom enough. Goals are a means to achieve something you want, not the end themselves. Form follows function. For example, I ride my bike about three days a week not because I have a goal to do so, but because I enjoy the experience of being outdoors and I appreciate the greater freedom I have when I am in shape. I often find that when people set aside their initial goals (form) there is more room for a deeper level of truth (function). It is what I call *GET* (*Goal Evaporation Theory*) in which many of the presenting problems people bring to coaching fall away as the real work to be done reveals itself in the process. It calls for coachees and coachees to stand still long enough to discern what is most true and what the latter are truly seeking. It calls for holding the space for people's stories before any attempts are made to change them or their stories (Gallwey, 1981/2009).

I saw this when teaching a class of graduate coaching students as a visiting lecturer. They had heard about my work and wanted to see how one could possibly coach without goals. The woman who came up front to be coached had a classic goal: to lose 5 more pounds. I accepted that story as it was true for her at that point and then spent about 8–10 minutes exploring the story with her.

At no point did we talk about how she was going to lose that weight or by when. We just held her idea lightly and non-judgmentally. What she came to realize was that her 'goal' was actually a familial and cultural construct about what she *should* weigh after having a child. She realized that she was happy and healthy as she was, and released her internalized goal to lose more weight.

This reflects narrative coaching's stance as a third-generation practice (Stelter, 2014a) with "a less clear and goal-oriented agenda [that] is hopefully more in-depth and sustainable, as coach and coachee create something together, . . . where both parties partake in a journey, and where new stories gradually take shape" (pp. 10–11). I tend to use intentions rather than goals in my coaching in helping people achieve what is important to them. Intentions involve setting a clear direction and the resolve to take an action or achieve an outcome—without the necessity of an ultimate goal or a defined path. Intentions work well with the four reconfiguration tools because they encapsulate what the person needs as they move in the direction of their new narrative: a clarity about when and where to pivot, a vision for where they are headed, and a guide for course correction along the way. They make visible the linkages between people's narratives, behaviors and results so they can adjust their strategies accordingly. This is why I teach narrative coaches to work in the moment with the unfolding narration and what 'is' rather than prematurely move to what 'could be' or 'should be'.

Having a clear intent also creates "an integrated state of priming, a gearing up of our neural system to be in the mode of that specific intention: we can be readying to receive, to sense, to focus, to behave in a certain manner" (Siegel, 2007, p. 177). When your identity and state are in sync with your intention, your actions are inspired and in flow because they are an extension of your being. When your identity and state are not in sync with your intention, your actions are often labored and less effective because it is all about your doing. As we shall see, this priming helps people notice when a pivot is called for, activates the resources necessary to move in the desired direction and instinctively act in line with their desired purpose.

> I used to play lots of tennis. I had a memorable experience of the power of intent when I won a free lesson with a top coach. Unlike all the others I had had in the past, he talked very little and invited me to focus on being in flow rather than on my techniques. I remember feeling my whole mind and body completely absorbed in what I was doing rather than worrying about if I was doing it right. There were no goals in sight. There was also no separation between my mind and my body, myself and my racket (or the ball). I soon was playing the best tennis of my life. *How could this be when he was not teaching me anything?* Or so I thought at the time. . . . My body already knew how to play tennis; the secret was to let it do so.

His approach, which mirrors how we work in narrative coaching, challenged me to trust myself and act from that intention. Paradoxically, I was able to achieve my desired outcome (play well) by releasing my attachment to and focus on it. This was certainly far more effective than setting a goal to improve my game by doing x, y and z. I find that focusing on distant goals often takes coachees into their head and out of their authentic experience and inherent trust—and, as a consequence, their performance drops. Narrative coaching starts with intentions as visualized, internal representations because they provide a way for people to stay grounded in themselves and be guided as they move forward. This approach aligns with Timothy Gallwey's (Gallwey, 1981/2009, 2001, 2009) great work on the "inner game" and newer versions of NLP in which you:

> 'set an intention' to do a particular behavior and you let your unconscious mind figure out how and when to do it. Setting an intention is different than goal-setting in that it is less focused on the outcome and more focused on the commitment. The theory is that if we are consciously

congruent when we set the intention, the unconscious will do the rest. (Tompkins & Lawley, 2001, p. 6)

Intentions are the proverbial 'red thread' that run through the narrative coaching process and the reconfiguration tools that are used along the way. The focus is on pivoting in the present in line with one's intentions more than setting goals for the future. Pivots work well because they provide a simpler focus and allow for more adaptive responses. If you do use goals with a coachee because it works for them, they should be set *at the end* of the coaching process in conjunction with the narrative reconfiguration tools you've used. Here are some of the differences between how goals are often used and what is possible with the use of pivots instead:

Goals	Pivots
• Require a target to shoot for	• Offer a focus to be guided by
• Have multiple meanings of term	• Have a simple, self-defined frame
• Take people out of the present	• Keep the present and future connected
• Define destination beforehand	• Define direction to head
• Define optima by which to plan	• Define values by which to be guided
• Define path and steps to get there	• Define triggers and practice opportunities
• Focus on comparisons with the future	• Focus on performing in the present
• Focus on execution and explanation	• Focus on experimentation and adaptation

In the end, whether you use intentions and/or goals as a resource in coaching, ensure the following:

- There is true conviction and commitment to any that are set (Locke, 1996);
- They are stated positively rather than negatively and in results or outcome language;

- They are stated in sensory-based terms and specific enough to guide behavior;
- They are co-developed in such a way that they will be recognized when accomplished;
- They can be initiated by the person and sustained until they are completed;
- They can be incorporated into all relevant situations; and
- They will generate the highest impact within reach of person's current repertoire.

Let's look now at four of the narrative reconfiguration tools you can use in coaching to support people's intentions and outcomes.

Using tools to bring new stories to life

The harder we try, the more confused things become. More often than not, we do not need more instructions; we need more nonjudgmental awareness, more clarity about the desired result, more trust in ourselves, and more willingness to act.
Tim Gallwey

Narrative coaches don't invest in trying to fix 'problems', but recognize instead that, "every expressed concern can be construed as an attempt to solve a problem, and every presenting complaint can be construed as a problem-solving effort gone awry" (Mahony, 2003, pp. 10–11). We are interested in how people have construed the problem, why they believed their attempt would resolve it, and what caused it to go awry. What coachees discover in exploring these questions points to the elements that need to be reconfigured in order to achieve more of their desired result. Therefore, invite your coachees to take greater accountability for their own awareness, attitude, and actions as they work with you to reconfigure their underlying narratives. In the end, narrative coaching is an iterative and developmental approach in which the most important factors are discovered in the process, learning and growth are central, and short-term and long-term needs are both addressed. This is part of a broader commitment in narrative coaching to focus at the start of sessions on the person, the relationship and the field rather than the presenting issue or goal.

I developed these narrative reconfiguration tools to provide a streamlined yet systemic approach to achieving transformative results. They are effective in part because they are simple, down-to-earth resources that reflect the DIYT (Do-It-Yourself-Together) spirit of our times. The tools (turning points, pivots, vectors of change and nudges) are designed to achieve the same outcomes as goals, but do so in ways that are more in line with the narrative approach, the lives we lead now, and the way many people naturally function. They support people's success by providing a flexible yet clear structure; tapping their intrinsic motivations; and keeping them in touch with themselves, their aspiration and their environment. They often enable people to move forward in ways they would never have imagined as possible— or seen at all—had they stayed within the narrow confines of goals set in advance. Each reconfiguration tool is particularly well suited for one of the thresholds and the developmental step it represents (see figure 13). For example, the first one (turning points) is most often found as people Separate and begin their journey.

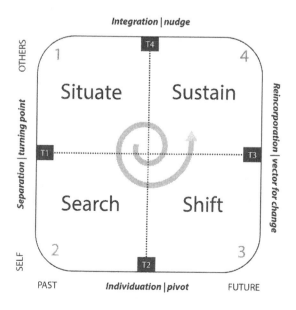

Figure 13. *The four primary reconfiguration tools*

You can use the four reconfiguration tools to assist coachees in seeing how their issues are often directly linked to stories that no longer serve them well. They are most effective when used with coachees who have moved beyond talking about their stories and are ready, willing and able to do the work. Everything up to that point in coaching is about preparing them for this awakening and reckoning. It is also important to remember that the energy tapped in the reconfiguration process must be equal to or greater than the perceived energy of the current narrative in order to bring about change. There has to be enough energy to make a difference, but not so much that it makes things overly complicated. The following is an outline of how to use the reconfiguration tools in coaching to guide people across the thresholds. The work done at each threshold in the process will come in handy at the next one, both as a source of material and as a resource for the next work to be done.

Guiding people across thresholds using the reconfiguration tools

T1: Notice the *Turning point* when the conversation shifts, signaling a potential change of direction that seems promising. Pause at this fork in the road to let its import be felt and to confirm the coachee's desire to take it. Invite her to articulate what she is leaving behind as she *Separates* and embarks on the *Search*.

T2: Work with her to fashion a *Pivot*—her old story on one side (drawing on what she left behind and is in Shadow) and the new story on the other side (drawing on her desires and core values at stake). Invite her to articulate what she gains as she *Individuates* and embarks on the *Shift*.

T3: Create a *Vector for Change* with three pivots (Behavior, Environment, Mindset) that is aligned around a shared Aspiration using integrative development theory. Invite her to articulate where she wants to *Reincorporate* first and who will help her as she embarks on *Sustain*.

T4: Use the Vector for change to help her identify a few meaningful *Nudges* she can use to move in the direction of her new story each day (and get back on track whenever necessary). Invite her to articulate how she will *Integrate* these changes into her life as she embarks on a new *Situate*.

Turning points

In times of great change, the learners will inherit the Earth while those attached to old certainties will find themselves beautifully equipped to deal with a world that no longer exists.
Eric Hoffer

This narrative reconfiguration tool is used most often in coaching to help people *Separate* and cross the T1 threshold from the *Situate* phase to the *Search* phase. Turning points[15] are often triggered by "inciting incidents" (see McKee, 2004) that reflect "breaches in the commonplace" (Bruner, 1986) where the status quo is disrupted. It is at these points where people turn or are turned off from their current trajectory and are now seeking another way forward as a result. Turning points can be found in the Story Spine in those "but one day . . ." moments as openings for a new narrative or story to emerge. In those moments people realize, "I used to think or do that, but now I want to or need to think or do this instead." We saw this in Nancy's example as she turned off from the story, "I'm just one of the gang" when she realized that was not true anymore. When people recognize they are at a turning point, the proverbial fork in the road, help them discover where they want to begin their exploration and what they are seeking in the process. Like all thresholds, these points in the coaching process are both powerful and fragile. Engage them with courageous and patient care. Images and themes that will end up playing a major role in their journey are often foreshadowed here. Reconfiguration is only possible for those who have stepped onto the path.

Reconfiguration is only possible for those who have stepped onto the path.

---

15   The names for the reconfiguration tools are not capitalized. They have heightened and specific meanings in this context, but they are positioned as a natural action done intentionally within narrative coaching.

As you begin exploring a coachee's turning point with him, pay particular attention to what he perceives he has lost or is losing and is now seeking to (re-)gain. Most coachees will frame this in tangible and familiar external terms at first. Go with it to build rapport and then invite them to begin the inner journey as well. It is important to let the story unfold fully because the more open people are to the process, the more fruitful it will be as they move through it. The full significance of a turning point is not likely to be revealed until later in the process. You can think of a turning point as an entrance into the conversation people most need as they start their journey. It is tempting to think we know what their stories mean and, therefore, where people and their stories are headed (or should head). Instead, be patient so their true purpose can reveal itself. Manage your respective anxieties so that neither of you prematurely forecloses on the process or the stories that are unfolding. Let them name the journey they are on as much as possible because they will be more committed to issues they have framed and solutions they have designed. Here is the first tool at work with one of my students:

> **Turning point:** After an initial conversation about her perceived lack of self-confidence after some time out of the job market, Rachel* realizes that she is at a turning point because her two young children are now old enough for her to return to work part-time.

Pivots

To have success in crunch time, you need to integrate certain healthy patterns into your day-to-day life so that they are completely natural to you when the pressure is on.
Josh Waitzkin

This narrative reconfiguration tool is most often used in coaching to help people *Individuate* and cross the T2 threshold from the *Search* phase to the *Shift* phase. The basic distinction that began as a turning point is now coming into more focus as they shift their attention from the past to the future and from deliberation to implementation.

For the person in our case story, it was the movement from being aware of her turning point to starting to think about looking for work. Pivots are a simple binary choice that people can make in the moment between thinking or acting in line with an old story (what they are leaving behind) and a new story (what they are moving toward). It is important to recognize that there is no need to discard the old story altogether. It still has value in certain forms and circumstances, and it can serve as a tempering agent for strengths and a source of compassion for those in similar situations. Coachees can use pivots to help them better self-regulate and choose well rather than lapse into reactive defaults. Pivots are *not* defined as a fixed and specific end point as one would with a goal.

Pivots radiate from a point in time with the old story along one arrow and a new story along the other. We saw an example in figure 5 which depicted the infusion of Shadow material to temper our strengths, and we can see three examples of regular pivots in figure 14. Whenever the person finds herself in a situation in which she would otherwise default to the old story, she now has a simple, memorable and actionable alternative she can choose in the moment. The more often she chooses the new narrative channel, the more those neural pathways and habits are strengthened, the more her identity comes in line with the new story, and the more her environment can relate to her in that way. It is important that the taglines for the two stories neither exceed too dramatically nor stay too timidly within the range of their current narrative schemas (Russell & van Den Broek, 1992) so they are seen as applicable and doable in coachees' everyday life. It is also critical for coachees to use words or key phrases from their own stories as they define the pivot's two arrows so they fit within their normal discourse and have emotional and somatic anchors.

> For example, a Lab participant developed a pivot based on an analogy in her story about a recent camping trip. She was having trouble getting her business going again after she had moved from the city to the countryside. She said it was like the procrastination she felt in getting out of her warm sleeping bag to go outside on the cold, damp mornings on her trip.

She identified her old story as "in the tent" and her new story as "out of the tent", and she used this pivot to help her make decisions each day. In a given moment, would she choose to go out of her 'tent' into the unknown to build her new life and practice or would she choose to stay inside and do something else? Either choice could be appropriate; the key was to be conscious in choosing which story to choose at that point in time—and nudge herself to 'get out of the tent' more often.

Here are three examples of pivots from work I have done. The old story is depicted horizontally to indicate that the situation will likely remain the same if nothing is done. The new story emerges from the same decision point, but rises up indicating it is moving in the direction of their aspiration.

Using a Pivot to change a team's mindset

NEW STORY: WE WORK FROM A COACHING MODEL
As a result: We empower families so they flourish (aided by our expertise).

OLD STORY: WE WORK FROM A MEDICAL MODEL
As a result: We deliver services to families as experts (irrespective of their experience).

Using a Pivot to change a career search strategy

NEW STORY: I AM LIBERATED BY WHAT I HAVE GAINED
As a result: I am myself and will make the most of this transition to create what I want.

OLD STORY: I AM DEFINED BY WHAT I HAVE LOST
As a result: I am a victim who is stuck in transition and has to start over from scratch.

Using a Pivot to change a leadership style

NEW STORY: IT IS IMPORTANT TO BUILD STRONG RELATIONSHIPS
As a result: I make space for our differences so we can grow and find the best solution.

OLD STORY: IT IS IMPORTANT TO ALWAYS BE RIGHT
As a result: I shut down our differences so I can stay on top and my team needs me.

Figure 14. *Three examples of a pivot*

It is helpful to have a stark distinction between the two story lines in a pivot, especially at first, so that there is no doubt. Later, people will need scaffolding to be able to do this on their own as the lines get farther apart—a reflection of the growing opportunities and challenges in living out the new story. It is also crucial that they develop a greater awareness of their inner experience and signals from their environment so they notice opportunities in the moment to choose the new path. This is particularly important when they feel triggered because their initial reflex is often to return to their old ways. As such, encourage coachees as they are starting out to practice the pivot whenever the choice presents itself, no matter how small the opportunity may seem. Invite them to notice and experiment with new ways of seeing, carrying and expressing themselves based in the new story. The more clearly and strongly people can hold their intention for the new story in their pivot, the more able they will be to "hold two contradictory experiences or memories in awareness at the same time . . . and intensify the focus on the positive memory while also remaining aware of the negative memory [they] have chosen to rewire (Graham, p. 121).

The aim is for coachees to increase their capability to "become more present to themselves in their social context and able to act with more impact within that context and to experience more congruence" (Vogel, 2012, p. 7). Pivots are generally triggered by experiential clues (e.g., place, time, body cue), which serve as an early warning system for our habituated narratives and responses (Silsbee, 2008). They give people both the circuit breaker they need and an alternative that has been primed and practiced. In many ways, it does not matter what the person chooses to pivot about as long as it has a meaningful connection with what the person is trying to achieve through coaching. Pivoting is an opportunity for coachees to learn a number of the meta-skills they will need, including being able to pause in the moment to reflect on their choices, observing reality and themselves without judgment, setting clear intentions, and learning through experimentation. In creating pivots with coachees, invite them to:

- identify actions (big or small) they already do frequently as points of practice,
- notice the pivoting choice in the moment,
- remind themselves of the likely consequences of each arrow, and
- make a new choice even if it feels awkward at first (which it most often does).

Often when I'm working with a coachee we will co-construct a visual diagram of the pivot on a whiteboard so that we can continue to refine the language and the significance of each of the two arrows as the session unfolds. I find this a very powerful way of working because of the synergies between the insights, the drawing, and their development—and the fact that it is being co-created and documented in real time. I often take the lead at first given my role as the coach but, at some point—often when I've got something not quite right—the coachee takes over and sees the process through to the end. This swapping of roles reflects the coachee's internal shift in taking more control of her own story and destiny. While pivots are designed to help coachees address specific situations or aspirations in their life, they also enhance their ability to self-regulate more broadly. Every time coachees practice their pivot they reinforce a new pattern not only for that issue, but also more broadly in terms of adjacent issues and their overall ability to pause and pivot. Here is the second tool at work with the same client:

> **Pivot:** After doing some archetype work, Rachel defined her pivot as "I am not visible in the market anymore" *(old story)* versus "I choose work that fits my life now" *(new story)*. The old story had kept her from reaching out to others because she was sure that she would not make it. As she began to rehearse the new story with her group, she started to build confidence in herself and also get contacts to help her get started.

Vectors for change

This narrative reconfiguration tool is most often used in coaching to help people *Reincorporate* and cross the T3 threshold from the *Shift* phase to the *Sustain* phase. It involves using the BEAM framework from integrative development theory to break down the original pivot into three components (*Mindset, Environment and Behavior*) (Drake, 2014a) to make it easier for the person to stay on track to reach her Aspiration (the fourth component). The three pivots are aligned in a vector for change to increase the number of signals that will activate the new story and the number of anchors to sustain these changes in the person's life. Vectors provide a performance structure in which people are more likely to feel connected with others, gain immediate benefit and enrich their sense of attachment security than with goals. They do so by enriching the *Environment* (providing a sense of a safe haven), guiding *Behavior* (increasing their sense of a secure base) and shifting their *Mindset* (creating a more resilient and mature working model) in order to fulfill their *Aspiration* (improving their abilities for empathy, exploration, engagement and execution).

Coachees can use their Vector to ask themselves: (1) How do I know I am at a pivot point? (2) Does the choice I am about to make move me closer to my new story or my old story? (3) What can I learn from this experience? (4) Where will I focus my attention in terms of the four BEAM elements to reinforce the new story? Vectors generally work better in coaching than linear and fixed action plans because they are more agile and responsive to changing conditions, opportunities, and understandings of the new story. A vector for change can be put into play once the pivots have become clear enough and the coachee has some trials under his belt from the *Shift* phase. Much of what people end up attracting or creating in the Sustain phase only appears once they turn the corner out of *Search* into *Shift*. However, it is essential at this juncture to connect the long-term *Aspiration* with sufficient short-term actions in order to get there. Vectors can be used to help people stay oriented toward their *Aspiration* while giving them room to flex on the specifics as their grasp of the situation, their progress, what matters to them, and what is required become clearer.

Vectors for change also have an advantage over goals in that the members of a team can all use the same vector to guide their choices and actions regardless of their ability to deliver on it, their level of contribution to it or their degree of accountability for it. In addition, they prompt teams to work on their collective narratives in order to support individuals as they make shifts in their personal narratives. In working with teams, I get them to imagine these shifts moving out across the vector as a wave, with more clarity and specificity close in and less so as it gets farther out in time. This gives people on the team the opportunity to ask the same two questions as for individuals: Does the choice we are about to make move us closer to our new story or our old story (or some version thereof)? Where should we focus our attention in terms of the four BEAM elements in order to be more in line with our new story more often? Vectors for change provide a simple yet powerful way for people to bring forward what has emerged from the coaching process as they move back into the world.

Coachees will be more successful in using vectors for change if their pivots are developed and organized according to the four integrative development elements, as seen in the figure below. Clarifying the *Aspiration* comes first and it serves as the North Star or Southern Cross for the process. *Mindset* is the first pivot because it reflects how people see their situation, make sense and meaning of it, and decide to take action. Without a new mindset as a starting point, most of us will revert to old behaviors and keep replicating old environments. Shifting the mindset is key to the formulation of a new narrative. *Environment* comes next. By shaping their environment, people will create a more receptive and fertile space in which they can naturally embody the new mindset and try out new behaviors. This is an important and often overlooked step that explains why most training and coaching initiatives on their own are not as impactful as hoped. Collective and structural narratives have a profound influence, for better or worse, on people's ability to sustain change. Determining which new *Behaviors* to invest in and how to best develop them comes near the end of the vectoring process not the beginning. At this point, new behaviors will seem like natural expressions of the new mindset and environment. Here is the third tool at work with the same student:

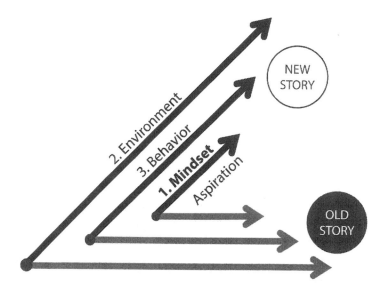

Figure 15. *Aligning the three pivots to create a vector for change*

Vector for change: Rachel worked with a peer on her original pivot which, as is often the case, was a *Mindset* pivot. She then decided on an *Environment* pivot that distinguished between "I have to do this all by myself" *(old story)* and "I will create the community I need" *(new story)*. Lastly, she drew on the archetype of the 'Queen' to identify her *Behavior* pivot that distinguished between "I will keep to myself since I am new to this" and "I will speak up as someone with a lot to offer". Her *Aspiration*: to find meaningful work with a healthy group of people that fit her other role as a mother.

Nudges

Pick battles small enough to win and big enough to matter.
Jonathon Kozol

This narrative reconfiguration tool is most often used in coaching to help people *Integrate* and cross the T4 threshold from the *Sustain* phase back to the *Situate* phase. It is the final step in the process as coachees embed their reconfigured narratives in their identities, stories, and lives. Nudges are the small steps they can regularly take to progress within the vector of change. They are important because as Silsbee (2008) notes, "We are creatures of habit . . . In order to replace what we've done for decades with something better, we have to practice new ways of doing until they are sufficiently stabilized in us to be available even when the worn grooves of old habits still call us" (p. 152). I think of nudges as tugboats with their deep, low motor and driven by captains with a keen sense of tides and winds; an experienced wisdom about where to push on a ship many times its size to get it to move in the right direction; and the patience to just keep nudging the boat to its destination—either to the right dock or out the right channel to the sea. Thinking like a tugboat, invite your coachees to

- recognize and take every opportunity (planned or unplanned) for practicing a pivot;
- take steps, no matter how small, which will move them forward along their vector; and
- appreciate what already works for them and use these to nudge and build momentum.

Thaler and Sunstein's (2008) research on nudges has led to the introduction of hundreds of applications that limit people's choices so as to guide them to the desired outcome with minimal effort. Well-known examples include placing "rumble strips" on highways that vibrate loudly to warn drivers they have drifted off the main pavement and switching your choice regarding organ donation on forms from *opt-in* to *opt-out* (Thaler & Sunstein, 2008). Narrative coaching builds on this by helping people identify simple nudges they can regularly use to reinforce their new narrative using all four BEAM elements (behavior, environment, aspiration and mindset). In a sense, we are helping people become their own "choice architects" (Thaler & Sunstein, 2008). People can deconstruct their current and desired behavior through experimentation in coaching sessions to determine the internal triggers and/or external signals they can use to define their nudges. For example, Rachel experimented with her posture in the workshop as part of trying on the Queen archetype. In the process, she found that paying attention to her low back was the best trigger. If she noticed herself unconsciously slouching, she used it as a gentle reminder to reactivate the Queen energy. This was often enough to bring back online all the other ways she was developing herself through this work.

Nudges are a very useful tool because they can be used wherever people notice opportunities to practice. This is quite handy for our busy lives where things don't always go according to plan. Tompkins and Lawley (2011) similar observed, "practice regularly and put yourself in contexts where the desired behavior is likely to be required and notice what happens" (p. 10). Brief therapist Bill O'Hanlon (2000) talks about it in terms of "What is one thing you can do differently?" Management scholar Karl Weick (1984) calls them "small wins" and writes that they "do not combine in a neat, linear, serial form, with each step being a demonstrable step closer to some predetermined goal. More common is the circumstance where small wins are scattered and cohere only in the sense that they move in the same general direction" (p. 43). Amabile & Kramer's (2012) research suggests that a sense of small wins and incremental progress is more important than big incentives in helping motivate people to engage and perform. This has been consistently demonstrated by experts such as K. Anders Ericsson and his colleagues (Ericsson & Charness, 1994; Ericsson, Krampe, & Tesch-Römer, 1993), George Leonard (1992) and Jim Loehr (2007) in their work on deliberate practice.

Here is the fourth tool at work:

Nudge: Rachel identified two nudges that would help her: (1) moving into her new *Mindset* just prior to calling a prospective client and (2) talking with one person on every train trip about what she did for a living.

A third serendipitously appeared when another narrative coaching student happened to see her on the station platform, waiting for the train into town for a follow-up workshop. She had shared at the previous program that normally she allowed herself to be "crowded-in". However, he quickly noticed that she was standing there as if she was a queen . . . and he shared with her that people were walking around her as if they could sense her regal energy. This was her first piece of evidence that the inner changes she was making were slowly yet positively changing her outer environment as well. She decided to add a third nudge, which was to stand like a queen whenever she was waiting for her train to work.

With each nudge, the reconfiguration of her stories solidifies and blossoms—and she is doing the same as a result. As a postscript: She secured a half-time coaching position a few months after the second workshop.

Coaches are like midwives who assist people in bringing their new stories to life through intention and attention. Their success is often a result of blended strategies formed around motivations and structures that are both mythological and mechanical in nature. Goals can be part of the formula if used well as markers, but outcomes are often best approached through clearly set intentions and a more iterative and integrative approach to change and development. In narrative coaching, we invite coachees to move (1) between externalization and internalization, (2) between soaring above the tree with clarity and descending down to it with conviction, and (3) beyond the dyad into the third spaces so they can reconfigure their narratives and fulfill more of their aspirations. The aim is to build up their self-awareness, self-regulation and self-efficacy so they can pivot in the moment again and again in service of their aspiration. You can use the narrative coaching model to help coachees plot a course *(pun intended)* to find what they have been searching for. You can use the four reconfiguration tools—turning points, pivots, vectors of change, and nudges—to help them develop themselves in the process of reaching their eventual destination.

Chapter 8

HOW NARRATIVE COACHING IS DONE

Those who can answer the essential question inside become more able
to handle the uncertainties around them.
Michael Meade

Up until now we have focused on the foundations of the narrative coaching model. This chapter offers an inside look at how it is used in practice, starting off with an overview of the whole flow. You will gain a deeper understanding of each of the four phases and how they work together to support people's growth. For each phase, you will learn valuable tips on what people commonly need, questions for your own reflection, common problems that are encountered, and contributions you can make to help people and the process move forward. We also explore how integrative development theory is woven into the process as a resource for scaffolding changes so they last. Lastly, an extensive case story is unpacked to show in more detail how the work is done. It is important to remember that the four phases are natural points along a spiral of change and development more than they are a sequence of steps to be taken. They are based in a circular view of development and the belief that at any moment we can be born all over again.

Narrative coaching begins with two key premises: (1) being aware of what is true right now is the prerequisite for any effort to bring about change and (2) everything you need is right in front of you. Your first order of business is to help coachees be present to themselves and the stories they are telling. Be a clear witness and a loving mirror so they can see their own stories and behaviors with more honesty *and* less judgment. Help them see their narrative logic and its consequences before they try to change anything. Otherwise, it is like building a castle on quicksand. For example, listen for implicit or explicit "if–then" statements by the coachee that bring their assumptions to light, e.g., *if* I work extra hard at pleasing my boss on this project, *then* I will get the promotion; *if* I have all the answers (or at least appear to), *then* people will respect me and need me (and never leave me). Allow yourself to see the world through their eyes because it is *their* understanding, not yours, that matters most in coaching. Let's turn now to the model and examine what the process looks like in action.

Allow yourself to see the world through their eyes because it is *their* understanding, not yours, that matters most in coaching.

Narrative coaching model

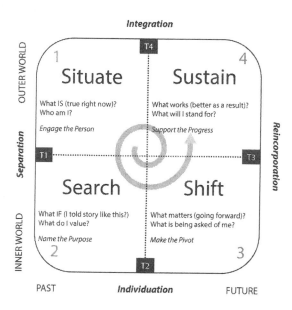

Figure 16. *Narrative Coaching model (expanded)*

This version expands on the basic model (figure 12) with its horizontal axis that spatially divides the outer and inner worlds and the vertical axis that temporally divides the past and the future. As noted before, this mirrors how our minds work and our stories are structured. Each of the 4 S's (Situate, Search, Shift, Sustain) is a phase in the coaching process and a phase in the person's journey.

- In spatial terms, the first and fourth phases (Situate, Sustain) are defined by what is *outer, profane* and *narrated;* and the second and third phases (Search, Shift) are defined by what is *inner, sacred* and *potential.*
- In temporal terms, the first two phases (Situate, Search) are defined by what *is*; the latter two phases (Shift, Sustain) are defined by what *will be.*
- The first two lines in each quadrant (focus, challenge) are written from the coachee's perspective and the third line (our role) is written from the coach's perspective.
- Each phase is characterized by a different degree of change readiness, so listen carefully for changes in people's language as signs they are ready to move on. The key is to match your actions with their level of readiness; e.g., what helps people get started is generally not what helps them get finished (Prochaska & Norcross, 2002).
- The spiral—the fifth 'S' if you will—is central to the narrative coaching process because people often need to circle the tree more than once to break through in their development or to their decision.

Each of the small black boxes indicates one of the four thresholds in the process and marks the transition from one phase to the next. Thresholds have both internal and external aspects in terms of what is required to cross them. For example, a coachee has started thinking about leaving his current role (outer world) to find one that is more aligned with his skills and passions. In crossing the first threshold (T1) he starts to gain a new clarity about his values (inner world) that will help him understand what he wants. Crossing a threshold enables and enriches the work of the next phase, e.g., the more a coachee allows the old story to disintegrate the more that becomes available for its reconfiguration. In so doing, you only need to go as deep as is necessary for what the coachee is trying to achieve and ready to address. At the same time, it is not uncommon for people to make significant changes based on the exploration of what seems at the time like a minor issue. The key is to notice when threshold moments appear—no matter whether they are big or small—and help coachees move through the doorway to what is on the other side. Before we look more closely at the four phases, here is a summary of the process from the coach's perspective:

The narrative coaching process:

1.   SITUATE | **Be curious.** What is going on?

     What are the *discourses and norms* in which her story sits? How is she *situated* in the conversation? In her story?

     Situate represents the beginning of the journey as the person acknowledges the reality of, and the desire for a departure from, the status quo. This phase is about developing trust in the coaching relationship and a willingness to engage in the process. Until then, the person is not yet onboard and she is likely to say, "I won't" or "I can't." (Prochaska & Norcross, 2002).

2.   SEARCH | **Be clear.** What does she truly want?

     What *challenges and forces* will she face? What is she *searching* for? What resources does she have and need?

     Search represents a period of exploration and evaluation as the person seeks greater clarity about herself and her situation in order to determine the value at risk and the purpose and motivation for change. It is important to help her stay in this phase long enough to see what is truly at stake and what she believes will restore order and fulfill her desire. Until the person is clear about that, she is likely to say, "I might."

3. SHIFT | **Be courageous.** What needs to change?

What *alternatives and resources* can she tap? What needs to *shift* so she can fulfill her quest and desire?

Shift represents a period of experimentation in preparation for taking new action and the consolidation of what the person has learned in the process. It is a time when she is developing a new sense of herself and a greater confidence as she moves on from the old story and lays the groundwork for a new story. This phase is about getting the person to a place where she can say, "I will."

4. SUSTAIN | **Be complete.** What is success for her?

What new *mindsets and actions* would help her move forward? What does she need, internally and externally, to *sustain* her gain?

Sustain represents the completion of the cycle as the person integrates the changes into how she identifies herself and acts with others. It is a time when new perspectives and habits and are formed and new ways of being and communicating start to take shape. By this time, you will likely hear the person say, "I am" and then, "I still am." And the cycle continues . . .

Guiding people through the four phases

1. Situate (Person)

It isn't that they can't see the solution. It is that they can't see the problem.
GK Chesterton

The people who come to us for coaching tell us their stories with the hope that we can help them. They want to better understand

their stories and themselves, see the truth of their lives more clearly
and bring about changes in their life and/or work. Our best gift to
them in this first phase is to embody the adage to 'be here now' and
invite them to do the same. As Henri Nouwen (1998) once wrote,
"Our most important question is not, 'What should I say or to do?'
but, 'How can I develop and offer enough inner space in myself and
outer space between us where their story can be received?'" (p. 69).
Coachees will be best served if you can (1) help them notice how they
are situated in themselves, in the conversation, and in their stories,
(2) stay within the frame, language, and experience of their stories as
much as possible, and (3) and identify the turning point and the call
to adventure that is before them. The irony of this phase is that the
more you and your coachees can be still in the beginning, the faster
they will achieve what they are seeking in the end.

It sometimes takes awhile for coachees to settle into this phase,
especially if they are used to more goal- or directive-styles of coaching. One of your key roles in the beginning, particularly when
coaching in high-paced environments, is to help coachees slow down
so they can show up. The quality of your work in this phase is measured not by the clock but by your presence, not by what you do but
how you are. That is why this section is shorter than the ones for the
other three phases. This phase is focused on deeply welcoming the
coachee and creating the field in which to work. That's it. There is
nowhere to go; there is nowhere to be but here and now. You can
often tell when a coachee is moving from Situate to Search because
he starts to exhibit signs that he trusts himself and the process,
and he has identified the turning point that defines the purpose
for coaching. Make sure both of you are in his story and not yours
before moving on.

Tips for working in the Situate phase

Aim
To fully situate them in the conversation and the story
Common needs for people
- A clear structure and frame for the process

- Greater attention to their basic human needs
- Greater awareness about themselves and their situation
- Feeling seen and heard for who and where they are now

Questions for the coach to reflect on
- How is this person doing?
- What support does she need in order to be here now?
- How is she defining the change?
- Why does she think the situation is the way it is?
- How would she describe what she has lost?
- What does she need to leave behind? Go in search of?

Common problems
- Gather too much information, most of which is not necessary
- Rush to a premature solution, which only provides symptom relief

Contributions from the coach
- Offer non-judgmental compassion, deep empathy, and genuine rapport
- Foster honest assessment, full awareness and existential acceptance
- Encourage self-reflection, e.g., through keeping a log or journal
- Build a platform of openness and trust for the work that is ahead
- Provide important facts (*not* advice) about benefits of the journey

2. Search (Purpose)

In order to come to the knowledge you have not, you must go by the way in which you know not.
St. John of the Cross

Once coachees have settled into the conversation, your next step is to help them get clear on what they are searching for and, within that, how they can best use their time in the coaching session. There are inherent tensions in this phase, e.g., between pursuing their aspiration and surrendering to what actually unfolds, between exploring the depths of their issue and focusing on what can be done today. You will often find your way to a suitable purpose for the conversation by noticing where the most energy is in motion. Once people are clear on the purpose for their session as part of a broader Search, they often realize that their aspiration and their surrender are two sides of the same coin. For example, I worked with a participant in one of our programs around the difficulties he was experiencing with his business partner. He became most animated and engaged around making more space for his book in their business. He realized in the conversation that he needed to surrender a story *he* had been telling himself about their partnership if he wanted to fulfill *his* aspirations. He went on to identify what needed to change for this to happen and what it would look like if he did. This reflects what I believe is the core maxim of this work: *Everything you need is right in front of you.*

Everything you need is right in front of you.

In this phase, coachees tend to suspend or transcend the problem as they have constructed it as they take on new perspectives from which to see their issues and alternatives in new ways. It is about stripping away false fronts to get at what they really want from the session. As McKee (2004) observed, the root of most problems in our stories (as well as in our lives) is confusion about our desires. Narrative coaching helps people resolve their confusion so they are much clearer about what they want and better prepared to cross the thresholds it will take to get it. They start to peel away the layers and identify the true nature and significance of their quest. In so doing, they become more open to exploring questions such as, "What am I trying to achieve with my story?" "How else might I tell it?" "How would that help me right now?" In the process, they start to surface their unspoken demands about how things 'should be' and their values at risk given that they are not. As McKee (2004) puts it, "What does the coachee want that, if you gave it to her, would stop the story?"

Many coaching methodologies focus on asking lots of questions based in the belief that the *coach's understanding* is essential for success and *information and analysis* will lead to good solutions. In contrast, narrative coaching is based in the belief that the *coachee's understanding* is essential for success and *experience and awareness* will lead to good solutions. This is why we invite coachees to literally enter their story as an immersive experience and work with it from the inside out. By this I mean both inside themselves as they are telling the story and inside the story as it is being told. It is not about role-playing, acting or re-enacting as if from a distance, but rather the incarnation of elements of their actual story in the moment. One of the techniques that works well here is freeze framing the story at critical junctures. By pausing in those moments, you can draw coachees' attention to what is unfolding in more detail, help them feel into the truth of the experience and the narration, and discover openings for change that might otherwise be missed. You will also uncover tensions and dynamics in coachees' stories that have a direct correlation to the issue(s) they are seeking to address in coaching.

The Search is ultimately defined and refined through exploring these 'complications'. For example, a coachee who wanted to create a better work/life balance came to see that the real issue was ultimately not his over-commitment to work but his fears about going home. We got to this new awareness by freeze framing his story about going home from work the day before—through which he realized that he was so stressed that he could not remember what he had for dinner, let alone if he even ate dinner. We now had an opening to explore his issue that was accessible for him yet significant enough to get to the heart of his issue (what he was blocking out by compulsively staying at work). The Search phase is about helping coachees wake up to these aspects of themselves and their lives where they have been asleep, and to explore these with an open mind and heart to see what else is possible. You can often tell that a coachee is moving from Search to Shift when they start talking about what they would like to do with their new insights, and they have identified a pivot that incorporates a clear distinction between the old story and the new story. In the process, make sure that the coachee has the important pieces of the story out on the table so they can be reconfigured in the next phase.

Tips for working in the Search phase

Aim

To clarify what they really want

Common needs for people

- Opportunities and openness to face themselves and confront reality
- Anchors, resources, and support from allies to move through the hard places
- Encouragement to stay in the flow rather than seek a quick fix
- Permission to let go so they can conserve energy to fight for what they want

Questions for the coach to reflect on

- What does this person value? What will motivate him to change?
- What does he most need to learn in order to move forward?
- What about his narrative is most in need of change?
- What is he attracted to, avoiding and/or anticipating?
- What does he desire? What is the critical choice to be made?

Common problems

- Analyzes too long, which leads to rumination and/or paralysis
- Avoids real issue, which leads down rabbit holes or to superficial change

Contributions from the coach

- Encourage candid self-reflection and whet his appetite for learning
- Help him explore his resistance and defenses as opportunities for growth
- Work with him to identify the benefits of change in his language

- Stay focused on his development and performance rather than fight his reactions
- Invite him to prove to himself that the benefits of the change will pay off

3. Shift: Pivot

Before you embark on any path ask the question, 'does this path have heart?' If the answer is no, you will know it and then you must choose another path. The trouble is that nobody asks the question. And when a man finally realizes that he has taken a path without a heart the path is ready to kill him.
Carlos Castaneda

In the Shift phase, people are preparing themselves to leave the liminal space and return to the world with a new narrative. They are putting together a resolution to the question that sent them on their quest in the first place. It is a time of sifting and sorting what they have learned thus far and experimenting with different configurations of their stories as they refine what they will bring to the world. As Poincare (1952) observed, "If a new result is to have any value, it must unite elements long since known, but still scattered and seemingly foreign to each other, and suddenly introduce order where the appearance of disorder reigned" (p. 30). What we are looking for in this phase are the points of leverage where a shift would make a significant difference in the coachee's narrative and life. Ironically, these are often the very elements a coachee wanted to avoid at first. A lot of your work in this phase is helping coachees discover what matters to them most from the Search phase, what it would take to bring it to the world and what they hope to gain in so doing.

Your patience, as measured by the quality of your presence not the quantity of your time, is important in this phase too. What coachees find in the end is often not what they were looking for in the beginning. This is one of the many reasons why narrative coaches do not set goals with coachees before this point in the process (if at all). Few of us can see what it is we need to do differently from the vantage point of the Situate and Search phases. It is only through completing the purifying and clarifying descent into liminality that people can round the corner, so to speak, at T2 to get the line of sight they need to see where to go from there. However, it is important to remember that this phase is still largely an inner one. The focus is on consolidating what they are learning, experimenting with what to bring back to their world and preparing themselves for the return. While there is often an excitement as coachees imagine a new life with their new story, there may also be a sense of disconnection and disorientation as their identities and relationships shift in line with their new directions.

This is because they are still in a liminal space even though they are increasingly orienting themselves toward their return to the world. To move through this phase, coachees need to practice the pivots they have chosen and experiment with what the new story would feel, look and sound like. You can support their success by helping them identify what may trigger the activation of the old story so they can strategize how to stay on track with and nurture the new story. This requires them to become increasingly able to notice when they are at the choice point, effectively self-regulate and make the new choice. Jungian psychoanalyst James Hollis (2010) offers two questions coachees can use here: "Does this choice diminish me, or enlarge me?" (p. 13) "Does this path, this choice, make me larger or smaller?" (p. 71). I also ask questions such as: "Does that decision or action move you closer or farther away from what you really want?" "What else would you need to address in order for this to work?"

While there is generally a cathartic release and a rising energy in this phase, it is important to temper that fire with the discipline the coachee will need in preparing themselves for the realities of the return. This is because their first attempts at reincorporating themselves into their world with a new narrative may not go as planned. As such, they need to be willing to adapt it as needed (without diminishing its purpose), find external allies and resources (starting with those who will be most receptive), use their energy wisely, and create the vectors of change and structures they need in order to succeed. As always in this work, encourage coachees to use their own frames and language in setting intentions, using the reconfiguration tools and making plans. Any knowledge that does not pass through their lived experience is seldom capable of bringing about deep and lasting changes (Carotenuto, 1985). As a coach, you can often tell that a coachee is moving from Shift to Sustain when they start to put more of their attention on others, the future and the world to which they will return.

Tips for working in the Shift phase

Aim

To experiment with the new story

Common needs for people

- Consolidation of learning and commitment in setting priorities
- Opportunities to experiment, make mistakes (with feedback), have early wins
- Support and reinforcement for the new ways of being and doing
- Access to related experiences to strengthen and guide the new story

Questions for the coach to reflect on

- What are this person's beliefs and assumptions about making this change?
- What will she gain from changing? Does she see it?
- What does she need to know in order to get started?
- What experiences might she need to have first?
- Who will be most affected by her changes?
- Can she address the key impediments to her progress?

Common problems

- Generating too many ideas, causing focus and energy to dissipate
- Avoiding moving into the future, not dealing with practicalities and realities

Contributions from the coach

- Investigate and address with her any barriers to change

- Invite her to formalize her pivots and write down her commitments
- Help her develop substitutions for old patterns while new ones take hold
- Ensure she has sufficient building blocks in place to get started
- Find examples of the desired mindsets and behaviors in her past
- Leave breathing room around her new stories so they can grow
- Connect her with relevant positive role models and opportunities

4. Sustain: Progress

Here I stand; I can do no other.
Karl Marx

In true narrative fashion, this last phase is not just about creating plans for the future, but also about identifying a plot line that connects the past, present and future in a new way. In order for new stories or a new relation between stories to be integrated into a coachee's life, they must evolve from, yet contain, elements of the old, 'familiar' stories (Sluzki, 1992). Any solutions she wants to take forward have to make enough sense to her within her stories-as-is and her world-as-is. The more coachees can bring about change using their own 'laws' (Kaplan, 2002) and their own narrative material, the more likely they will be able to sustain their change. This phase is about helping people integrate what they have gained through a conscious use of cumulative nudges. Invite them to practice in their current world as much as possible, especially as they start, rather than seek out too much that is new. For example, most coachees would more reliably be mindful as they brush their teeth than in trying to start a meditation practice for the first time.

Many of the steps coachees take in this phase involve their relationships to significant others in their life or workplace, e.g., renegotiating relational agreements, releasing aspects of their life that no longer fit, making more space for their new choices and creating new structures of support. People's new narratives are more likely to survive if they can negotiate or create conditions in which they and their stories can flourish. Otherwise, it becomes too hard to bridge between their old and new worlds. Therefore, ask yourself:

- Do they have what they need to bring the new story to life?
- Does the energy flow better now or are there places where it is still stuck?
- Do they have strong allies who can provide safe places to practice?
- Who will support and challenge them as they bring their new narrative into the world?
- Do they still have old loyalties (to people or narratives) that hold them back?

One of the most striking features I notice when people have dropped into the Sustain phase is their profound and visceral sense of 'coming home.' For most of them the telltale sign is the softening of their face as the tension and defenses drop away and they can be more authentic and transparent. Isn't that what we all really want in our heart of hearts? "To return to some resting place inside ourselves, outside of all frantic activity, outside of time, that we sense is waiting for us, calling to us at every moment of our lives?" (Moody, 1997, p. 156). Take time in this phase to help coachees reflect on and celebrate how far they have come—both for its own sake and as the foundation for what is to come next. You can often tell that a coachee is moving from Sustain back to Situate when they start to exhibit signs of increased intrinsic motivation and an internal locus of control; their identity, language and behaviors are reorganizing to incorporate the change; others recognize a difference; and new results are appearing.

Tips for working in the Sustain phase

Aim of this phase
To integrate changes and manifest the gift

Common needs for people
- Discipline and recognition to practice consistently and deliberately
- Provisions for lapses and external challenges in order to keep on track
- Self awareness, self-regulation and simple practices as nudges
- Ways to remember the new choices in the moment
- Opportunities to hone and demonstrate mastery
- Accountability for making decisions and taking action

Questions for the coach to reflect on
- What has changed the most for him?
- What can he do now he could not as well before?
- How will this benefit him and others?
- What will help him sustain the change?
- Is his story rich enough to sustain his new future?

Common problems
- Making plans that are difficult to implement and/or not acted on
- Failing to prepare for challenging responses from significant others

Contributions from the coach
- Help him identify and connect with key supporters early on
- Send him reminders of his new stories with queries about his discoveries
- Prepare him for the collective narratives into which he will return
- Identify likely obstacles and challenges and how to address them
- Craft further experiments to explore and experience his new narrative
- Invite him to make new connections in line with his new stories
- Develop the means for him to recognize lapses and respond effectively
- Establish new routines and support networks to reinforce the new behaviors

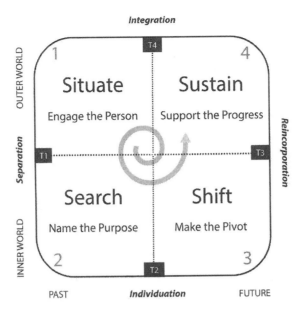

Figure 17. *Narrative coaching model (teaching version)*

Taking a closer look: A case study

Wayne[16] was a man in his early forties who came to coaching to sort out some career issues. In particular, he was neither satisfied in his current role nor clear about what to do next. He had a vague sense of déjà vu in assessing his current dilemma and was curious how he could forge a new path for himself in his career. He had been seen as a top talent in his early corporate career, but had migrated to smaller firms over time. Along the way, he had developed significant expertise, but continued to struggle with finding suitable and satisfying employment.

One of the key themes to emerge was the similarity between his interpersonal patterns within his family of origin and his choices

---

16 The case has been altered to preserve anonymity; a version of it first appeared in Drake & Stelter, 2014, pp. 83–87.

of roles, leaders and workplaces. Early in our sessions he identified what he saw as the crux of the matter: "I notice whenever I go into really downward spirals in my career it's been around injustice—in situations where healing and flow were being blocked by power and unfairness." We co-created experiences in which he could experiment with other ways of being that would attract situations more likely to fulfill his deeper desires around work and self-expression. The key elements in Wayne's coaching journey across four 90-minute sessions are organized using the four phases in the narrative coaching model as a reflection of the broader arc of his journey in coaching. There were also smaller spirals through the entire model within each session. The model was used as a frame for the sessions and for interpreting the data from the transcripts. I've included representative text from him, brief descriptions of what I did as the coach, and some comments and reflections on the process (*in italics*).

Situate ('what is' true right now)

We spent much of the first session reflecting on an initial dream about paddling his boat upstream to no avail and gathering stories about his family and career path. We were able to get beyond the feelings of anger and betrayal that emerged by remaining non-judgmental about the characters in his stories and non-assumptive about what they meant. *In narrative coaching, all characters are welcome at first, because it is too early to tell which ones will end up being critical to discovering and/or implementing the resolution.* We explored related stories as the key themes started to emerge in order to develop a deeper understanding of his narrative patterns and dynamics. The primary focus in this first phase was situating him as the narrator and protagonist and on developing a rich field in which new experiences and stories could emerge. One of the core themes that appeared early on in the following comments from Wayne:

> I felt my family [of origin] life was unstable; I wanted to leave, but couldn't; I often felt stuck in the middle. I went on a number of long journeys in search of what I perceived I lost (or on behalf of what I perceived others lost), but I'm not sure where to go, often get blocked or lost along the way, and often feel like an exile.

We explored key phrases such as "being stuck", "being lost" and "being an exile" so they came alive for him in a palpable way and could be used in creating subsequent experiences in our sessions. We worked with these narrative elements so that he had the full sense of those experiences, how he positioned himself in those stories and the impact of doing so. We also explored his continual efforts to return 'home' in the workplaces he chose in an attempt to redeem his unfulfilled quest on behalf of himself and others. He became aware early on in our work together of the price he had paid and the payoffs from staying stuck in this cycle as well as his strong desire to change this pattern. He had been here before, but this time he was looking for a new pattern and path.

We worked in depth with a story about being a kid in his front yard and feeling torn between home (his house) and the world (across the street)—and his subsequent sense of wanting to keep a foot in two worlds and thereby holding himself back. As he put it, rather than become the king (a man in his own right) and proclaiming his innate right to be here, he often abdicated his space or overspent his energy. He talked about these issues this way:

> Part of what keeps me stuck is a sense of the binary nature of my life—the sense that I have one foot in this camp and one foot in another—and a lack of faith that I can generate prosperity on my own. There is a sense of being trapped, a fear that if I turn one way I will be 'sucked back into the evil empire' so need to keep it at arm's length, but if I go in the direction of my true values I can't be generative enough.
>
> If I could just find the right place, then my gifts could flourish. So everything is about the drama of finding the right place. And I go black and white over it. This is not the right place any more. Now I've got to leave, but where do I go? It's almost like if I find the right place then I'll know what my gift is or what my work is.

The last line foreshadowed what was to come soon in our conversation, a reflection of the recursive nature of narratives as temporal Mobius strips. By this point we had assembled a rich palette of narrative images and elements to work with. *It is important at this phase to get a few key stories on the table in a focused fashion, then circle back to the key themes to better understand their dynamics and the developmental opportunities they may signal.*

Search ('what if' I told my story life this)

As we moved deeper into his issues, I asked Wayne to keep a journal of his dreams as they often shed light on what is at stake. *Dreams can be particularly useful in the Search phase in surfacing the Shadow and opening up new possibilities.* Wayne reported that:

> Images of leprosy, dissolution, letting go, unlocking doors behind which sits a sense of vitality (and danger) kept appearing in my dreams and stories—signaling to me that something important was happening.

There is often a quickening of the pace as coachees move through this phase—and new energy that had been locked up in old stories starts to become available. We created an experiential activity to help him embody his perceived binary choice between: (1) staying in the family pattern (e.g., in the front yard), thereby losing himself but gaining rewards; or (2) leaving the family pattern (e.g., crossing the street), thereby gaining himself but losing rewards. The basic structure for the experience was drawn from the images and language in his actual stories, and unfolded based on what he/we noticed as he stepped into the story in the coaching room. The aim was to give him a visceral sense of what it was like for him to live out these two stories, how it felt when he made these sensations conscious, how it sounded in hearing himself talk about them out loud, and what he would like to be and do differently. The latter emerged from his experience in the activity and the story itself, not by stepping outside the experience to analyze it or offer advice. *As was noted earlier, everything—including the new story—was right in front of us and already there.*

We spent most of our time in this session working with the two primary obstacles that kept appearing in his stories and dreams: the 'rock' to which he had been attached and the 'fence/wall' he kept trying to break through. We set up an experience in which he tried to move away from the rock—which he discovered symbolized his parents and the stories surrounding them—and towards a new life.

As he began to release the ties he felt from the rock, he sensed a chasm in front of him—not too dissimilar to the street in front of his house as a boy—that he would need to cross in order to more fully attend to his own family, life and career. The persistent desire to break through the fence/wall was also captured in his urge to cross this chasm. In guiding him through the process, I moved between active guide and present witness positions as well as between facilitator and character roles depending on what was called for. In the end, he gained a palpable sense of renewed energy by cutting the ties to the 'rock' (with gratitude for them) and naming the chasm and then breaking free to cross it. Once there, I helped him to solidify his new place so that he had enough of a foundation to begin embodying the new story.

He came to recognize in doing this exercise that the fight for him was not to change or redeem the others—to whom he often felt indentured for rescuing him from the pain of feeling trapped—but to acknowledge them and fight for what is important to him. We then could move on to explore what would have to change within himself and in his relationship with others in order to bring these new stories to life. Around this time, Wayne was having some initial conversations with another firm as part of his desire to move to a new job. At the next session, he shared:

> I noticed my old patterns appearing as I went through the interview process for a senior role with [this firm]. I began to connect the dots between that opportunity and my family pattern. I used what we have done in coaching to name the narrative drama I would have entered if I took that position, the peacemaker role I would have ended up playing yet again, and how it would likely end for me. As a result, I turned down the offer.

It felt like a major victory for him to not take on that role and an honoring of the developmental journey he had been on. He was feeling empowered to open himself to discovering new aspects of himself and new ways of being in the world. *This phase is about clarifying the deeper purpose for the coaching work, channeling the new insights and energy that have been liberated and beginning to bring them to life. It requires patience and perseverance on the part of the coach and the coachee as it is often tempting to want to skip this challenging work in an unfortunate rush to get to the end. However, skipping this vital step generally results in outcomes that are shallow and less sustainable. It is important in this phase to have a clear purpose for the conversation and yet not get overly attached to where it is headed or what it will mean in the end. As we noted earlier, it is quite often the case that neither the coach nor the coachee know what the latter's story or process is really about until it resolves.*

Shift ('what matters' most going forward)

As he began to name what mattered to him most from the previous session, he shared:

> I was particularly struck by the return of energy, the thrumming, that came into my legs when I did the work with the 'rock'. Somehow the phrase, 'cut off at the knees' came to mind in thinking about my past. I now feel I can claim more of my right to stand on my own two feet, on my terms—and with this claim comes a new sense of energy.

I suggested that perhaps it was time for him to honor that 'thrum' in his heart and body and to explore what that would mean for him in making new choices about his work. I reminded him of what the 'rock' had 'said' in the powerful experience he had had in the previous session, "You have our blessing to go embrace your own children and your life." We spent a fair bit of time letting that blessing sink him so he really felt it and owned it. He began to imagine a new place for himself in relation to others at work as he increasingly freed himself from old narratives and the roles he unconsciously felt obligated to take as a result. *As noted earlier, this accountability and anchoring is important because new behaviors flow more easily from identities (and their stories) that support them.*

We developed a profile for what kinds of work environments would bring out the best in him and support his efforts to live out a new story of himself at work. This became a template by which he gauged potential opportunities, particularly in terms of the relationships with key figures on any executive team with whom he would work. He was able to see the compensatory nature of many of his previous roles and was curious about how to do it differently. In doing this work he moved beyond the earlier fantasies about a place for him based on 'if only'. As a result, he was able to attain a significant breakthrough in how he was approaching his search for suitable work and his life as a whole. It came when he said:

> It seems like maybe what I'm being asked right now is the opposite of what I thought for a long time: *I need to own my gifts and the right place will come to me [rather than the other way around].*

As is often the case in narrative work, there was no need for goals at this phase. He was starting from a new sense of himself and he had some key pivots, fresh experiences with trying new ways, a strong intrinsic motivation to chart a new path, and a template to use in making healthier choices about work. He ended this session by saying:

> There is a greater lightness and sense of freedom that is emerging. There were some wonderful moments near the end of our sessions when I felt much more in flow and could take an observer's stance on my own stories rather than being enmeshed in them.

Sustain ('what works' better as a result)

As we reached the final session, the focus was on consolidating his gains from our work together and identifying next steps for him. He decided to forego the job search for a while but quit his position, with a plan to do contract work while he sorted out the various aspects of his life that had been built up around the old story, e.g., like some important conversations with his wife and kids. I referred him to a colleague who specializes in career strategies to get some tactical support in searching for a new job when he was ready. He also sought out opportunities at home and with colleagues where he could practice living from his new story. He concluded the final session with:

> I feel such relief in beginning to put down all these burdens I

have carried. I feel freer now to pursue a path that is healthier for me. I recognize that these are just the first steps of a longer journey.

As a postscript to this case story: I recently had the opportunity to work again with Wayne. He still wrestles with vestiges of the old narrative, but far less than before and with much more insight and resilience now. I noticed that, while some of the old language crept in a few times, he was starting from a much stronger place and he pivoted much more quickly now. *It was a reminder again that narrative coaching doesn't solve problems as much as it accompanies people as they circle the tree again and again—with increasing maturity and wisdom—so they can live in greater congruence with their authentic self and their deepest aspirations. The problems don't ever fully go away in a sense because they are part of the human condition and our character. Instead, their energy is transmuted over time such that, hopefully, they are less of an impediment.* Wayne has set up his own practice and has developed a rubric based on our work that he uses to determine which clients would best suit him. It struck me how much more clarity and energy he has now that he is not tied up fighting old narrative battles. What more could you ask for?

Using integrative development to support change

One of the benefits of narrative coaching is that people are developing themselves in ways that are directly related to what they will need to resolve their issue. As a result, by the time people get to the Sustain phase they are better prepared to successfully implement what they decide. For example, they will have reached a much clearer understanding of how they got to this point in the Situate phase, released old narratives that no longer serve them in the Search phase, and rehearsed new narratives that are in line with what they truly want in the Shift phase. I created Integrative Development (Drake, 2014a) and the four BEAM factors (see figure 15) as a theoretical frame for understanding how best to support people through the four phases. It offers a systemic view of change you can use in coaching through the vector of change tool and a broader commitment to scaffolding at multiple levels. As we saw in the previous chapter, BEAM stands for Behavior, Environment, Aspiration and Mindset; and they are arranged below in the sequence in which they are generally addressed. As you read through this section, think about how you can support your coachees in a more integrative manner.

Aspiration: A common challenge in sustaining change is that people lose sight of their initial aspiration and, as a result, the insights and enthusiasm from the coaching experience wilt under the pressures of returning to the 'real world.' To help with this, narrative coaches focus on fewer things in coaching sessions, identify strong and authentic leverage points, ensure coachees have a very clear purpose, and offer them the four reconfiguration tools to keep the aspiration front of mind. Australian psychologist Daphne Hewson offers an important distinction that can be used to help people sustain their fledgling aspirational story—especially if they are facing headwinds in their environment. She (1991) writes:

> The new story is not a turn-off from the old road, but the continuation of a different, old road—one on which the person had been traveling without previously recognising they were doing so. I started to realize the importance of reconstructing a past history of the new story, rather than creating a new story that is simply a deviation from the old one. But, even then, it was easy for the new story to be mainly present and future based, with only the old, problem-saturated story having a recognized past history.
> (p. 5)

Mindset: In my experience, helping people develop and sustain a new mindset is often the most significant contribution I can make to their journey and their growth. New mindsets and new behaviors must co-evolve if coachees are to sustain the changes they begin in coaching. Each one must be experienced as a natural byproduct of the other. They must be able to see themselves as the new person they are becoming, even if only in glimmers in the beginning. It is easy in the Sustain phase to slide back into old mindsets because they are familiar paths to getting things done. Narrative coaches help people develop the new habits of mind as well as the resilience and resourcefulness they will need to continue nudging themselves along the lines of the new story. Otherwise, they may naïvely move ahead and be unprepared for the emotional turmoil or challenges that await them. Mindsets are important because people can only see as far as their stories will take them, and they can only act as far as their stories will back them.

Environment: Any new story told in a coaching session—even if it has served as a transformational vehicle for the coachee in that setting—must survive the retellings that will occur in other contexts if coachees want to sustain change. Narrative coaching looks beyond the individualistic psychologies at the core of most coaching methodologies by overtly addressing the social and contextual issues that shape people's narratives and lives. It is based in the firm belief that no one heals without community (Mehl-Madrona, 2010) and no communities heal without the people in them. There is little value in sending a changed person with new stories back into an unchanged environment. One of the key contributions of integrative development to coaching is making a place for the significant impact of the environment—past, present and future—on people's mindsets, identities and behaviors. Shadow coaching, peer coaching and self coaching are used a lot in narrative coaching and narrative leadership projects because they offer just-in-time support for people in their environment.

Behavior: New narratives and stories must be both *believable* (i.e., linked to existing life conditions as the coachee understands them), and *actionable* (capable of being put into daily practice) if they are to be enacted. Coaching sessions provide a safe space where people can deeply experience and experiment with new stories before they have to try them with others. The aim is to get them to begin building up the neural pathways and muscle memories associated with their new narrative. Your role in the end is to help coachees identify where they would like to first test out the new story with people who will welcome it, support it, and give good feedback on it. The focus is on continuing and extending the practices they started in coaching, in ways and places that will nourish them and embed what they have started. The more coachees can integrate what they have learned in how they act and interact, the greater the degree of freedom and maturity they can attain.

Closing

The velocity necessary for success exceeds the rate of reflection. The faster events move, the faster we move to try to keep up with them until we are overwhelmed by the escalating pace.
Sam Keen

Many coaching models are centered around (1) the imposition of a structure on the coaching conversation, (2) a linear progression toward goals and (3) what the coach should do. In contrast, the narrative coaching model is centered around (1) the immersion in the story as it unfolds in the coaching conversation, (2) a circular progression toward new awareness and action, and (3) what the coachee is experiencing. Those who struggle at first to coach or be coached this way generally do so because they are stuck in their preconceptions about what coaching is 'supposed to be'. It works best to imagine the model as a window through which you can look at a coaching conversation rather than as a set of steps to which you must adhere. It works best when you can fundamentally trust the field as you work rather than act as if you are responsible for driving the process. Otherwise, it is like trying to help a garden grow by constantly fertilizing and watering it rather than respecting its natural rhythms and needs.

Coaching this way involves a (1) *narrative understanding of people* as narrators in supporting their development and performance; (2) *narrative structure* for use in listening to and reconfiguring the material that is narrated; and (3) *narrative approach to practices* in guiding people across thresholds so they can re-enter the world with a new story. The narrative coaching model integrates these three into a unified process of change and enables people to transform their stories and their lives at the same time. Narrative coaching helps people break free to engage more fully in reality as it *is*, develop more mature narrative strategies, and more consciously choose the stories they live by. Along the way, you can help coachees be more aware of where they are in their process, to seek out what they need to move to the next phase, and to determine what they will do once they are there. The more you have circled your own 'trees' in your life and work, the more you can genuinely and effectively help others do the same.

It is important to note, however, that developing a higher consciousness does not inherently resolve your psychological issues or take away your anxiety, but does enable you to find greater freedom for yourself and others. Find ways to raise your level of consciousness that work for you in your life and practice so you can hold bigger spaces for people and work with them at more levels. The more you can embody radical presence with coachees the more they will relax, engage with the real work to be done, and resolve the questions that brought them to coaching. Your role is to provide a strong enough container and a robust enough process to meet them wherever they are and help them move forward. What my own journey has taught me is that the more courageously and fully I step into my own experiences and encounters, the stronger and more compassionate I am with the fellow human beings who entrust me with their stories. At its core, narrative coaching is about (1) declassifying, demystifying, and democratizing transformation and (2) being willing to walk along side people as they find their way to new stories about who and how they want to be in the world.

IV. NARRATIVE PRACTITIONERS

Chapter 9

HOW TO HOLD SPACE

We have a choice . . . to be technicians or artists, or strive to be both.
Each will reveal some aspects of change and deny others. But if the
whole is to be held and respected as living process then some form of
artistry is requisite. We will not understand until we trust ourselves
enough, and quieten ourselves enough, to hear the silent melodies of
spirit playing on the instruments of matter.
Allan Kaplan

This final section of the book is about you as a narrative practitioner.
While a number of the key narrative coaching skills you will need
are addressed in these three chapters, the emphasis is ultimately on
you. It is about coaching from essential principles not from elaborate
methods. As such, it is about your *being* more than your *doing*. This
first chapter is on holding space for people and their stories; it is
the lifeblood of narrative coaching around which everything else is
built. We will look at how you can tap the power of radical presence,
create a container, and work in the field to enrich your ability to hold
space in a generative manner. In so doing, I stand on the shoulders
of giants such as Carl Rogers (1961) who wrote about his work as
follows:

> It is my purpose to understand the way he feels about
> in his own inner world, to accept him as he is, to create
> an atmosphere of freedom in which he can move in
> his thinking and feeling and being, in any direction he
> desires. How does he use this freedom? It is my experi-
> ence that he uses it to become more and more himself. He
> begins to drop the false fronts, or the masks, or the roles,
> with which he has faced life. He appears to be trying to
> discover something more basic, something more truly
> himself. (pp. 108–109)

Rogers truly believed that a therapist's presence and empathetic listening constituted the most powerful sources of help and support one human being can provide for another. He (1961) was instrumental in developing our understanding of how to work this way. He noted the paradox that when people can accept themselves just as they are, then they can change. This stance became a cornerstone of narrative coaching and other related practices. For example, he demonstrated the importance of *authenticity* as a practitioner—"It does not help, in the long run, to act as though I were something I am not" (p. 16), *accountability*—"Am I secure enough within myself to permit him his separateness?" (pp. 52–53) and *acuity*—"Can I let myself enter fully into the world of his feelings and personal meanings and see these as he does?" (p. 53). This same commitment lives on in narrative coaching in one of our core questions, "What does this person need most from me right now?" and in the way we hold space for coachees and their stories. Linda Graham (2013) shares a line she heard once which makes this point, "All this talk . . . is just an excuse to hang out long enough for the relationship to do the healing" (p. 132).

"What does this person need most from me right now?"

Heather Plett (2015) described holding space as being "willing to walk alongside another person in whatever journey they're on without judging them, making them feel inadequate, trying to fix them, or trying to impact the outcome." It is about using your body, voice, presence and energy to create a sense of safety which is at the same time quite alive with potential. Holding space is a sacramental act that supports people in coming home to themselves and to what is calling them. It is a phenomenological activity (Ihde, 1977) in which there is heightened attention to the experience of the field that has been created and the energies that are in play. In part this means generating experiences within held space that enrich people's attachment security so they are better equipped to self-soothe, self-regulate, and self-direct. The more we can be with people this way in coaching, the more powerful their experience and outcomes will be. I see this in my workshops when participants drop their anxiety about 'doing it right' and allow themselves to relax, pay attention and support what emerges.

This attention to the here-and-now of a situation can be seen in *epoché* as an open approach to phenomenon through a suspension of judgment and a bracketing of one's immediate judgment and interpretation of a situation. Depraz, Varela, and Vermersch (2000) describe the three phases of this process as: (1) suspending our habitual thoughts; (2) converting or reorienting our attention from the external to the internal; and (3) letting go in order to respond to the immediate experience and the knowledge found there. This describes well what it means to hold space in narrative coaching, as does Carnabucci and Anderson's (2012) suggestion that:

> The [coach] must maintain a state of relaxed inner stillness throughout the complex process which requires a great deal of skill. There should be an open awareness of all sorts of things—and not only the energies in the field but also thoughts and images that appear—while toggling back and forth between pre-existing . . . theory, personal experiences and the information of the present moment while bracketing preconceptions, beliefs and assumptions. Just like the meditator returns to the present with each breath, the [coach] stays alert to distractions and refocuses attention (p. 38).

A narrative coach helps people dive into their own *lifeworld* (Husserl, 1931; Merleau-Ponty, 1945/2013), its existential nature (see Spinelli, 2010) and their phenomenological experience of it. This focus is served well by a narrative approach since that is what stories are designed to communicate. It is also why we place more emphasis on experiences and less on a rush to interpretation, meaning or action. It is about directly engaging the elements of the stories even as we subtly attune ourselves to the context in which they are narrated. It is about staying as much as possible within what I call *story time* and *story space* (the felt experience of the story as if it is happening right now, not the literal sense of chronological time or physical space) when working with coachees and their narrative material. Otherwise, it is too easy for both coaches and coachees to rush toward premature coherence as a defense against their "anxiety of sitting with undigested elements of experience until they take meaningful shape, however transitory or provisional that shape may be" (Josselson, 2004, p. 125).

Your role as a coach is to hold up a clear and loving mirror for coachees so they can openly share their stories and find the resolution they are seeking. This here-and-now focus in holding the space for people has many advantages. It provides a safe laboratory in which coachees can experiment with new behaviors, experience new voices before trying them in the world (Anderson, 2004; Yalom, 2000), and embed any shifts in awareness or capacity in their life as an anchor for change (Drake, 2007). When you hold space for people it creates more spaciousness in you and them and, as result, there is more spaciousness for new stories. As a result, they discover there is much more in their stories than they realized and more options of stories to be told. For example, in telling the story of what happened, they are often struck by some new element or aspect of the narrative of which they had not been previously aware (Grafaniki & McLeod, 1999). In the end it is about the confident humility to trust that it is the space you create with coachees that is the primary contributor to change.

For example:

> I was asked to coach a key contributor in a manufacturing company to help her address some difficult relational and performance issues. Her initial stories were of anger at her employer and her colleagues. However, through exploring her story more fully she was able to reframe the issue as one in which she felt her professional passion and expertise had been compromised as the company had grown significantly. Her willingness to engage in these deeper truths emerged from a conversation about a pet and, with that, what 'home' meant for her. We held that space for quite some time until she allowed herself to feel

into her truths—one of which was that work no longer felt like 'home' as it had in the beginning.

In the end, what she wanted was the chance to leave with dignity and the courage to return to her craft. To do so, she needed to shift from what she came to call her "they don't appreciate or respect me" story to her "I want to do what I love" story. In the end, she left the organization, moved to a new city, and found a new job where she could thrive again in doing want she loved. I helped the VP of HR reflect on how much the culture had changed over the years and what they could do to better retain and leverage their legacy talent.

Tapping the power of radical presence

Be so still inside [yet vibrant] that you can listen at every moment to what life is offering you.
David Steindl-Rast

A few years ago I was asked to present on my narrative work at a coaching psychology conference. I used the occasion to reflect on how I was using this work in moving through a time of great transition in my own life. One of the advantages of being in a liminal space myself was that it gave me more direct access to and new insights on the deeper dimensions of change. I used my own life as a laboratory in which I could explore how to distill coaching to its essence and develop more advanced practices. I also drew from my observations of the profound things that were happening for people in the Narrative Design Labs I had started to run. What emerged was a provocative proposition about coaching: "Radical presence is enough to facilitate growth and the desired outcomes most of the time." This became the core around which the six principles of narrative coaching solidified, and it has had a profound effect on how I teach and coach. Radical presence is the embodiment of a fundamental trust in your state of Awareness, Being and Connectedness in the field to affect change.

> Radical presence is the embodiment of a fundamental trust in your state of Awareness, Being and Connectedness in the field to affect change.

We can see parallels in engaged Buddhism (see Kramer, 2007), *relational flow* (M. Moore, Drake, Tschannen-Moran, Campone, & Kauffman, 2005), the pursuit of mastery (see Leonard, 1992; Sennett, 2008) and Silsbee's (2008) work on mindfulness in coaching in which, "presence evokes changes in others" (p. 5). It comes from a disciplined wisdom and a deep connection with oneself and the energy and flow of what is happening. It is analogous to what Josh Waitzkin writes about chess Grandmasters, "[M]uch of what separates the great from the good is deep presence, relaxation of the conscious mind, which allows the unconscious to flow unhindered. . . . The Grandmaster looks at less and sees more, because his unconscious skill set is much more highly evolved" (pp. 142, 143). Kohut (1971) talks about masterful psychologists in the same way:

> Her oscillating attentiveness is focused on barely perceptible cues that signal a change in state, in both patient and therapist, and on nonverbal behaviors and shifts in affects. The attuned, intuitive clinician, from the first point of contact, is learning the nonverbal moment-to-moment rhythmic structures of the patient's internal states, and is relatively flexibly and fluidly modifying her own behavior to *synchronize* with that structure, thereby creating a context for the organization of the therapeutic alliance. (p. 317)

What this means for narrative coaching is that we let go of our preconceptions about what ought to occur so that we can be fully engaged and nonattached with what is actually occurring. Working for a particular outcome provides structure for a coaching session, but it also subverts other processes and outcomes (Brown, 2004) which are often more appropriate and impactful. As a result, we teach coaches to not try so hard, but instead to notice and focus their energy on what is unfolding in the moment. The more you can hold space for your coachees—no matter what energies have been stirred up in the process—the more they will be able to do the same for themselves. The coaching relationship becomes a practice ground to develop their attachment-related capabilities such as self-regulation, trust and authentic communication. By providing these experiences and responding differently than has often been the case with others in their life, you are helping people change their patterns of narration and behavior (Wachtel, 2008) and attain greater mastery in their life.

With greater presence, you can more fully immerse yourself in coaching conversations without losing yourself or the coachee *and* you can stand back to see the gestalt of what is unfolding. This ability for multidimensional apprehension has been described as "evenly suspended attention" (Freud, 1912/1961) and as "free-floating" and "poised attention" (Reik, 1954). It is characterized by a temporary suspension of expectations about what people should or might experience or communicate as well as assumptions about the relevance and meaning of whatever thoughts and feelings may arise for either party during the session. This state of attentiveness can be thought of as *generative uncertainty*. It requires relinquishing your needs for control and understanding as the basis for moving forward in coaching and, instead, leaning into the uncertainty with both rigor and vigor. It is about listening for the authentic voice wherever it is found—in the coachee, a character in his story, in you or in the room. To do this, focus on your presence and let go of your preconceptions of the 'right answer' or the 'good outcome'. Listen instead as an "instrument of the speaker" (Charon, 2006); trust and be present to the developmental process that is already underway.

This state of attentiveness can be thought of as *generative uncertainty*.

Mindfulness

Make your state of mind more important than what you are doing.
Hugh Prather

You can think of radical presence as *engaged mindfulness*. It enables you to circle up and down the proverbial tree as you coach—all the while staying present to yourself, the other person, the moment and the arc of the conversation and beyond. To be engaged means to be present, available, and not to turn away. . . . [It] implies a nonjudgmental openness, a trust in the ultimate workability of *all* experience" (Morgan, 2005, pp. 140–141). "It is not about achieving a different state of mind; it is about settling into our current experience in a relaxed, alert, and openhearted way" (Germer, 2005, p. 16). In mindfulness, "our relationship to experience is one of engaged equanimity. We can release the tension between what is and what 'should be' that leads to suffering (Siegel, 2007); stop trying to fix things long enough to see what is (Fulton, 2005); and view situations from multiple and novel perspectives (Langer, 1997). The equanimity and self-regulation we develop through somatic and mindfulness practices are essential to remaining present to our coachees and open to what emerges.

Helping coachees approach their issues with greater mindfulness helps them in a number of ways. Mindful awareness "allows us to step back from the experience of the moment and observe it from a larger field of awareness that is not any of those experiences, that is larger than any of those patterns. With that awareness, we can begin to see different possibilities for responding" (Graham, 2013, p. 52). Cavanagh and Spence (2013) describe it as, "A motivated state of decentered awareness brought about by receptive attending to present moment experience" (p. 117). When people are present to their stories with more mindfulness they are paradoxically able to move deeper into them for insight and release them as illusion. Both are part of the process of development as people need to notice how they got into something before they can get out of it. Mindfulness enables people to do that with more regularity and ease. An engaged and empathetic mindfulness is important for both coaches and coachees so they can work more openly and deeply with the latter's issues. It enables them to tune in to themselves, each other and the conversation. It also enables coachees to access more energy and take more conscious and focused action as they return to the world.

Mindfulness is about becoming more:
- *Aware:* We are not separate, so we can be accepting of all experience. This helps Situate coachees in themselves, their stories and the conversation.
- *Awake:* We are not asleep, so we can remain present with sensations and feelings. This helps coachees Search inside themselves and their stories.
- *Alive:* We are not on automatic pilot, so we can harness and focus our energies. This helps coachees release old stories and reconfigure new ones in order to Shift.
- *Agile:* We are not reactive, so we can act from a conscious, accountable state. This helps coachees learn how to Sustain their new stories in the world.

Creating the container

In the degree that I am governed by fear I become breathless and rush everything. I think about the next move rather than remaining in the experience of the moment—which is sufficient unto itself.
Sam Keen

The greater our presence as a coach and the more mindfulness we can bring to our coaching, the stronger the container will be in which coachees can do their work. It is what Christina Baldwin calls "holding the rim." It involves positioning yourself as a "good enough" and available caregiver when you coach so that coachees can experience a secure attachment orientation and relax into themselves as a result. This is analogous to the ways in which good-enough parenting supports children so they can go 'inside' and rest in imagination and the experience of self (Stern, 1985). Along the same lines, Winnicott (1962) suggested that a child's sense of self consolidates during periods of quiescence when she feels safe and calm in the presence of her caregivers. I find that many coachees have the same need. The notion of a "container" is useful here as a safe yet vibrant space where people are free to work on their issues. I find it useful to think of them in terms of the three primary elements of secure attachment: safe haven, secure base, and working model.

In creating the container, we are offering coachees a *safe haven*, a "holding environment" (Winnicott, 1971) in which it is "safe to be nobody and thus to begin to find the self . . . and to be, instead of always having to do" (Stevenson, 2005, p. 39). People will look for this as they start the coaching process as the basis for trust and will look for it again whenever they surface difficult aspects of their stories or lives. Holding space in this way helps people to feel accepted and cared about, heard and validated, and understood and connected (Howe, 1996; Mikulincer & Shaver, 2007). I find that people's issues often resolve themselves when we masterfully attend to these three needs when we coach. It is based in a trust that the resolution is already present and the subsequent belief that my role is primarily to support the person's system to recalibrate itself.

It is based in a trust that the resolution is already present and the subsequent belief that my role is primarily to support the person's system to recalibrate itself.

We can also see the container as providing a *secure base* from which people can explore and grow. It is a function of the relationship and can best be understood as a vessel in which the coach holds difficult affects (Levine, 2010) and painful mental states (e.g., anxiety, frustration, anger) (Bion, 1967) the coachee is not yet able to tolerate or understand until such time as the coachee is able to do so. Your ability to stay with, process, and communicate difficult emotions and uncomfortable experiences helps coachees to engage them more fully and in new ways (Stadter & Scharff, 2000). Therefore, alternate between confrontation and affirmation (Cozolino, 2002; Wiener, 1994) so that coachees feel safe enough to stay present and consolidate what is happening, but not so safe as to lose momentum or the motivation to change. It is about communicating to coachees, "I see you as you are right now and I see who you want to be."

Lastly, we can see the container as a space where people can upgrade their *working models*. One of the ways we can do that is to make room for what Fritz Perls (Perls, Hefferline, & Goodman, 1951) called "safe emergencies" where people can be with their unintegrated and deregulating thoughts and feelings—and gain some tools and nurturance with which to integrate these experiences. Perls and his colleagues also talked about the vital role of frustration in the container as an experience that often occurs at the intersection of confrontation and affirmation. They argued that our role as professionals is, in part, to frustrate the person in such a way that he is forced to "find his own way, discover his own possibilities, his own potential—and to discover that what he expects from the [coach], he can do just as well himself" (F. S. Perls, 1992/1969, pp. 56–57). A key step is to invite coachees to notice what frustrates them and how much of their energy goes into manipulating the world in response instead of using it to grow. You can then accompany them in expanding their windows of tolerance and maturing their working models so they can function at higher levels across more situations.

In this way, narrative coaching can be seen as a maieutic process because "everything new needs to be held, a place into which it can be born" (Tarrant, 1998, p. 175). *Maieutics* is the science and art of midwifery, of attending to the process of giving birth. "Psychological maieutics, then, is the science and art of facilitating the psyche's transformation and the emergence of new psychological structures" (Stein & Stein, 1987, p. 298) through which new stories can be

born. It is important to remember that as a coach you are supporting a natural process that is already under way, with or without you.
People "have periods when they need a cradle in which to experience
rebirth; they also have periods when they need a grave in which to
experience the warrior" (Paris, 2007, pp. 154, 155). Like a good crucible, a strong container for coaching holds space for the yin and yang
of the feminine and masculine, action and reflection, and confrontation and affirmation. When we are good stewards of the container
with coachees, we are more able to constellate a productive 'field' in
which to work together.

Working in the field

*Real human freedom is our willingness to pause between the events in our
lives and the response we choose.*
Rollo May

Within the broader notion of holding space, we have looked at your
presence as a coach and at the container for a conversation. We
now turn our attention to the 'field' that emerges when it all comes
together. It is not something we make happen as it is already present;
rather, it is something that we can enrich and utilize as coaches. A
field in this context can be defined as "a defined space with a felt
sense of heightened energy related to what has transpired (or is
transpiring) there which influences those who enter." I would like to
begin with a story that illustrates the palpable sense of a field.

> While in Vienna a couple of years ago to run a narra-
> tive coaching workshop, I went out for a long walk to
> explore the city as I generally do when I arrive in a new
> place. One of the destinations on this particular walk was
> to visit the museum that is housed at Sigmund Freud's
> apartment. The museum had been successful in retrieving
> many of the original furniture items that had been scat-
> tered around the world in the years following his death in
> 1939. After exploring the first few rooms, I came around a

corner . . . and there in front of me was the famous living room, re-assembled as it once had been. Many of the pioneers of psychology had sat on those couches and in those chairs in the formative years of the early 20th century. It felt so palpably real, almost as if their conversations were happening right in front of me at that moment. The energy was electric, and I was so moved by the experience. I noticed a distinct shift in myself, as if I were both elevated and grounded as a professional.

I want people in my coaching sessions and workshops to have a similar experience. I believe that the field is the conduit for much of the work in coaching. I see our role as learning how to attune ourselves to it, notice what is present without worrying about how it got there or what it means yet. In a field, "our intention, body, and mind become integrated together. You start to be aware of perception happening from the whole field, not from within a separate perceiver" (Scharmer, 2007, p. 149). It requires that we move beyond an atomistic view of coaching and human interaction in general to take a more systemic view. For example, "Can we recognize when there is enough trust in the field to ask a more daring question? Can we trust the field to hold the energy that it stirs up? Can we trust that the resolution is already present in the field?" Once I shifted my attention from worrying about what I would do next to observing what was already there, my effectiveness as a coach increased dramatically as did the level of change my coachees could attain. Support for the notion of a 'field' can be found in other disciplines as well.

Kurt Lewin (1951) saw a field as a topological construct. He viewed situations as maintained by a set of forces that interacted to create a field in which groups and individuals operate. He defined a field as, "the totality of coexisting facts which are conceived of as mutually interdependent" (p. 240). He believed that changes in people's behavior stem from changes in the forces within the field. Narrative coaching builds on this notion of fields by accentuating their sensory, emotional and nonconscious dimensions and by leveraging the integrative nature of these forces. We help people reconfigure the relationships between (1) their stories about themselves and their experience in their environment, (2) themselves and the characters in their stories and life and (3) their personal stories and the larger narratives through which they are defined and by which they act. Lawley and Tompkin's (2000) work on *Clean Language* offers a similar view on fields:

> As symbols form and their relationships to each other become clear, the whole Landscape becomes psychoactive: that is, the coachee has thoughts and feelings in response to the symbols and events. After a time the Landscape becomes a four-dimensional, multi-layered, systemic, symbolic world which with uncanny accuracy represents and reflects how the coachee experiences, behaves and responds in 'real life'. (pp. 17–18)

Margaret Wheatley (1994) believed that, "Fields encourage us to think of a universe that more closely resembles an ocean, filled with interpenetrating influences and invisible structures that connect" (p. 52). Edmund Husserl (1931) wrote about fields as phenomenological experiences and Rupert Sheldrake (2009) described them as unseen structures, occupying space and becoming known to us through their effects. Psychologist Nathan Schwartz-Salant (1998) noted that the field "contains all of the past stories, individual and collective. The field is affected by the inner life of each person" (p. 160). He (2007) later wrote about his belief that, "only this palpable realization of a mutual field quality has a creative potential" (p. 49). Author Harriet Rubin (2000) offers some good advice on how to work in fields, what she calls "third realms": "It's a matter of intentionally letting go of your focus, of your sharp focus, and of letting yourself see with your imagination" (p. 340). All of these point to the importance of preparing for and attending to the field that is constellated in coaching.

Understanding the nature and power of fields is important because, as noted earlier, all problems are problems of the present. Therefore, I think of the space in which I am coaching as a stage and use it in whatever way would support the transformative process. I make use of whatever props are available and slowly turn the profane space into a sacred space—and then back into profane space as coachees prepare to 'go home'. In Greek, the word is *temenos*, the ancient idea of a "sacred space within which special rules apply and in which extraordinary events are free to occur" (Nachmanovitch, 1990, p. 75). It refers to a "psychic and physical area that has been ritually set aside, 'cut off,' so to speak, from the mundane, so that one may focus on the unsaid" (Kailo, 1997, pp. 195–196). It is much easier to constellate a strong field in which to work if you treat the space around you, *wherever you are*, this way. It is your being and your blessing that affirms its sacred nature not the location itself. The field's power came not from Freud's furniture as separate objects. It came from the constellation that was re-created in that particular space and from my experience as someone who appreciated its significance.

I think of the space in which I am coaching as a stage and use it in whatever way would support the transformative process. I make use of whatever props are available and slowly turn the profane space into a sacred space—and then back into profane space as coachees prepare to 'go home'.

You can access more of the power in the field by diving *into* coachees' experience as opposed to diving *under* their experience in search of an explanation. For example, be alert for moments in their stories in which new dimensions of experience can be accessed as they often serve as a gateway to another world (Milton & Corrie, 2002). These opportunities often emerge at unexpected moments and in unexpected ways for coachees as they are telling their stories. They can be discerned through sensing ripples in the field. For example, you notice there suddenly is a sense of sadness in the air. It is like the feeling you have when you walk into a room and can feel tension or excitement in the air. A heightened ease and vitality in your body and the sense that the characters in the story feel alive in the room (Badenoch, 2008) often indicate you are at such a point. Sometimes you have to pause when you are coaching and rewind to when you first sensed a shift in the field. I offer coaches and coachees the same advice to help them stay present to their experience in the field, "Relax and have faith; you don't have to push. The current will carry you, even if it feels like you are in the dark" (Tarrant, 1998).

A story-based approach to coaching is well suited for working in the field because the two-way traffic between implicit and explicit dimensions, between signs and the signified, is inherent in the very nature of narratives. When coachees immerse themselves in the experience of their current or potential story they have a rare (and often cathartic) opportunity to experience the emotions of an event and its meaning in the same moment (McKee, 2004). This means they can directly experience it and process it at the same time, which thus makes it possible to experiment with new possibilities *in the session*. This is powerful because it brings together the emotions perceived by the right hemisphere of their brain (body sensation, and affect) and the meaning of those signals from their left hemisphere (language and thoughts) (Graham, 2013). Narrative coaching really shines in these moments as an accelerated development tool that brings forth more of the whole person and more of the whole story.

The here-and-now focus inherent in a field-based approach has many advantages. It imparts a sense of immediacy to coaching sessions and provides more accurate data than "relying on patients' imperfect and ever-shifting views of the past. . . . Moreover, the here-and-now provides a laboratory, a safe arena, in which a [person] can experiment with new behaviors before trying them in the world outside" (Yalom, 2000, p. 149). This may require several circles of the tree with a coachee. For example:

> I remember the time when an old friend who was in my workshop shared with the group what she had written as part of one of the practices. The first time through she seemed unconvincing, so I invited her to speak to her discovery again. What came next was much closer to the ground truth she had been avoiding. When she was done, she said with a warm smile and a tear

in her eye, "I hate you, David." As she reported, it was actually an expression of endearment for seeing her into more of what was really true for her. While it was tempting to invite her into another round, my sense was that we had done enough for now.

My invitation for you is to hold space for people with a fierce tenderness and a warm tenacity. Remember that it is their journey not yours. Sometimes this means believing in them in ways they can't yet for themselves; sometimes it means walking alongside them as they move through big experiences; and sometimes it means standing behind them and cheering them on. What makes all this possible is a willingness to be radically present to your coachees, to build a sufficient container as a crucible for their transformation, to meet them in the field to discover what else is possible and to offer them what they and their stories most need in the moment. This is why in our programs we focus on developing the practitioner first before everything else. You are your greatest instrument as a coach bar none. When in doubt, keep returning to holding the space and noticing what is happening in the field.

My invitation for you is to hold space for people with a fierce tenderness and a warm tenacity. Remember that it is their journey not yours.

Tips on holding space

Be radically present
- Be open so that you can move into whatever role would be most advantageous in the process.
- Let your perceptions and the process itself unfold and ripen according to their own rhythms.
- Remain oriented and open to the unknown so there is more spaciousness for both coachees and their stories to reveal themselves.

Build a strong yet fluid container
- Remember that people will only recognize the truth that awaits

them when they are ready and will benefit most if they can bring it forth in their own terms.

- Make room within yourself for the thoughts and feelings that a coachee finds unpleasant, frightening and/or shameful so you can help them do the same.
- If you find yourself feeling really tired after coaching it may be a sign that you are working too hard. Remember, everything you need is right in front of you.

Sense and engage with the field

- Think of sessions as a stages for improvisation in which the cardinal rule is "yes, and" and the primary aim is to advance the action or story (Johnstone, 1981, 1999; Spolin, 1999).
- Honor the 'white space', the 'empty space'. Be open to shift your perspective between the 'objects' in the space and the space itself, each of which is important.
- Focus on the field and let go of the compulsion to solve a problem, be clever, be powerful, or be omniscient.

Chapter 10

HOW TO LISTEN TO STORIES

Do you have the patience to wait
until your mud settles and the water is clear?
Can you remain unmoving
until the right action arises by itself?
Masters don't seek fulfillment.
Not seeking, not expecting,
they are present, and can welcome all things.
Lao-Tzu

In the last chapter we looked at the three core skills involved in holding space as coaches play: being radically present, building the container, and working in the field. While a narrative approach may seem passive to coaches who are used to more directive and verbal methods, it is actually a very active and dynamic process. What makes it distinct is that a narrative coach's energy is primarily invested in sensing into the conversation not steering the conversation. Our role is observing and listening to an unfolding narrative that is slowly revealing itself, not talking to make things happen. This requires a light yet disciplined touch, a commitment to slow development and deep attention, and a fundamental trust that everything is already present and right in front of you. As Rachel Naomi Remen writes, "The most basic and powerful way to connect to another person is to listen. Just listen. Perhaps the most important thing we can ever give each other is our attention. A loving silence often has far more power to heal and connect than the most well-intentioned words."

> Our role is observing and listening to an unfolding narrative that is slowly revealing itself, not talking to make things happen.

This chapter will focus on engaging with silence (both for itself and for what it can offer), seeing coaching as relational mediation, understanding what it means to listen narratively and using the Narrative Diamond to listen at four levels. As you read, start to imagine what it would be like to use silence and what you hear as *the* organizing principle for your coaching, not just something you do in the wake of deploying your techniques. One of the core images I use in describing and teaching this work was inspired by John Freeman's (1964) description of Carl Jung's writing:

> Jung's arguments spiral upward over his subject like a bird circling a tree. At first, near the ground, it sees only a confusion of leaves and branches. Gradually, as it circles higher and higher, the recurring aspects of the tree form a wholeness and relate to their surroundings—a persuasive and profoundly absorbing journey. (p. 10)

I was taken by this image of a bird circling a tree and came to realize it was a fitting analogy for what narrative coaches do as they listen and inquire. Sometimes we help coachees find the 'thermals' and rise above the confusion to see the bigger picture, recognize patterns and/or get a new perspective. It opens up more space in their stories (and identities) and increases their awareness and alternatives. Sometimes we help coachees descend to find a new branch on which to land, consolidate their gains and make decisions. It narrows or shifts the focus of their stories (and identities) and increases their clarity and ability to take new action. These spirals are the hallmark of narrative coaching and central to our approach to listening. They are measured by the quality not the quantity of either time or words. Mindfully "circling the tree" as you listen to people's stories enables them to get closer to the core dynamics of their issue and make more powerful changes in the end.

In my experience, it does not matter which stories peoples choose to share first. They will begin at the level at which they are ready, and the critical themes will be forthcoming regardless of where they begin. Any story or set of stories can be a portal into the larger issues at play and the path for people to reach their resolution or aspiration.

There is no need to rush to get to a 'bigger' story; start with whatever you get. For example, one of my most touching coaching conversations ever was a brief demonstration that began with "I've moved house", stayed focused on the moving boxes in the story, and ended 10 minutes later with a powerful revelation by the coachee about why the kitchen was still unpacked. There are many roads to the top of the mountain. What matters more than where you begin is how well you walk alongside people as they discover where their stories are leading them.

In listening to coachees this way, attuning yourself to them, and staying with them in their stories and their world, you are "hearing them into speech" (Morton, 1985). It is about providing "a pure, objective, loving witness to what is happening within and without" (Brown, 2004, p. 14). I think of it as *360° listening*: it encompasses the whole space in which the conversation is being held, not just the exchange of content between two people. It is about listening to yourself, the other person, the stories and the field *all at the same time*. Your ability to truly hear the other person is diminished when you overly focus on any one dimension. Therefore, worry less about what to ask and focus more on just deeply listening to people's stories at four levels:

- what is the *context* (who is saying it, in what setting),
- what is the *content* (what is said/not said, at many levels),
- what is the *construct* (how it is said, within what frame), and
- what is the *consequence* (why is it said, with what impact).

> I think of it as *360° listening*: it encompasses the whole space in which the conversation is being held, not just the exchange of content between two people.

While this might seem like it would require extra effort and prompt us to try harder, it is actually an invitation to listen with what I call 'soft eyes' and 'soft ears'. It is analogous to how much more you can see at night when you are out in nature by turning off the flashlight and allowing your eyes to adjust. Taking a 'softer' approach enables you to perceive the invisible wholeness that lies beyond the parts; read narrative threads that are often subtle and gradual; intuit underlying movements; and stay open so that the story reveals its inner secrets to you and the storyteller (Kaplan, 2002). This allows you to access more of your senses as a listener, create a greater sense of spaciousness when coaching, and avoid the temptation to grasp for interpretation. For example, it enables you to hear not only what is in the words, but also hear what the words do not say. As Indira Gandhi once said, "You must learn to be still in the midst of activity and to be vibrantly alive in repose." Let us turn now to silence and the Narrative Diamond as two of the key elements in a narrative approach to listening.

Engaging with silence

Do not speak unless you can improve upon the silence.
Ram Dass

An ability to embrace silence—and the stillness and clarity it brings—is essential as a coach. However, it is important to state up front that being silent is more than just not talking. As Max Picard (2002) writes beautifully, "When language ceases, silence begins. But it does not begin because language ceases. The absence of language simply makes the presence of Silence more apparent" (p. 15). Silence is not merely empty space, a place of nothingness; it is an open space you can move into, a place of discovery and full of potential (Baker, 2002). Silence is a place in which your restless minds, internal chatter, and fragmented attention can find the stillness you need to listen well. It is from this stillness that you can observe and hear the coachee at multiple levels at the same time. When you are still, the non-essential drops away and underlying truths surface—pointing you toward right action (Scott, 2002). We can learn a lesson here from research on blind adults that suggests that "their auditory superiority occurs not at the level of detecting when a sound has arrived but in higher-order processing of language, sorting out a conversation they're paying attention to from background chatter" (Begley, 2007, p. 97).

Joan Chittister (2010) observes: "Silence is the lost art in a society made of noise . . . But until we are quiet and listen, we can never, ever know what is really going on—even in ourselves" (p. 106). Silence is one of life's greatest teachers. It often brings people face to face with some deeper truth and, in so doing, reveals and amplifies what they have not yet resolved within themself or manifested in their life. As a result it can feel awkward and even frighten us at times. To make fuller use of silence in coaching, think of listening as receiving and noticing what is already present, rather than as something you do to make things happen. Be willing to engage coachees with silence and engage the silence itself. Listen for what is in the silence, e.g., unspoken words, missing details, omitted events, unmentioned characters. Be alert to the significance of such omissions, for the narrative secrets to which they might point. Only speak when you can improve on silence. Silence is like a down pillow on which you can lay your head. Sink into it and all that it has to offer.

To make fuller use of silence in coaching, think of listening as receiving and noticing what is already present, rather than as something you do to make things happen.

A question I am often asked is, "How does my silence help people get the outcomes they want?" In my experience, effectively using silence benefits both the coach and coachee by:

- fostering a stronger trust in themself and each other so they can both show up in the conversation with more consciousness, compassion and candor;
- equipping them to 'sit' with issues long enough to gain a truer awareness and a better understanding of what is happening rather than rushing to action;
- enabling them to better self-regulate in the midst of challenging emotions and create a stronger platform for what the coachee wants to achieve;

- supporting a sense of safety so there is more somatic awareness, willingness to experiment, certainty of what truly needs
to be done and more honesty about progress.

Again, it is important to remember that silence is not the absence
of talking, but an active and generative practice in its own right.
Your use of silence signals your trust in the process and your willingness to remain radically present so the coachee can do what he
needs to do.

Be a mindful PRO

One of the tools I've found the most helpful in developing myself
and my use of silence comes from the work of a colleague, Gregory
Kramer. He developed and teaches insight dialogue in which
people move between meditation and dialogue—with each deepening the other and the people involved. The stillness that emerges
from meditation supports a deeper connection and sharing in the
dialogue, and what emerges in dialogue can be brought back into
meditation to deepen the insights. I have adapted this process for
coaching to teach people how to listen in a way that moves between
fertile silence and dialogical inquiry. It is made possible through
the commitment in narrative coaching to hold space for people,
their stories and their journeys. The following chart brings together
the *inner and outer responses* in his core framework (Kramer, 2007),
the *energy* associated with each pair of responses (Drake, 2012),
and the *results* that may come from the process (Gallwey, 1981/2009,
2001, 2009).

Internal response → External response → Energy → Result
Pause → Trust emergence → Consciousness → Less judgment,
more awareness
Relax → Listen deeply → Compassion → Deeper connection,
more attention
Open → Speak the truth → Courage → Authentic choices, more
accountability

Here are some tips for you on the power of listening in coaching from a place of proactive silence.

1. As you listen, notice your own state and breath as a reminder to *Pause* before you speak so that you can be more conscious, aware, and without judgment in the moment. Pausing is at the heart of your ability to self-regulate. It enhances your capabilities as a coach and models for coachees how they can do the same. More than just a welcome respite, pausing and settling into the silence are in themselves transformative. By suspending your habitual reactions and responses you began to unbind the neural networks that would otherwise be reinforced, allow your stress to diffuse, and open up more space for what the Buddhists would call lovingkindness. As Kramer (2008) observes, "When *Pause* uncovers difficult matters, it needs the support of *Relax*[17]" (p. 204).

2. The more you *Pause*, the more you can *Relax* and (a) be awake to and accept what you are experiencing, (b) listen more deeply and compassionately to yourself and others, and (c) form deeper, more attentive connections. This reduces your need for striving as a coach and enables you to more fully trust your presence. Relaxing can then mature into deep acceptance and compassion. "Over time, meeting troublesome inner phenomena with stillness means that they are not fed; their energy begins to drain out of them" (p. 205).

3. The more you *Relax*, the more you can courageously *Open* and speak your truth in the moment, make more authentic choices in the session, and be more accountable for yourself (Kramer, 2007). This enables you to get to the heart of the matter much sooner. In part this is because, as Kramer points out, "Just as the *Pause* is where stillness meets reactivity, in *Relax* love meets suffering. When this happens, healing happens. It happens on the spot" (p. 127)—and *Openness* emerges as a place from which to connect, speak, or act.

---

17 Italics added.

Listening narratively

If you want to understand what other people are saying, you have to assume that what they are saying is true. So then you have to figure out what's going on within their view of the world that makes it true.
George Miller

Listening to people's history is less about gathering the facts and more about surfacing the fictions by which they live. For example, what are the internalized relational worlds that guide their daily choices (Badenoch, 2008) and shape their identities? This question is important because people can do no other than to begin in their own world—and so you might as well meet them there. They will only be able and willing to travel with you to new places—and consider new stories—if you can be with them just as they are right now and without judgment. Any judgment from you or them excludes aspects of the present moment and thereby makes them unavailable for the work at hand. As coaches, we have a professional responsibility to listen to coachees with our expertise and experience AND to stand in their shoes and engage them with compassion and acceptance at the same time. Kaplan (2002) describes it as follows, "To apprehend [what is going on], we have to move into a different state of being—one which is simultaneously inside and outside, participant and observer, analyst and artist" (p. xvii).

It reflects what John L. Johnson called "catching the edge" as the place in a good story where the listener's awareness fades in and out, where dream or fantasy can step in. We are often most effective as coaches when we work with the critical narrative material at the edge of the coachee's awareness or consciousness. This is often necessary because people's stories have their own internal logic and coherency that often makes changing them hard, particularly if we try to approach them straight on (Bridges, 1980). I find in my own practice it involves both intently listening to what is being said, while at the same time being peripherally aware of micro-shifts in the field that warrant closer attention. This involves using both defocused attention and focused attention—operating like a camera with a wide depth of field in which the foreground and background are both in focus. To do this, you need to be simultaneously attentive to both the explicit verbal content and the implicit experience (Stern, 2004). It involves being on the lookout for the unconscious intents, the subtexts, of stories that are often not visible or accessible at first.

The more you can listen at multiple levels to people's stories, the more you hear and the more roles you can play as their coach. This reflects what Bion (1961) described as the need for *binocular vision* to hold together knowing and not-knowing. Bateson (1982) used the same term to refer to the convergence of two perspectives which vary slightly different from each other. Listening in this way will enable you to be more accurate within a single dimension of a person's story (like his emotional state) and to add dimensions to the overall vision of what is going on (like the connection between movement in his story and his somatic expression). LeCompte (1993) writes about narrative research in the same way whereby "with one 'eye,' [researchers] record what they 'see' the subject doing, creating a record of the participant's activities—often in the participant's own words. With the other, they record a whole range of other data, including what they themselves are doing and what everyone involved in the research setting is feeling and doing" (pp. 16–17). Listening narratively gives you a sense of depth perception that it is easy to miss otherwise.

Theodore Reik (1998) described it as listening beyond the spoken word with what he called "the third ear". By this he meant not only to listen to what the other person is saying (and not saying, but thinking and feeling), but also to our own inner voices. It requires thinking of yourself as a sensor to pick up clues about what is happening in the field not so much as an interpreter who is planning what to do next. Listening with a 'third ear' enables you to hear more of what is happening at symbolic, somatic, and unconscious levels. Fulton & Siegel (2005) described it as listening to "the unspoken, the avoided, and the accidental—to find the reality that lies imperfectly revealed and imperfectly disguised in thought" (p. 36). This is valuable in narrative coaching because as Reik (1998) also observed, the facts people tell about their lives lose a lot of their significance as the sessions progress; and "events, thoughts, and impulses on the fringes of their attention acquire an unexpected importance" (p. 273).

Here are some skills that will help you listen this way as a coach:

- paying careful attention to the circumstances that seem to trigger the telling of a particular story by the coachee (Edelson, 1993);
- listening for different voices in her stories as a means to elicit different aspects of her self, particularly the silenced ones (Gilligan & Brown, 1991);
- uncovering the patterns that have grown up to choke off her inner knowing to help her recover her existential sense (Bugental, 1990); and
- generating experiences and moving toward the *not known* more than gathering information and moving toward the *known*.

Using the Narrative Diamond

Almost every encounter in life presents possibilities for growth. But these transformations require that a person be prepared to perceive unexpected opportunities. Most of us become so rigidly fixed in the ruts carved out by our conditioning that we ignore the options of choosing any other course of action.
Mihaly Csikszentmihalyi

I share Ricoeur's (1988) interest in the fact that the *space of experience* (the narrator) and the *horizon of expectation* (the story) mutually condition each other. This is important because

> the way we select which events are included in (and excluded from) our narratives, the main themes around which we organize them, the characters we regard as significant or nonsignificant, the voices one privilege or silence all shape both our identities and our life stories. (Botella & Herrero, 2000)

I developed the Narrative Diamond to teach people how to coach with these considerations in mind. One of the highlights of the framework is the role that characters play in working with people's stories. We can think of stories as people's implicit and explicit conversations with other characters, and we can assume that if a story mentions an event or character, this element is in some way relevant to what the protagonist is seeking (Mar, 2004). Many of the tensions in people's stories in coaching can be traced to disparities between the narrator's point of view and that of certain other characters. These disparities often literally or figuratively mirror tensions in their life (and vice versa). As such, the characters in people's stories often provide the key to transforming their stories and resolving their issues. Any resolutions attained between the characters in a coachee's story often have strong connections to the resolution the coachee can attain related to this issue in her life (and vice versa).

People are more able to face important challenges, answer essential questions, and make hard choices (McKee, 2004) if they can see the connections between their inner stories and their outer lives. In narrative coaching, we do that by listening to people's stories as a way to bring their internal narrative processes into the room so they are more accessible to change. This allows the coachee to move between the author's stance and the protagonist's stance—as well as the stances of the story, other characters and the field—in order to gain new perspectives on and new options for their stories. If people can create some distance from their story they can often see it more truthfully and engage with it more viscerally. It is often easier for people to be more accountable for their narration and its impact if it first becomes more malleable and approachable. After working with their stories out in the open, coachees can take what they've experienced and learned in the session and put it 'back in themselves' (albeit transformed) as a guide for moving forward in a new way.

The more you can picture people's inner community, the easier it becomes to understand how they see themselves and others as well as act and communicate—and the more fully you can track and support their development (Badenoch, 2008). The very act of telling their story in safe space like coaching enables people to "observe, correct, and comment on the self that is being portrayed in and shaped by their stories" (Josselson, 2004, p. 112). This includes inviting the coachee to separate his role as the narrator *of* his story from his role as the protagonist *in* his story (Linde, 1993) so he can appreciate the difference and make adjustments as so desired. I find that sometimes it is enough to help coachees even recognize there is a distinction and make new connections as a result, e.g., "I see myself as a strong person yet I seem to be acting like a victim in my story." However, it is important to remember that it is not about where you think the story is going or should go, but rather about where the story wants to go. What is it seeking? What is it asking of the coachee? What is it calling for in the session?

The framework

The Narrative Diamond is based in the fundamental premise that the characters (e.g., people, objects, metaphors and analogies, events) that appear in coachees' stories are systematically related to each other and correspond with aspects of their lives in ways to be discovered. Each story serves as a stage in which the narrator locates and positions the characters relative to herself and the others within a fluid interpersonal field (Drake, 2003; Osatuke et al., 2004; Riessman, 2002). This is important because "Two paces east or west and the whole picture is changed" (Durrell, 1988, p. 210). As a matter of fact, I have seen the meaning and outcome of a narrative coaching process hinge on mere inches, like when we work with the Three Chairs. This framework for listening provides a way for you to track the positions of and relationships between characters involved in the issue at hand as well as to guide explorations with coachees about what most needs to shift.

> The Narrative Diamond is based in the fundamental premise that the characters (e.g., people, objects, metaphors and analogies, events) that appear in coachees' stories are systematically related to each other and correspond with aspects of their lives in ways to be discovered.

As with the broader narrative coaching model, the Narrative Diamond reflects both the process of how stories are formed and the process of how to work with them in coaching. The true nature of the coachee and the characters in his story is often revealed as they face difficult dilemmas and need to make difficult choices and take new actions. We can generally tell if something is amiss in a coachee's story when something about a character doesn't seem quite right. It is similar to the reaction we have in a movie when one of the characters acts completely 'out of character'. Whereas in a movie that might turn us off, in a coaching session it alerts us to the fact that there is an element of the story that is trying to get our attention. As Hillman (1983) observed, "the action is in the plot . . . and only the characters know what's going on" (p. 59). Find ways to join with coachees in exploring what these characters are doing in the story and how they might contribute to (or challenge) the resolution of their issue.

Working with the characters in coachees' stories is quite useful because they often arise from unconscious sources within the coachee and, as such, bypass their more habitual and defended patterns of narration. What you are after is getting past the "every day" version of the story to discover the "but one day" turning points that will yield new material with which to work. These often emerge first from the characters, particularly those playing a projective role in the narration. Richard Seel (2003) offers a number of questions you can use to help coachees get inside their own stories, including:

- Which character resonates with you most?
- What is the character feeling?
- What are the character's assumptions and agendas?
- What are their values and what do they care about?

I would add:

- Which character(s) trigger an adverse reaction in you?
- Which character has the most to teach you?

Each of the four elements of the Narrative Diamond framework corresponds with one of the four phases in narrative coaching: The Situate phase tends to focus on the Narrator, the Search phase on the Story, the Shift phase on the Characters and the Sustain phase on the Field in returning to the Narrator. Together, they reflect the hermeneutic nature of narrative coaching and its search for meaning in the *declarative* space of the coachee as narrator, the *narrative* space of the story, the *projective* space of the characters and the *generative* space of the field. You can use this framework to bring the initial story further into the field, surface aspects of the story as seen in the characters but not previously recognized or allowed as part of the narrator, and support the emergence of a new narrative from within the field. In the diagram, the listener is depicted off to the side, away from the usual dyadic position across from the narrator. This is done deliberately to demonstrate a more fruitful position from which you can engage narrators, the stories and the characters in the field.

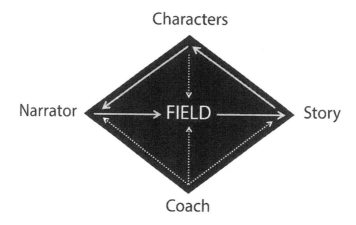

Figure 18. *The Narrative Diamond framework for listening*

The flow of the framework follows the solid arrows in the diagram, from the Narrator to the Story, the Characters and back to the Narrator. The dotted arrows radiating out from the coach and the characters represent the support you can offer throughout a coaching conversation to bring material into the field and work with it there. There are four modes of listening in this framework, one for each of the four elements, and each one is used most often with its respective phase in the narrative coaching process (see figure 19):

1. Welcome the *Narrator* (coachee) and pay attention to what *is being said* as a way to build the rapport that is required for coaching. This is important in the Situate phase because the primary aim is to be mindfully empathetic with a fellow human being.

2. Advocate for the *Story* and pay attention to what *is not being said* as a way to discern what is missing or lost, what is truly at stake and desired. This is important in the Search phase because the primary aim is to identify the agenda for change.

3. Engage the *Characters* and pay attention to what *wants to be said* as a way to determine what the new story is trying to communicate and what needs to change as a result. This is important in the Shift phase because the primary aim is to envision and experiment with new options.

4. Work in the *Field* and pay attention to what is already shifting and being *said differently* as a way to design a supportive structure for the new story and bring it to life. This is important in the Sustain phase because the primary aim is to develop a path that works.

While listening in a certain way can be particularly useful at different points in the coaching process, it is important to remember that listening narratively is not linear or sequential. Do your best to listen in ways that are in sync with wherever the coachee is in his process and what he most needs from you as his coach. Otherwise, for example, if you ask lots of questions early on, you may end up with lots of unnecessary information about the situation without really understanding what the coachee wants to be different. If you get too caught up in the story itself, you may not leave enough time or energy to help the coachee identify next steps. The framework also provides a useful structure for literally and functionally re-positioning yourself in coaching conversations as they unfold and for shifting how you listen as a result. When I work, I imagine the framework being projected onto the space in front of us to physically anchor the work and to determine where to position my chair relative to the four elements as the process unfolds.

I imagine the framework being projected onto the space in front of us to physically anchor the work and to determine where to position my chair relative to the four elements as the process unfolds.

Example of how it can be used

The following case story is about a coaching client whose presenting issue was her frustration with and judgment about her boss. It shows a summary of the key insights she had in the session as framed by the four phases of the Narrative Diamond and the narrative coaching model. A key step in the process was getting her to own and be accountable for the story as hers. It reflects one of the key maxims in this work: You can only coach the person in the room.

1. Narrator | Situate | Listening for what is being said

I am feeling very frustrated. I'm upset because the leader in charge of this project regularly points out small mistakes in our team's reports, but he doesn't acknowledge what we are doing well or how hard we are working.

2. Story | Search | Listening for what is not being said

When I hear myself talk about about what it is like to put together these reports every two weeks, I realize that I am not putting in as much effort as I used to and, on top of that, I frankly don't like working at this level of detail anymore.

3. Character | Shift | Listening for what wants to be said

When I look at my situation from the perspective of the reports, they feel like a heavy burden. I was thinking I wanted coaching to help move on, but I see now that this was just a reactive response. What I really want is to figure out how to talk with my boss about communicating with us in a very different way.

4. Coach | Sustain | Listening for what is being said differently

I am noticing a shift in myself from blaming and reacting to my leader to a deeper appreciation for the real issue and how I want to move forward. This has helped me realize that I actually enjoy most of my current job. I'm excited to stretch myself by presenting this request to my boss and working on a solution with him.

More on using the framework

The Narrative Diamond is useful for mapping coachees' stories in sessions and where they place themselves in these stories and in their storytelling. James Lawley and Penny Tompkins (2000) made the same observation, "[W]here coachees sit and where they want you to sit is often determined by their dominant lines of sight. . . . Coachees naturally place themselves where it is most appropriate for them to explore their symbolic world" (p. 93). This attention to physical arrangements can be found in the work of psychotherapists such as Harry Stack Sullivan who would sometimes sit next to a patient so they could look out together at the problem troubling the person. It can also be found in some Native American traditions in which people would face each other to build sufficient relationship and agreements for a conversation, turn in the same direction to look out at the issues and develop a shared resolution in that space, and then turn back to face each other to make new agreements for moving forward.

Given the spatial nature of stories and narrative coaching sessions, it is no surprise that the notion of positioning is important in this work. Every position provides a particular point of view that shapes what we think we see, what we think it means, what experiences we have as a result, and the stories we tell about it. As such, be curious about the positions your coachees adopt relative to their issue and their stories. You can use the Narrative Diamond framework to help coachees' explore their stories from multiple points of view in order to increase their awareness, understanding, and alternatives. For example: How would the *character* with whom you had the argument see the situation? What is missing from the *story*? How do *you* feel as you tell that story? Why are you telling *me* this story? What are you noticing in the *field* now? It is about helping people establish new relationships between existing elements in their stories and/or introduce new elements (Hermans, 2004) in order to better align their narratives and stories with what they are trying to achieve. Look for opportunities to co-create experiences with coachees in which they can experiment with new positions.

When I work, I often shift my position relative to the coachee and the story as it is being told based on what seems to be called for. It is a dance between responding to what is present and proposing what may be on the cusp of what's next. For example, I might start out facing the coachee to build sufficient rapport and trust, shift to be more at an angle as I explore the narrative material with him, and move in closer again if a stronger relational connection (e.g., due to increased vulnerability) or a new experience is needed. I often invite coachees to try out other positions in relation to me and/or the story as well in order to open up new ways of seeing themselves and their stories, others in their stories, and the coaching relationship. I usually take more of the lead in the conversation at the start of a session, but then support the coachee to take more of the lead as soon as they show signs of wanting the 'baton'. The aim is to see where the coachee and the story want to go as they seek resolution and a return to greater wholeness. The insights gained in the process largely determine where the conversation goes.

You can use the Narrative Diamond to work with the person's constructed self (how his past makes its way into the present), or the person's imagined self (how the future makes its way into the present). However, regardless of which timeframe the story comes from, it is important to bring it into the present moment in the session. In so doing, you can draw from Stern's (2004) insight that there are actually three present moments when people tell their story—each of which deserves our attention as we listen: "(1) the present moment of getting the original experience into verbal narrative form; (2) the present moment created in the teller during the telling of it to someone; and (3) the present moment evoked in the listener during the telling" (p. 192). The first informs how we listen to the narrator, the second informs how we listen to the story and its characters, and the third informs how we listen to ourselves and the field as we coach. When a coachee tells you his story, he is telling more than he can know at the time. Your role is to reflect back to him—sometimes frame by frame—what he said and did not say as well as how it affected you and may affect others.

Narrative coaching is ultimately about the depth of your radical presence, the astuteness of your sensory observations, and the non-attached yet full engagement you bring to your listening. The more mindfully aware you can be, the more you can step back from the experience of the moment, be immersed in it and observe it from a higher level of awareness—all at the same time (Graham, 2013). Consequently, narrative coaches make far greater use of silence, the field, and the narrative material than other approaches. This requires listening with a 'third ear' so that you can hear the subtle yet powerful clues about the path to and nature of new stories. Therefore, develop your ability to access your Four Gateways so that you can truly listen in a 360° manner:

LISTEN WITH . . .

- *Open head:* Be curious rather than analyzing or judging what the person is saying.
- *Open heart:* Be compassionate rather than pulling away to distance yourself emotionally.
- *Open hara:* Be courageous rather than muting your instincts or taking on what is not yours.
- *Open hips:* Be centered rather than trying to figure out how to fix the person or situation.

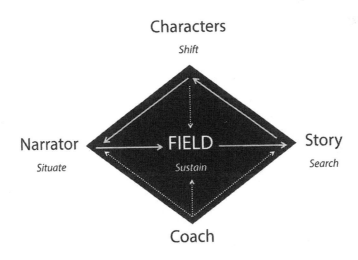

Figure 19. *The Narrative Diamond (expanded)*

Some tips for you as you listen

- Create a rich field, notice what appears, remain connected even in silence, and actively engage with coachees' narration as it emerges.

- Invite them to stay in their stories as they unfold. As they do so, the critical elements will become more apparent and more available for renegotiation.

- Stay attuned to the field and use what you find there to help coachees more clearly see their current reality and what they want to do about it.

- Put more emphasis on generating experiences and less on rushing to interpretation, meaning, or action. Remember to pause, relax and open.

- Invite coachees to explore other perspectives, reframe their experiences or try new ones in order to reconfigure key elements in their story.

- Listen for the gaps between intention and action, expectation and results, and body and mind in their stories. Listen for what would help seal these leaks of energy.

Chapter 11

HOW TO INQUIRE INTO STORIES

The patient needs an experience, not an explanation.
Frieda Fromm-Reichmann

One of coaching's greatest strengths is its use of powerful questions for getting to the crux of matters with people. You can often tell when a question really hits home for a coachee because of the pregnant pause that follows. In developing narrative coaching, I took it one step further in asking, "What if that profound pause was already present, and it is the pause that makes these questions possible and powerful—not the other way around?" Our role as coaches, then, is to inquire into this silence and what is happening in the field. Most of the time it is better to ask questions that increase coachees' awareness of what is already present than to ask questions that introduce new material into the conversation. Most of what you need in the session is already in the person's stories, both in terms of the sources of their suffering *and* the sources of their transformation. Inquire *into* not *about* people's stories when you coach so that you keep the conversation in the present moment as much as possible.

Inquire *into* not *about* people's stories when you coach so
that you keep the conversation in the present moment as
much as possible.

In this chapter we will look at deepening your capacity for inquiry through the Four Gateways, using a simple structure for inquiry, and working with metaphors and analogies. In narrative coaching, inquiry is seen as both a mindset and an act of communication. We are curious about:

- What essential questions is the coachee trying to answer?
- Are these still the right questions?

- If not, what is the essential question now? Really?
- What would change if the coachee asked it?

The primary focus in narrative coaching is on generating illustrative experiences through your questions rather than using them to gather information or probe for explanations. This is based in the premise that there are no 'correct' explanations and, even if there were, there is little evidence to suggest a strong correspondence between having more information and attaining personal growth (beyond a rudimentary level). This is a welcome respite for many coachees who, in addition to information overload, are awash in a sea of explanations and labels.

Another appeal of narrative coaching is its focus on the lived human experience and the available narrative material rather than on normative diagnostic measures and canonical professional discourse. The aim of our inquiry is to help people expand their frame and shift their narrative so that more becomes possible for them (F. Barrett & Cooperrider, 2002). In keeping with Erickson's 'utilization principle', we use the coachee's own language as much as possible in our inquiry to minimize resistance and maximize impact. Doing so not only enhances rapport, but it also enables coaches and coachees to more readily stay in the present moment and to have anchors for what emerges. As Alexander (1961) put it:

> The key lever of change lay in direct experience that has contradicted long-held expectations rather than in interpretations that explained them as rooted in the past. . . . In this view the emphasis shifts from insight to experience, although the role of insight as a secondary but often powerful consolidating factor is by no means denied. (p. 307)

The key is to ask questions that keep coachees grounded in the experience of their own narration as opposed to detached through analysis or premature planning. For example, instead of asking, "What could you do differently next time?"—which takes people into an imaginary future—first ask, "What is happening for you right now as you talk about the future?" This supports people to develop themselves *at the same time* they are addressing their issue so they can resolve it (and others like them). Narrative questions tend to be more vertical in nature—rising above or diving into the present situation—as opposed to the typical horizontal approach to questions in which each one leads to another like fence posts across the prairie. It is not about taking the person or the conversation somewhere with your questions, but about using them to make the most of each and every moment. For example: Where does the coachee invest the most energy? Where does she turn for guidance? Where is the energy stuck or misplaced? What is truly calling for our attention right now in this conversation?

Think of your questions as invitations to coachees to develop a new relationship with their internal and external experiences (Carotenuto, 1985) in order to resolve their issues in the most elemental way. Otherwise, you and your coachees often end up trying to solve the wrong problems and, as a result, the issues persist. In the process, it is important to remember: Your understanding of what is happening is secondary and, ultimately, seldom necessary for the coachee to achieve their purpose in coaching. The fundamental purpose of your inquiry is for them to become clearer. Your understanding is a beneficial byproduct, but is not essential. This is why narrative coaches experientially investigate what's in the stories rather than clinically analyze them. What does the story want to be asked? Coaching is seldom about gathering more information—much of which will not be relevant in the end and is often more for our own needs—but about using our inquiry to create new experiences for coachees that open new doors. As Moore (2000) describes it, "I've no intention of tracking down a culprit. I only want a fuller story" (p. 66).

> **Your understanding of what is happening is secondary and, ultimately, seldom necessary for the coachee to achieve their purpose in coaching.**

Therefore, think of inquiry as a way of being *with* people, a deep and attuned curiosity, more than just the act of asking questions. It is about coming alongside coachees to inquire into their stories *with* them, rather than standing outside their stories and asking questions *to* them. This requires us to bring our questions into the profoundly here and now and to be more courageous in what we ask. Tompkins and Lawley (1997) offer a great example, "What's the next question the coachee would really like to be asked?" At the same time, recognize that he may be dreading it as well because he knows at some level that if he truthfully answers that question it may serve as a threshold from which there would be no going back. *Ask anyway.* This is why it is important to provide enough time and space for coachees to settle into the conversation and into themselves. Many people are slow to recognize what they are actually feeling or wanting, let alone putting words to their feelings or wishes. If you rush them or they feel you are somehow interrogating them, it will trigger most people to withdraw aspects of their stories and themselves. Instead, help people access and express their fullest self so they can access and express their fullest story.

A common way this is done in narrative coaching is to invite people to access aspects of their story that are hidden by their conscious mind but present in their body. I've increasingly incorporated somatic methods and questions in narrative coaching to help people be more present in their body. I ask questions such as, "What do you notice in your body as you are telling this story? What do you think this means?" "What happens if you speak with your hand on your belly? While standing like a warrior?" This often leads people to immediately scan their body and, in so doing, they often discover new aspects of their stories that warrant their attention. Ginette Paris (2007) observes, "What the psyche refuses to acknowledge, the body always manifests. Whenever the body says 'no more,' it is sending a message that should get our attention; it may be inviting us to a voyage of descent" (p. xii). It is often a powerful and moving experience when people slow down so they can experience more of the truth in their story. Inquiry is about walking with them on that journey, and trusting that what they are seeking is already present. The following is a process I use to help people access more of their stories and their knowledge in coaching.

Using the Four Gateways

I developed this simple process as a way to help coaches and coachees drop into their bodies (Drake, 2011a) as they work together. It is based on the system of chakras found in a number of philosophical traditions. These gateways represent access points to the flow of energy (or lack thereof) in the body and each one can be seen as associated with a different type of knowledge. The use of energy as a construct finds support in the neuroscience of attachment patterns and self-regulation, and it provides a way to ground intuition and increase self- and other-awareness. The gateways can be used to develop your ability to 'read' the situation and to support coachees in making more informed choices. I primarily focus on these four gateways since they are generally the most accessible for people; but with more advanced students I introduce an additional four gateways to deepen their capabilities.

The Four Gateways		Level of knowledge
Think	*Put hands on head*	Mental
Feel	*Put hands on heart*	Emotional
Be	*Put hands on hara (gut)*	Spiritual
Do	*Put hands on hips*	Physical

When using this as a process of inquiry with coachees, start by drawing their attention to their hands as a way to get in touch with their body's knowledge. I find the use of the hands especially helpful for coachees who have a harder time sensing what is going on with them physiologically. The act of focusing on their hands is in itself helpful because it gets coachees out of their heads. You can then guide them to place their hands at each of the four spots on their body, one at a time at first, while focused on their question or decision. With each of these gateways, the question is the same for coachees, "What does this part of me, this way of knowing, have to say about my question?" You can guide them to move up and down these four gateways as needed to gain the knowledge they are seeking. What often transpires is an emerging awareness of energy (information) that is blocked at a gateway or between gateways. I then work with the person to explore what is happening at that gateway: "What is missing? What do you notice? What would it take to restore the flow here?" When they feel complete and there is a restored sense of flow—or at least a sense of what is needed to restore flow—they are more ready to do the work at hand.

For example:

1. Using the *head* gateway, the coachee notices that his story is jumbled as he tries to think about whether or not to stay in his current role.

2. Using the *heart* gateway, he feels a sense of sadness and loss he had not been aware of before and he associates it with a realization it may be time to move on.

3. Using the *hara* gateway, he first senses fear but then, as he breathes deeper into it, he discovers a sense of adventure he had been stifling.

4. Using the *hips* gateway, he becomes aware of a new energy as he imagines himself exploring other options.

5. Moving back through the gateways he feels the clarity and alignment he needs to start looking for a new role.

One of the primary reasons coachees struggle to make decisions or act in new ways is because they get stuck in their heads. Using the gateways helps people access more sources of knowledge they can then use to get unstuck and make better decisions. I find that in our fragmented and distracted world, coachees can access more of their truth and make better decisions by using their head last rather than first. Otherwise, the executive function of their mind is often overwhelmed and not nearly as effective. However, I tend to start the gateways process with the head because that is where most people begin as they tell their stories in coaching. Many people discover in focusing their attention on their head that the energy and knowledge there is often unclear (or clear but flat). Ultimately, it is about helping people to inquire into their whole self and how they are truly doing so they can access more energy and knowledge in support of their new choices and new actions.

You can use the gateways in the narrative coaching process to help coachees:

1. quiet the noise in their *head* so they can see how they are *Situated* in a new way;

2. notice in their *heart* what values are at stake so they can clarify their *Search;*

3. breathe fully in their *hara* so they can *Shift* to a deeper sense of what is true for them;

4. adjust their *hips* and overall stance so they can act with more confidence and *Sustain* their intention; and

5. return to their head so they can confirm their course of action and be more grounded and confident as they start out because the rest of their body is aligned.

An example from coaching supervision:

1. You notice that you don't voice your concerns about a coachee to her directly, but talk abstractly about them with your supervisor instead (*head*).

2. You explore your emotions (*heart*) around what happens for you in those moments when you want to speak up to your coachee.

3. You check in with your gut (*hara*) to get to the core of what you really want to say and the energy that arises when you envision saying it directly.

4. You practice it out loud with your supervisor (*hips*) until you find your message, stance and authentic voice so you can communicate with your coachee.

5. You rehearse the moment when you will speak to your coachee to ensure that the flow is aligned and anchored, you feel ready and the message works. (*head*)

You can use one or more of the gateways as needed: e.g., invite the coachee to put her hand on her heart to name a feeling, put one hand on her heart and the other on her hara to ground her grief, or put one hand on her hara and the other on her hips to gather more strength to make a tough decision (and act on it). You can also invite the coachee to notice if there is a sense of deadness in any of the gateways and reflect on what that might signify in terms of their needs. Louis Cozolino offers a simple way to remember this; it works along the same lines and fits well with the analogy of the bird circling the tree. I sometimes use it when I am feeling stuck with a coachee or I notice I am off track in my formulation:

- Move **up** into your mind when you feel triggered by the coachee, are reacting from old habits, need to put words to images/sensations you are experiencing or need to shift the frame of the conversation.
- Drop **down** into your body and heart when you feel disconnected, distracted, lost or confused by what the coachee is saying, or are uncertain what the coachee is feeling.

The first Lab in our training series is exclusively focused on participants' personal development. They learn the basics of the work by applying it to themselves through guided experiences and peer coaching. Once they have experienced it for themselves and seen what it can do, they are in a much stronger place to be able to offer it to others. So, make sure you are doing the work for yourself so that you can remain present to people and curious wherever their journey in coaching takes them. This is important because coachees are generally not able to travel farther in sessions than you are willing to go. Working somatically also provides great modeling for coachees and significantly enhances the quality of the conversation and its outcomes. Both coaches and coachees can use the gateways to help them drop deeper into their embodied experience so they can bring more of their whole self to the process. The inquiry will be more powerful, the conversation will be more transparent, and the outcomes will be more transformative the more they can do so.

Coachees are generally not able to travel farther in sessions than you are willing to go.

Moving up and down the tree

It's not that I'm so smart. But I stay with the questions much longer. . . .
If I had one hour to solve a difficult problem, I'd spend the first 55 minutes
defining the problem.
Albert Einstein

As we have seen throughout the book, narrative coaching is a mindset—or what my Dutch colleagues call an "attitude"—more than anything else. This is as true for coachees as it is for you as a coach. Much of the initial work in narrative coaching is about helping people surface, explore and adapt their mindset so they are able to narrate their experiences in new ways. As a result, they are not only able to resolve their presenting issues but they also increase their maturity and capability as a foundation for moving forward. A narrative approach to inquiry is well aligned with brief methods in this regard. We are not invested in either a need to understand the problem or an assumption that the solution is somehow connected with eliminating the problem (Hoyt, 1996). Instead, we ask questions to increase coachees' clarity about what they most want to be different and how they will know they have been successful (W. O'Hanlon, 1998). In this section we will return to the analogy of coaching as a bird circling a tree to describe the types of questions we tend to ask in narrative coaching.

A narrative approach to inquiry in coaching aligns with the shift from deconstructive listening to deconstructive questioning in certain forms of psychotherapy. *Deconstructive listening* is about accepting and understanding people's stories as they are—without reifying them—and seeking openings for aspects of their narratives that haven't yet been storied (Freedman & Combs, 1996, p. 46). Once there is enough of a shared understanding, there is a shift to asking questions. *Deconstructive questioning* invites people to see their stories from different perspectives, notice how they are constructed (or even *that* they are constructed), note their limits, and discover there are other possible narratives. In moving between listening and questioning, we are searching for elements in the story that are amenable to challenge, redefinition, or re-interpretation (Coulehan, Friedlander, & Heatherington, 1998) but are close enough to the coachee's current experience and narrative so as to be seen as approachable (Grafaniki & McLeod, 1999). Overall what this means is that narrative coaches tend to ask far fewer questions, particularly in the beginning.

I also think it is important to make the same distinction we did with the classic rites of passage model by adding the vertical line here as well. I have added *Constructive listening* and *Constructive questioning* to represent a more complete cycle in coaching. The addition of constructive listening is a reminder to stay in Situate long enough to get to the real questions; the addition of constructive questioning is a reminder to stay in Sustain long enough to ensure the outcomes are integrated. These additions highlight the unique proposition in narrative coaching that listening drives inquiry not the other way around. You can see the four approaches in the following figure. Each of these modes of engaging with coachees relates to one of the four phases of the narrative coaching model and one of the four elements of the Narrative Diamond. As before, these are phases along a spiraling path not necessarily linear steps in a process.

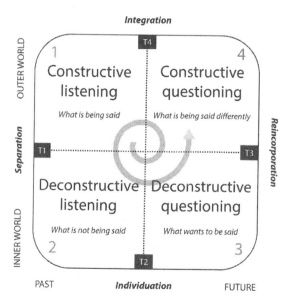

Figure 20. *Using deconstructive and constructive approaches in coaching*

The initial focus in coaching is on the coachee and using *constructive listening* to track what is being said (Situate). Next, the focus is on the story and using *deconstructive listening* to help the coachee explore what is not being said (Search). We don't ask many questions that elicit the recall of the old story, as it is likely to increase the person's commitment to that story. Instead, if need be, we ask questions about experiences of the desired new story in the past to strengthen it as a foundation for the present and the future (Hewson, 1991). Once the coachee has determined what she wants to change, you can shift to *deconstructive questioning* to help her discover what wants to be said and what needs to shift to bring about the change (Shift). Lastly, you can use *constructive questioning* based on what is already being said differently to help the coachee prepare for how she wants to bring her new story to life (Sustain). For example:

1. Constructive listening—Noticing "My team doesn't deliver the results I want."
2. Deconstructive listening—Exploring "I don't think they understand what I want."
3. Deconstructive questioning—Discovering "I wonder if I am not being clear with them."
4. Constructive questioning—Addressing "I need to make my requests more concrete."

While this framework mirrors the flow of narrative coaching, feel free to move between the types of listening and questioning based on what best serves the needs of the coachee and the conversation. In so doing, I often position my questions "on the razor edge between love and power and [seek to] be both supportive and uncompromising" (Heron, 2001, p. 62). This often proves quite effective, both as a technique and as modeling for coachees about authentic communication. If you get caught up in listening for too long, coachees often remain stuck in the problem and their own rumination and procrastination; if you rush to questioning too soon, coachees often prematurely choose a project they are not ready for and/or is not at the right level. When in doubt as you move between listening and questioning, return to your breath, to the moment. Come back to presence. When you feel called to inquire, here are some tips for you.

Ten tips for narrative inquiry
- Trust that the resolution is already present.
- Let your questions emerge from the silence and what you hear.
- Ask questions to generate experiences not pursue or provide explanations.
- Stay in the story and the present moment even when asking about the past or future.
- Position yourself relative to and in support of the unfolding story.
- Move toward the unknown more than the known with most of your questions.
- Ask open questions to connect and closed questions to invite them to choose.
- Ask one question at a time. Keep them short, simple, and to the point.
- People can only intervene in their life at the level at which they can make distinctions.
- Recognize that your understanding is not essential for their progress.

When you are formulating a question, ask yourself, "What purpose am I hoping it will serve?" While there is no formula for calculating exactly which question to ask or when, there is a sense in narrative coaching that certain types of questions are better asked at certain points in the conversation. You can draw on the core narrative coaching analogy, that of a bird circling a tree, as a guide to help you do so. Imagine yourself starting with the coachee's experience on a branch in the thick of things as he begins his story, then moving up the tree and into the sky to help him get a better perspective. You can stop on the upward spiral as needed to help him name what he has discovered. Once the implications of the current story and the desires for a new story are clear, imagine yourself moving down into the tree again to help him determine how to put his new story and/or decision into action. The underlying questions are always the same: At what level—relative to the tree—is the coachee right now? What is the next level for him? How can we get there? In doing so, be inspired by the infamous line from Albert Einstein that you can't solve a problem at the level at which it was created.

I use the following natural flow to teach practitioners how to move and up and down the tree with their questions based on what they are hearing and sensing in the conversation. I created it for a partner development program in working with PwC Australia to build a coaching-based culture. It is now one of people's favorite experiences in my programs. You can also use it when you coach to assess where coachees are relative to their issue and where they need to move next in terms of the level of inquiry. I have included sample questions for each level; I encourage you to find ones that work for you. I start with some version of question #1 at the bottom of the left column; then move up to the top of that column. You can then bridge to question #5 at the top of the right column to ground the person, invite them to name their discovery, and help them prepare to move down through the tree to take action. When you are done, you will have guided the coachee in a complete spiral from Situate to Situate. It is often quite powerful to ask them to reflect on how far they have traveled and where they have ended up.

Moving up above the tree

5. How is it affecting you? What is its *meaning* for you?

4. What is important about it to you *(values)*?

3. How do you *feel* about it?

2. What do you *think* about it? What story are you telling about it?

1. What *happened*? Is happening?

Moving down to the tree

5. What is true and important for you now?

4. What is your motivation to do it differently?

3. How will you track your progress?

2. What do you need in order to get started?

1. How will you know you have been successful?

Working with metaphors and analogies

This is what keeps you doing things you don't want to do. You do them because you're out of touch with the place where your actions come from.
James Bugental

Metaphors and analogies represent unique opportunities in coaching because they act as 'side doors' into people's narratives and identities. They tend to be less defended because they are generally framed as common phrases, images or experiences which seem innocuous at first. They can be seen as attempts of our unconscious to surface images through which we can notice aspects of ourselves that warrant our attention. It is as if our unconscious and unspoken lives press for recognition in these narrative fragments (Phillips, 1994). They often "mark the living presence of important narratives that constitute one's sense of self" (James L. Griffith & Melissa E. Griffith, 1993) and, as such, often reveal larger issues at stake for us. This is why in narrative coaching we work directly with the metaphor or analogy itself rather than psychologize it. We inquire *into* it rather than *about* it. Metaphors and analogies:

- Offer heuristics and linguistic shorthand by which we operate everyday
- Provide access into the coachee's world, into the spaces in between their stories
- Bridge the symbolic and the literal, the emotive and the logical
- Draw on and combine resources from both the left and right hemispheres
- Bridge between literal and symbolic, cognition and affect, conscious and unconscious[18]

---

18 Adapted from Marshak, 1993, pp. 44–45.

They connect the world as lived *in* the tree and the world as seen from *above* the tree, and they enable people to make associations that we would otherwise not make. They communicate by "juxtaposing two not entirely comparable elements, thereby inducing the hearer to extract from the somewhat discordant image a new vision of the primary element" (Bassler, 1986, p. 158). They sit on the doorstep between worlds and offer people an opportunity to move in and out of perspectives on their situation and/or themselves. One of the ways you can capitalize on this juxtaposition is by inviting coachees to bring their metaphor or analogy to life and immerse themselves in it as is if it were real. By animating their metaphors and analogies —and participating in them as coach or character—you can help coachees gain a fuller understanding of their situation, its meaning and significance, and their path to resolution. This often yields more robust outcomes because the whole brain is activated and the whole person is engaged. "When the metaphor evolves, behavior changes in the client's 'real' world" (Tompkins & Lawley, 1997, p. 1).

For example, for a coachee who felt "stuck in the mud" I pressed her feet down as she tried to walk across the room—to give her a visceral experience of its impact in her life. In processing the experience, we explored how it was that she kept finding herself in this place and what would need to shift for her to walk freely. A Lab participant described himself as a "lone wolf", so I invited him to stand across the room away from the group and notice what happened for him and the group. We all stood there in silence for a minute or two to let his sudden separation from this group sink in. In the dialogue that followed, he began to see where this behavior came from and how he wanted to be more in balance. We also talked with the group about what came up for them in the experience. Bringing metaphors and analogies alive is more powerful than just talking about them. It enables coachees to subjectively experience their issue rather than try to objectively explain it. When I am working, I tend to pause if the person uses a metaphor or analogy that seems significant and explore it then and there. Often it becomes the focus for the work in that session.

When you are working with people who are literal in nature, you can ground them in the tangible aspect of the metaphor or analogy before exploring its symbolic meaning. When you are working with people who are imaginative in nature you can ground them in its symbolic aspect before exploring with them its more literal implications. I enjoy working with metaphors and analogies because they call for serious play and, as such, provide access to the core dynamics of coachees' issues. There is often a point in working with them where you can freeze frame the moment to capture the essence of the issue. For the "stuck in the mud" person it was the moment she tried to lift her foot from the floor. For the "lone wolf" it was lifting his head and seeing the group across the room.

These experiences can often be quite powerful for people, particularly if they are followed all the way through and given time to fully process. I recommend not debriefing or discussing big experiences straightaway because it dilutes the energy and the transformative potential. Let the person sit in silence or quietly walk outside so the new awareness can start to settle. Having another person they trust quietly hold space for them as they do so is often appreciated. The changes that began in the process will continue to ripple through the person for hours if not days if they are cared for well. For the same reason, I don't plan after big experiences, as it tends to prematurely thrust the person back into the world before their new story has gelled. If I offer any instructions it is to simply notice what is unfolding and to nurture themselves.

Closing

Have care; there is something here that matters.
Alfred North Whitehead

In this chapter we have looked at inquiry as it is conceptualized and used in narrative coaching. Following the flow of the model, you can use your curiosity and questions to open up and expand new lines of inquiry with people, explore what emerges as important and in need of attention, and focus and narrow the conversation in preparation for implementation. In so doing, you are in essence creating zones of proximal development for people in which they can learn what is required to make the passage across the next threshold. Your coaching can offer them the scaffolding they need as they move into, though and out of each phase. They start in what they know in Situate, move toward the unknown when there is a breach in the known and then cross the first threshold to move into Search. The unknown continues as they start their explorations, but at some point they develop a greater sense of the known as they progress through this phase. Eventually, they move toward the big unknown at the second threshold where the focus on the past and the release give way to a focus on the future and the return. They enter the Shift phase and the pattern starts again—and continues for the rest of the spiral.

This chapter offered you some tools you can use to help people on this journey. The four gateways can be used to fine tune your presence with people and your ability to tap multiple sources of knowledge as you coach. I use it often with coachees and participants to help them access their own inner knowing and to ground them in the moment, particularly if they are working on a major decision. It is a powerful, simple way to connect people with themselves and the process that is underway. We also used the analogy of the bird circling the tree as a frame for thinking about the nature of the questions you ask in coaching. What seems important here is the foundation of generative silence and a deep curiosity about what is happening with the person and her process. As a result, your questions neither lead nor follow the conversation but accompany it as you circle the tree. This can be readily seen in working with metaphors and analogies that bridge between worlds. In the end, remember that it is your presence that often matters most—not whether or not you ask the perfect question. Trust that everything you need is right in front of you.

CONCLUSION

If you ever find yourself in the wrong story, leave.
Mo Willems

Narrative coaching draws on rich traditions that predate coaching, incorporates practices that transcend traditional coaching and offers glimpses into what coaching could become. As I thought about how to conclude this book, I realized that parables and fables have been used as a teaching device for thousands of years because they communicate the moral of the story in simple terms. They are built around two questions, "What is the main message I want you to take away?" and "What common experience can I use as a reference point?" As I thought about this book in those terms, I began with some provocative questions: What if we released the word "coaching" and thought in terms of transparent connection, authentic communication, and transformative purpose? What if coaching was a magnificent scenic overlook and there is more road ahead? What if coaching was just the way we lived? My main messages would be:

- Be radically present to yourself, the other person and the conversation.
- Help people discover the truths and the illusions in their stories. Both will be liberating.
- Remember that the power to change is in the pivot in this moment, again and again.

I would like to conclude by offering a brief summary of what we have covered so far, the six core principles of narrative coaching, a narrative bill of rights for coachees and a glimpse into what is next for this work. The first section of the book on *narrative psychologies* showed how the narrative coaching process is based in a deep understanding of how our brain develops and our mind works, how we form relationships and identities, and how we learn and grow over time. It does so with a deep respect for the preverbal, unconscious and embodied nature of our narratives and stories. The second section on *narrative processes* offered a look at the function and structure of stories and the act of narration and formulation as resources in coaching. These are important in learning what to listen for in people's stories, witnessing them as narrators and advocating for the stories themselves. Two of the essential skills for doing so are pattern recognition and sense making. At the heart of the process is a commitment to stay in the present moment and within the stories as they are being narrated as much as possible.

The third section on *narrative practices* explored rites of passage as the underlying structure for narrative coaching as a change and transition process. The narrative coaching model was introduced with a solid overview of where it came from, each of the four phases and how they can be used in sessions for optimal results. The final section on *narrative practitioners* offered three of the key skills in narrative coaching—holding space, listening and inquiry—and why each is framed and done differently than in more traditional approaches. The use of silence, the field and the whole self in coaching are of particular importance. The integrative nature of narrative coaching is evident as you look back over these sections, their respective four-phase models and how they are connected in a unified process. Narrative coaching works well because the process mirrors how people naturally transition, develop and tell stories. Narrative coaching is also unique in that it is organized around the coachee and her stories not the coach or even the problem/solution.

Coachees have arrived where they are right now along the songline of their life. It could be no other. The choice for them now is, "Which stories will I continue to tell? Which stories will I change or release? What new stories might I want to bring to my life?" At the same time, it seems important to acknowledge that their stories are formed out of material from larger narratives that existed before they were born and will continue on in some form after they die. Narrative coaching is one of the few methodologies that moves beyond the individual to address these larger narratives and forces that shape their identities, mindsets and behaviors. It offers a process through which people can awaken more fully and achieve more of what matters most as a result. When I work, I see myself as a channel for wisdom and energy that is passing through me in service of the process and the person. I am actively holding the space rather than actively driving the process. My experience and expertise strengthen the channel more than they structure the process. Similarly, the model is a reflection of how people naturally transition and develop, not a recipe that is imposed on the conversation. The more you develop yourself, the stronger your channel and the more powerful yet simple your coaching will become.

This book is a culmination of a long personal and professional journey. It is also an invitation to you to help create what comes next with this work. I hope that the book has been a rich and rewarding start to your journey with narrative coaching. In the end, it is about helping people to

- become more aware of and awake to their own stories,
- recognize that these stories are personally and socially constructed,
- recognize that they are formed in relation to larger narratives,
- understand how these shape their identity and behavior,
- be more authentic and authorial in how they narrate and live, and
- relate to others and their narratives with a wider window of tolerance.

It does so not by offering a prescriptive methodology, but by grounding itself in an integrative philosophy and a set of clear principles.

Principles

Narrative coaching is built around a robust model and it offers a distinct and powerful methodology. Fundamentally, though, it is a philosophy and set of principles for purposeful conversations. One of the things participants most appreciate is how this work enables them to integrate their prior knowledge, experience and modalities —and at a higher level. They find that they can let go of a lot of what they thought coaching had to include and, as a result, they end up de-cluttering the way they work. They come to see the wisdom in only adding to the coaching conversation when it feels essential to do so. One colleague described what I am doing with narrative coaching as "helping people reboot their human operating system." Another one remarked in the midst of a Lab, "It can't be this simple, can it?!"—and then affirmatively answered her own question a few minutes later. Narrative coaching can work this way because it is based in the following:

The six core principles of narrative coaching

- *Trust that everything you need is right in front of you.*
  This is the cornerstone of narrative coaching. It means staying out of our heads—worried about what to do next—and trusting that the resources and resolution are already there. It means moving toward the unknown and letting go of our need to be in control or clever so that we can:
- *Be fully present to what IS without judgment.*
  This is about being radically present even as we observe what is unfolding using our expertise and wisdom. It means serving as a loving witness and accepting what is true for coachees before attempting to make changes—so they can do the same for themselves. Therefore:
- *Speak only when you can improve on silence.*
  This is about using the power of generative silence to build rapport, activate the field and make more space for the whole story. It means staying in the moment, listening at many levels and being guided more by what we hear and sense than what we say. From that place we can:

- *Focus on generating experiences not explanations.*
  This is about literally bringing people's stories into the room. It means inviting them to take new action now—rather than analyzing and planning for later. This allows them to experiment with trying out new ways of being, acting or speaking. To do so:
- *Work directly with the narrative elements in the field.*
  This is about inviting people to address, reframe and reconfigure elements in their stories to evoke insights and move them closer to their aspiration. It means staying within their frame and language so that changes are more likely to stick. This is especially important when we are called to:
- *Stand at the threshold when a new story is emerging.*
  This is about noticing when people are approaching a developmental breakthrough and choice point—either of which may come first. It means ensuring they are prepared to cross, safeguarding their traverse and welcoming them and their new story on the other side.

Working from these principles requires a commitment to a strong ethic in relation to people and their stories. This is reflected in the fact that people often comment on how respectful narrative coaching feels. This is so important because they often have far more invested in and tied up with their stories than you or they realize at first. It is analogous to the observation by the American naturalist John Muir, "When we try to pick out anything by itself, we find it hitched to everything else in the Universe." A story is just a story. A story is also way more than a story. Therefore, in narrative coaching we tend to move slowly at first. It gives people the time and space to soften their grip on their stories before releasing or reconfiguring them when they are ready. I use the following set of ethical principles to guide me when I coach or teach other coaches[19]. They are based in a fundamental belief that when you coach people you are a guest in their narrative 'home'.

A story is just a story. A story is also way more than a story.

A narrative bill of rights in coaching

- People have the right to a safe space for their story-telling. Respect them and their stories before anything else.
- People have the right to be heard in a nonjudgmental and non-assumptive manner. Take their communal and cultural stories seriously.
- People have the right to tell their own story their own way. They are accountable for the impact of their stories on themselves and others.
- People have the right to understand and interpret their own stories. They are responsible for changing their stories, lives and selves if/as they choose.
- People have the right to expect coaches to manage their own stories, agendas and participation. Be an exemplary steward of the process and the field.
- People have the right to make sense and meaning of what happens in coaching. They are responsible for what they choose to do as a result.

---

19 I have been inspired by the work of Paul Costello and his commitment to ethics in narrative work.

What's next for narrative coaching

What story is worth your life?
Lisa Marshall

I believe that narrative coaching and what it stands for are even more vital today for both coaching and our world. I am more committed than ever to deepening my understanding of both the dynamics of change and the potential for this work. At the same time, I am equally committed to democratizing this work so that its principles and practices become more accessible. Narrative coaching is well suited to do so because it doesn't need certitudes; instead, it precipitates an acceleration of consciousness (Paris, 2007). When all is said and done, we are all part of one human story. As Jung observed, many of the issues in our life are a result of becoming separated from our stories. Therefore, narrative coaching's mission includes reuniting people with their most authentic stories about who they are and how they want to be in the world. I see at least three trajectories for this work in the near future:

- innovating how and where it is applied,
- inquiring into its foundations and impact, and
- increasing the global community of practitioners.

We live in a time that is deeply in need of more integrative methods that are both profoundly personal and proactively social. I developed the following variation on the core model to capture the essence of where I think narrative coaching is headed. It centers around accelerating three fundamental shifts this work has always stood for: (1) using coaching to bring about change not just respond to change; (2) connecting personal and social transformation as one process not two (or more); and (3) seeing mindfulness as a collective enterprise not just a personal resource. Each of these is captured in the graphic below.

> We live in a time that is deeply in need of more integrative methods that are both profoundly personal and proactively social.

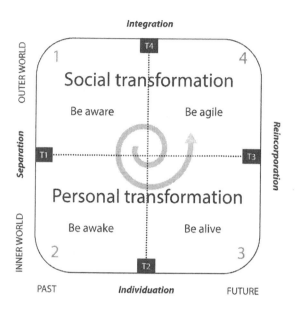

Figure 21. *Narrative coaching as an integrative development process*

For example, each of the four outcomes of mindfulness from page 257 are linked to one phase in the integrative development and change process.

1.   The first step is to help people become more Aware of their current Situation so they can plant the seeds for social transformation as they Separate. *We are not separate, so we can be accepting of all experience.*

2.   The second step is to help people become more Awake in their Search so they can prepare for their personal transformation as they Individuate. *We are not asleep, so we can remain present with sensations and feelings.*

3. The third step is to help people become more Alive through their Shift so they can manifest their personal transformation before they Reincorporate. *We are not on automatic pilot, so we can harness and focus our energies.*

4. The fourth step is to help people become more Agile in how they Sustain so they can contribute to social transformation as they Integrate with their new narratives. *We are not reactive, so we can act from a conscious, accountable state.*

Innovating how and where it is applied

I will continue to train practitioners to use narrative coaching in their work with individuals and teams. At the same time, there is an increasing focus on the integration of these principles and practices in larger projects[20]. I believe that coaching has to scale if we are to address the complexity of global issues such as climate change. While coaching will continue on as a discrete activity in many forms, it must now also become an integral part of how everyone operates. Given that stories are at the core of what makes us human, I believe that narrative coaching has a role to play in making this transition. This will include finding more ways for our stories to unite us (based in love) not divide us (based in fear), and preserving our connection to nature as technology increasingly shapes our lives. I've identified four levels at which coaching will increasingly work as it evolves, and listed them below along with their narrative type, their integrative development element (BEAM) and a few insights on what it might include. These represent the next frontier for this work and for our larger human narrative.

---

20 Learn about our Narrative Design Partners program at www.narrativecoaching.com.

Level	Narrative type	BEAM element	Insight
Cellular	Epistemological	Behavior	How can coaching be used at a micro-level and in real time to support desired behaviors? Wearable technologies and advances at the biological/technological interface are examples of what is to come.
Consciousness	Ontological	Mindset	How can coaching be used for a greater awakening when external forces are making this more difficult? The need to urgently address issues such as climate change will challenge people to operate at a higher level and with a more resilient mindset.
Cultural	Ecological	Environment	How can coaching be used in a more integrative fashion so people and the systems in which they live and work can co-evolve? As institutions like government, education, health care are less able to meet collective needs, how can we work together to build what is next.
Creative	Cosmological	Aspiration	How can coaching help shape a more inclusive, generative and sustainable narrative around which we can align and fully contribute? There is a growing need to make transformative tools available to everyone as part of what I call a DIYT (do-it-yourself-together) era.

Inquiring into its foundations and impact

Narrative coaching is a developmental methodology through which people can resolve their issues at a number of levels using their own stories. Because narrative coaching is seen as a rite of passage, we work with both sacred and profane spaces, personal and collective narratives, and conscious and nonconscious dynamics in people's stories. I see tremendous potential growth for narrative coaching and its impact in the following three areas:

- How to work holistically with narratives—e.g., how can integrative development help us better understand how to turn insight into action through reconfigured narratives?
- How to develop contemporary rites of passage—e.g., how would they look using non-western, non-masculine and ecological frames (Bynum, 1984)?
- How to develop practitioners who can work across a wide spectrum of modalities and interventions—e.g., how can we address issues that will be increasingly systemic in nature?

What all this seems to be signaling is a call for a more pronounced weaving together of the threads that are already in place. I believe this will be increasingly important as we move into a difficult period of transition as a planet. It calls for more people to move out to the edges to provide leadership wherever it is needed and support leadership wherever it is present. Instead of standing behind others, cheering them on, I see a need for us to move more toward the front to help lead the way. This means that we as coaches have to do our own work so that we can do the same for others. This will require simple things like diversifying our service portfolio and more demanding things like diving deeper into our own development. As Metzger (1992) notes:

To reconstruct a self, an old self may have to be shattered. Sometimes the world-vessel must be pulverized. To discover who we are, we may have to divest ourselves of everything, go beyond the imagined limits of ourselves. We may have to leap out of the familiar, jump off a cliff, go to the very edge of the world where all the dragons live. (p. 71)

The good news is that you will find others out there in those narrative fields, engaging their 'dragons' in order to come more fully and courageously alive. You can find out more about the third trajectory, increasing the global community of practitioners, on page 336.

I developed narrative coaching, in part, because I believe we need more people who can go to these deeper and more difficult places within themselves and with others if we are to rise to the challenges before us. This means creating more space for our full humanity; e.g., our pain and suffering *and* our joy and fulfillment. For example, what if we brought narrative coaching to hospices to help people bring closure to the Narrative that is a life. This is a time that calls all of us to do the real work of our quest and to join with others who are doing the same. Listen deeply into the silence, the earth and the hearts of others. Look unflinchingly into your own soul to see what is calling you. Engage the younger generations to see what they are trying to tell us as they prepare to take the mantle of leadership from us. Given that, what are the events in your life right now preparing you for? What do you sense is yours to do? In the end it comes down to the question, "What story do you most want to bring to life right now? I am heartened that you have chosen to read this book and I look forward to hearing where it takes you. Travel well . . .

REFERENCES

Abma, Tineke A. (1999). Powerful stories: The role of stories in sustaining and transforming professional practice within a mental hospital. In Ruthellen Josselson & Amia Lieblich (Eds.), *Making meaning of narratives* (Vol. 6, pp. 169–195). Thousand Oaks, CA: Sage.

Ainsworth, Mary, & Bowlby, John J. (1991). An ethological approach to personality development. *American Psychologist, 46,* 331–341.

Alexander, Bobby C. (1991). *Victor Turner revisited: Ritual as social change* (Vol. 74). Atlanta, GA: Scholars Press.

Alexander, Franz Gabriel (1961). *The scope of psychoanalysis.* New York, NY: Ronald Press.

Allport, Gordon. (1955/1968). *Becoming: Basic considerations for a psychology of personality.* New Haven, CT: Yale University Press.

Amabile, Teresa M., & Kramer, Steven J. (2012). The power of small wins. *Harvard Business Review, 7.* Retrieved from http://hbr.org/2011/05/the-power-of-small-wins/ar/1

Anderson, Timothy. (2004). "To tell my story": Configuring interpersonal relations within narrative process. In Lynne E. Angus & John McLeod (Eds.), *Handbook of narrative and psychotherapy: Practice, theory, and research* (pp. 315–329). Thousand Oaks, CA: Sage.

Anzaldua, Gloria. (1987). *Borderlands | La frontera: The new Mestiza.* San Francisco, CA: Aunt Lute Books.

Augustine, Saint. (400/2009). *Confessions* (Henry Chadwick, Trans.). Oxford: Oxford University Press.

Austin, James T., & Vancouver, Jeffrey B. (1996). Goal constructs in psychology: Structure, process, and content. *Psychological Bulletin, 120*(3), 338–375.

Badenoch, Bonnie. (2008). *Being a brain-wise therapist: A practical guide to interpersonal neurobiology.* New York, NY: W.W. Norton.

Bakan, David. (1966). *The duality of human existence: Isolation and communion in Western man.* Boston: Beacon.

Barrett, Frank, & Cooperrider, David L. (2002). Generative metaphor intervention: A new approach for working with systems divided by conflict and caught in defensive perception. In Ron Fry, Frank Barrett, Jane Seiling, & Diana Whitney (Eds.), *Appreciative Inquiry and organizational transformation: Reports from the field* (pp. 121–145). Westport, CT: Quorum

Barrett, Terry, Cashman, Diane, & Moore, Diane. (2011). Designing problems and triggers in different media. In Terry Barrett & Sarah Moore (Eds.), *New approaches to problem-based learning* (pp. 18–35). New York, NY: Routledge.

Bartel, C., & Dutton, Jane E. (2001). Ambiguous organizational member-ships: Constructing organizational identities in interactions with others. In M. A. Hogg & D. J. Terry (Eds.), *Social identity processes in organizational contexts* (pp. 115–130). Philadelphia, PA: Psychology Press.

Bassler, Jouette M. (1986). The parable of the loaves. *The Journal of Religion, 66*(2), 157–172.

Bateson, Gregory. (1972). *Steps to an ecology of mind.* New York, NY: Ballantine Books.

Bateson, Gregory. (1982). Difference, double description and the interactive designation of self. In F. Allan Hanson (Ed.), *Studies in symbolism and cultural communication* (Vol. 14, pp. 3–8). Lawrence: University of Kansas.

Begley, Sharon. (2007). *Train your mind, change your brain.* New York, NY: Ballantine Books.

Berger, Peter L. (1963). *Invitation to sociology.* New York, NY: Doubleday.

Berger, Peter L., & Luckmann, Thomas. (1966). *The social construction of reality.* New York, NY: Doubleday.

Bergum, Vangie. (1997). *A child on her mind: The experience of becoming a mother.* Westport, CT: Bergin & Garvey.

Bernstein, Jerome S. (2005). *Living in the borderland.* New York, NY: Routledge.

Bion, Wilfred R. (1961). *Experiences in groups and other papers.* London, UK: Tavistock.

Bion, Wilfred R. (1967). Notes on memory and desire. *Psychoanalytic Forum, 2*(3), 271–280.

Bluckert, Peter. (2010). The Gestalt approach to coaching. In Elaine Cox, Tatiana Bachkirova, & David A. Clutterbuck (Eds.), *The complete handbook of coaching* (pp. 80–93). London, UK: Sage.

Bly, Robert. (1988). *A little book on the human shadow.* New York, NY: HarperCollins Publishers.

Boa, F. (1988). *The way of the dream: Conversations on Jungian dream interpretation with Marie-Louise von Franz.* Boston, MA: Shambhala.

Boje, David M. (1998). The postmodern turn from stories-as-objects to stories-in-context methods. *Research Methods Forum.* Retrieved from http://www.aom.pace.edu/rmd/1998_forum_postmodern_stories.html

Boscolo, Luigi, & Bertrando, Paolo. (1992). The reflexive loop of past, present, and future in systemic therapy and consultation. *Family Process, 31*, 119–130.

Botella, Luis, & Herrero, Loga. (2000). A relational constructivist approach to narrative therapy. *European Journal of Psychotherapy, Counselling & Health, 3*(3), 407–418.

Bowlby, John. (1969). *Attachment* (2nd ed. Vol. 1). New York, NY: Basic Books.

Bowlby, John. (1973). *Separation: Anxiety and anger* (Vol. 2). New York, NY: Basic Books.

Bowlby, John. (1982). *Loss: Sadness and depression* (Vol. 3). New York, NY: Basic Books.

Bowlby, John. (1988). *A secure base: Clinical applications of attachment theory.* London, UK: Routledge.

Boyd, Brian. (2009). *On the origin of stories.* Cambridge, MA: Harvard University Press.

Brehony, Kathleen A. (1996). *Awakening at midlife.* New York, NY: Riverhead Books.

Bridges, William. (2001). *The way of transition: Embracing life's most difficult moments.* Cambridge, MA: De Capo Press.

Bridges, William. (1980). *Transitions: Making sense of life's transitions.* Reading: Addison-Wesley.

Brimhall, Andrew S., Gardner, Brandt C., & Henline, Branden H. (2003). Enhancing narrative couple therapy process with an enactment scaffolding. *Contemporary Family Therapy, 25*(4), 391–414.

Brown, Molly Young. (2004). *Unfolding the self: The practice of psychosynthesis.* New York: Helios.

Bruner, Jerome. (1986). *Actual minds, possible worlds.* Cambridge, MA: Harvard University Press.

Bruner, Jerome. (2002). *Making stories: Law, literature, life.* Cambridge, MA: Harvard University Press.

Bruner, Jerome, & Luciarello, J. (1989). Monologue as narrative recreation of the world. In K. Nelson (Ed.), *Narratives from the crib.* Cambridge, MA: Harvard University Press.

Buck, Stephanie. (2004). *Home, hearth, and grace: The archetypal symbol of threshold on the road to self.* Paper presented at the 2004 International Conference: Jungian Society for Scholarly Studies, Newport, RI.

Bugental, James, F.T. (1990). *Intimate journeys: Stories for life-changing therapy.* San Francisco, CA: Jossey-Bass.

Burke, Kenneth. (1969). *A grammar of motives.* Berkeley, CA: University of California Press.

Bynum, Caroline Walker. (1984). Women's stories, women's symbols: A critique of Victor Turner's theory of liminality. In R. L. Moore & Frank E. Reynolds (Eds.), *Anthropology and the study of religion.* Chicago: Center for the Scientific Study of Religion.

Campbell, Joseph. (1968). *The masks of God: Creative mythology.* New York, NY: Viking.

Campbell, Joseph. (1973). *The hero with a thousand faces.* Princeton: Princeton University Press.

Carey, Maggie, Walther, Sarah, & Russell, Shona. (2009). The absent but implicit: A map to support therapeutic enquiry. *Family Process, 48*(3), 319–331.

Carnabucci, Karen, & Anderson, Ronald. (2012). *Integrating psychodrama and systemic constellation work.* London, UK: Jessica Kingsley.

Carotenuto, Aldo. (1979). *The spiral way: A woman's healing journey* (John Shepley, Trans.). Toronto, Canada: Inner City Books.

Carotenuto, Aldo. (1985). *The vertical labyrinth: Individuation in Jungian psychology.* Toronto, Canada: Inner City Books.

Carr, David. (1986). *Time, narrative, and history.* Bloomington: Indiana University Press.

Carson, Timothy L. (1997). *Liminal reality and transformational power.* Lanham, MD: University Press of America.

Casement, Patrick. (1991). *Learning from the patient.* New York, NY: Guilford Press.

Cavanagh, Michael J., & Spence, Gordon B. (2013). Mindfulness in coaching: Philosophy, psychology or just a useful skill? In Jonathan Passmore, David B. Peterson, & Teresa Freire (Eds.), *The Wiley-Blackwell handbook of the psychology of coaching and mentoring* (pp. 112–134). West Sussex, UK: John Wiley & Sons.

Chafe, Wallace. (1990). Some things that narratives tell us about the mind. In Bruce K. Britton & A.D. Pellegrini (Eds.), *Narrative thought and narrative language* (pp. 79–98). Hillsdale, NJ: Lawrence Erlbaum.

Chaiklin, Seth. (2003). The zone of proximal development in Vygotsky's analysis of learning and instruction. In A. Kozulin, B. Gindis, V. Ageyev, & S. Miller (Eds.), *Vygotsky's educational theory and practice in cultural context* (pp. 39–64). Cambridge: Cambridge University Press.

Charon, Rita. (2006). *Narrative medicine: Honoring the stories of illness.* New York: Oxford University Press.

Chiron, C., Jambaque, I., Nabbout, R., Lounes, R., Syrota, A., & Dulac, O. (1997). The right hemisphere is dominant in human infants. *Brain*(120), 1057–1065.

Chittister, Joan. (2010). *Illuminated life: Monastic wisdom for seekers of light.* Maryknoll, NY: Orbis Books.

Clandinin, D. Jean, & Connelly, F. Michael. (2000). *Narrative inquiry: Experience and story in qualitative research.* San Francisco, CA: Jossey-Bass.

Clutterbuck, David, & David, Susan A. (2013). Goals in coaching and mentoring. In Susan David, David Clutterbuck, & David Megginson (Eds.), *Beyond goals: Effective strategies for coaching and mentoring* (pp. 21–34). Farnham, UK: Gower.

Corrie, Sarah, Drake, David B., & Lane, David A. (2010). Creating stories for complex times. In Sarah Corrie & David Lane (Eds.), *Constructing stories, telling tales: A guide to formulation in applied psychology* (pp. 320–352). London, UK: Karnac.

Coulehan, Robin, Friedlander, Myrna L., & Heatherington, Laurie. (1998). Transforming narratives: A change event in constructivist family therapy. *Family Process, 37,* 17–33.

Coyote, Peter. (2014, August 12). Robin Williams' last gift. Retrieved from https://www.facebook.com/peter.coyote.3?fref=photo

Cozolino, Louis. (2002). *The neuroscience of psychotherapy: Building and rebuilding the human brain.* New York, NY: W.W. Norton.

Cozolino, Louis. (2006). *The neuroscience of human relationships: Attachment and the developing brain.* New York, NY: W.W. Norton.

Cozolino, Louis. (2010). *The neuroscience of psychotherapy: Healing the social brain* (Second ed.). New York, NY: W.W. Norton.

Cross, Susan, & Markus, Hazel. (1991). Possible selves across the lifespan. *Human Development, 34,* 230–255.

Crossley, Michelle L. (2002). Introducing narrative psychology *Narrative, memory and life transitions* (pp. 1–13). Huddersfield: University of Huddersfield.

Czarniawska, Barbara. (1998). *A narrative approach to organization studies.* Thousand Oaks, CA: Sage.

Czarniawska, Barbara. (2004). *Narratives in social science research.* London, UK: Sage

Day, David D., Harrison, Michelle M., & Halpin, Stanley M. (2009). *An integrative approach to leader development: Connecting adult development, identity, and expertise.* New York, NY: Psychology Press.

Dayton, Tian. (2005). *The living stage: A step-by-step guide to psychodrama, sociometry and experiential group therapy.* Deerfield Beach, FL: Health Communications, Inc.

de Shazer, Steve. (1988). *Clues: Investigating solutions in brief therapy.* New York, NY: W.W. Norton.

Deegan, Mary Jo, & Hill, Michael R. (1991). Doctoral dissertations as liminal journeys of the self: Betwixt and between in graduate sociology programs. *Teaching Sociology, 19,* 322–332.

Depraz, Natalie, Varela, Francisco J., & Vermersch, Pierre. (2000). The gesture of awareness: An account of structural dynamics. In Max Velmans (Ed.), *Investigating phenomenal consciousness: New methodologies and maps* (pp. 121–138). Amsterdam, The Netherlands: John Benjamins.

Doige, Norman. (2007). *The brain that changes itself: Stories of personal triumph from the frontiers of brain science.* New York, NY: Penguin Group.

Dougherty, Nancy J., & West, Jacqueline J. (2007). *The matrix and meaning of character: An archetypal and developmental approach.* London, UK: Routledge.

Drake, David B. (2003). *How stories change: A narrative analysis of liminal experiences and transitions in identity.* (dissertation), Fielding Graduate Institute, Santa Barbara.

Drake, David B. (2004a). Creating third space: The use of narrative liminality in coaching. In Irene Stein, Francine Campone, & Linda

J. Page (Eds.), *Second ICF Coaching Research Symposium* (pp. 50–59). Quebec City, Canada: International Coaching Federation.

Drake, David B. (2004b). *Creating third space: The use of narrative liminality in research and practice.* Paper presented at the Narrative Matters Conference, Fredericton, Canada.

Drake, David B. (2004c). *Once upon a time: Depression as an expression of untold narratives.* Paper presented at the Narrative Matters Conference, Fredericton, Canada.

Drake, David B. (2005a). *Creating third spaces: The use of narrative liminality in organizational coaching.* Paper presented at the Western States Communication Association Convention, San Francisco, CA.

Drake, David B. (2005b). *Narrative coaching: A psychosocial method for working with clients' stories to support transformative results.* Paper presented at the Second Australia Conference on Evidence-Based Coaching, Sydney, Australia.

Drake, David B. (2007). The art of thinking narratively: Implications for coaching psychology and practice. *Australian Psychologist, 42*(4), 283–294.

Drake, David B. (2008a). Finding our way home: Coaching's search for identity in a new era. *Coaching: An International Journal of Theory, Research and Practice, 1*(1), 15–26.

Drake, David B. (2008b). Thrice upon a time: Narrative structure and psychology as a platform for coaching. In David B. Drake, Diane Brennan, & Kim Gørtz (Eds.), *The philosophy and practice of coaching: Issues and insights for a new era* (pp. 51–71). San Francisco, CA: Jossey-Bass.

Drake, David B. (2009a). Evidence is a verb: A relational view of knowledge and mastery in coaching. *International Journal of Evidence Based Coaching and Mentoring, 7*(1), 1–12.

Drake, David B. (2009b). Identity, liminality, and development through coaching: An intrapersonal view of intercultural sensitivity. In Michel Moral & Geoff Abbott (Eds.), *The Routledge companion to international business coaching* (pp. 61–74). London, UK: Routledge.

Drake, David B. (2009c). Narrative coaching. In Elaine Cox, Tatiana Bachkirova, & David Clutterbuck (Eds.), *The Sage handbook of coaching* (pp. 120–131). London, UK: Sage.

Drake, David B. (2009d). Using attachment theory in coaching leaders: The search for a coherent narrative *International Coaching Psychology Review, 4*(1), 49–58.

Drake, David B. (2010). What story are you in? Four elements of a narrative approach to formulation in coaching. In Sarah Corrie & David Lane (Eds.), *Constructing stories, telling tales: A guide to formulation in applied psychology* (pp. 239–258). London, UK: Karnac.

Drake, David B. (2011a). *An introduction to the Four Gateways.* Paper presented at the Narrative Design Lab, San Francisco, CA.

Drake, David B. (2011b). Moving from good to great: A narrative perspective on strengths. Paper presented at the Positive 2012, Wollongong, Australia. http://www.uow.edu.au/content/groups/public/@web/@gsb/documents/doc/uow122223.pdf

Drake, David B. (2011c). A narrative approach to coaching. In Leni Wildflower & Diane Brennan (Eds.), *The handbook of knowledge-based coaching: From theory to practice* (pp. 271–278). San Francisco, CA: Jossey-Bass.

Drake, David B. (2011d). *Using the five elements of mastery to develop ourselves as supervisors*. Paper presented at the ANSE Summer Institute, Stavanger, Norway.

Drake, David B. (2011e). What do coaches need to know? Using the Mastery Window to assess and develop expertise. *Coaching: An International Journal of Theory, Research & Practice, 4*(2), 138–155.

Drake, David B. (2012). *An introduction to narrative design*. Sydney, Australia: Center for Narrative Coaching & Leadership.

Drake, David B. (2014a). *Integrative Development: A narrative approach to growing leaders*. Petaluma, CA: Center for Narrative Coaching & Leadership.

Drake, David B. (2014b). Narrative coaching. In Elaine Cox, Tatiana Bachkirova, & David A. Clutterbuck (Eds.), *The Sage handbook of coaching* (2nd ed., pp. 117–130). London, UK: Sage.

Drake, David B. (2014c). Three windows of development: A post-professional perspective on supervision. *International Coaching Psychology Review, 9*(1), 36–48.

Drake, David B., & Stelter, Reinhard. (2014). Narrative coaching. In Jonathan Passmore (Ed.), *Mastery in coaching: A complete psychological toolkit for advanced coaching* (pp. 65–96). London, UK: Kogan Page.

Drake, David B., & Stober, Dianne R. (2005). *The rise of the postprofessional: Lessons learned in thinking about coaching as an evidence-based practice.* Paper presented at the Australia Conference on Evidence-Based Coaching, Sydney, Australia.

Durrell, Lawrence. (1988). *The Alexandria quartet* (8th ed.). London: Faber.

Dweck, Carol S. (2008). *Mindset: The psychology of success.* New York, NY: Ballantine Books.

Edelson, Marshall. (1993). Telling and enacting stories in psychoanalysis and psychotherapy. *The Psychoanalytic Study of the Child, 48*, 293–325.

Eliade, Mircea. (1959). *The sacred and profane: The nature of religion.* New York, NY: Harcourt.

Ellis, M.J. (1973). *Why people play.* New York, NY: Prentice Hall.

Ericsson, K. Anders, & Charness, Neil. (1994). Expert performance: Its structure and acquisition. *American Psychologist, 49*(8), 725–747.

Ericsson, K. Anders, Krampe, Ralf Th., & Tesch-Römer, Clemens. (1993). The role of deliberate practice in the acquisition of expert performance. *Psychological Review, 100*(3), 363–406.

Erikson, Erik H. (1950). *Childhood and society*. New York, NY: W.W. Norton.

Eron, Joseph B., & Lund, Thomas W. (1996). *Narrative solutions in brief therapy*. New York, NY: Guilford Press.

Evanoff, Richard. (2000). The concept of "third cultures" in intercultural ethics. *Eubios Journal of Asian and International Bioethics, 10*, 126–129.

Feldenkrais, Moshe. (1972). *Awareness through movement*. New York, NY: Harper & Row.

Fitzgerald, Stephen P., Oliver, Christine, & Hoxsey, Joan C. (2010). Appreciative Inquiry as a shadow process. *Journal of Management Inquiry, 19*(3), 220–233.

Fosha, Diana. (2003). Dyadic regulation and experiential work with emotion and relatedness in trauma and disorganised attachment. In M. F. Solomon & D. J. Siegel (Eds.), *Healing trauma: attachment, mind, body, and brain* (pp. 221–281). New York, NY: W.W. Norton.

Foss, Sonja K., & Foss, Karen A. (2003). *Inviting transformation: Presentational speaking for a changing world* (Second ed.). Prospect Heights, IL: Waveland Press.

Fox, Hugh. (2003). Using therapeutic documents: A review. *International Journal of Narrative Therapy and Community Work, 4*, 26–36.

Francis, Sophie (2012, September 15). [personal communication].

Frank, Arthur W. (2010). *Letting stories breathe: A socio-narratology*. Chicago: University of Chicago Press.

Frederickson, Barbara. (2006). The broaden and build theory of positive emotions. In M. Csikszentmihalyi & I. Csikszentmihalyi (Eds.), *A life worth living: Contributions to positive psychology*. New York, NY: Oxford University Press.

Freedman, Jill, & Combs, Gene (1996). *Narrative therapy: The social construction of preferred realities*. New York, NY: W.W. Norton.

Freeman, John. (1964). Introduction *Man and his symbols* (pp. x). New York, NY: Doubleday.

Freire, Paolo. (1970). *Pedagogy of the oppressed*. New York, NY: Seabury Press.

Frye, Northrop. (1957). *Anatomy of criticism: Four essays*. Princeton: Princeton University Press.

Fulton, Paul R., & Siegel, Ronald D. (2005). Buddhist and western psychology. In Christopher K. Germer, Ronald D. Siegel, & Paul R. Fulton (Eds.), *Mindfulness and psychotherapy* (pp. 28–51). New York, NY: Guilford Press.

Gagan, Jeannette M. (1998). *Journeying: Where shamanism and psychology meet*. Santa Fe, NM: Rio Chama Publications.

Gallwey, Timothy. (1981/2009). *The inner game of golf*. New York, NY: Random House.

Gallwey, Timothy. (2001). *The inner game of work.* New York, NY: Random House.

Gallwey, Timothy. (2009). *The inner game of stress.* New York, NY: Random House.

Gergen, Kenneth J. (1973). Social psychology as history. *Journal of Personality and Social Psychology, 26*(2), 309–320.

Gergen, Kenneth J. (1994). *Realities and relationships.* Cambridge, MA: Harvard University Press.

Gergen, Kenneth J., & Kaye, John. (1993). Beyond narrative in the negotiation of therapeutic meaning. In Kenneth J. Gergen (Ed.), *Refiguring self and pyschology.* Aldershot, UK: Dartmouth.

Gergen, Mary, & Davis, Sara N. (2005). Dialogic pedagogy: Developing narrative research perspectives through conversation. In Ruthelen Josselson, Amia Lieblich, & Dan P. McAdams (Eds.), *Up close and personal: The teaching and learning of narrative research* (pp. 239–257). Washington, DC: American Psychological Association.

Gergen, Mary M., & Gergen, Kenneth J. (2006). Narratives in action. *Narrative Inquiry, 16*(1), 112–121.

Giddens, Anthony. (1991). *Modernity and self-identity: Self and society in the late modern age.* Stanford: Stanford University Press.

Gilligan, Carol. (1982). *In a different voice: Psychological theory and women's development.* Cambridge, MA: Harvard Business School Press.

Gilligan, Carol, & Brown, Lyn Mikel. (1991). Listening for voice in narratives of relationships. In Mark B. Tappan & Martin J. Packer (Eds.), *Narrative and storytelling: Implications for understanding moral development* (Vol. 54, pp. 43). San Francisco, CA: Jossey-Bass.

Gioia, Dennis A. (1986). Symbols, scripts, and sensemaking. In Henry P. Sims Jr. & Dennis A. Gioia (Eds.), *The thinking organization* (pp. 49–74). San Francisco, CA: Jossey-Bass.

Gluckman, Max. (1962). Les rites de passage. In Max Gluckman (Ed.), *Essays on the ritual of social relations* (pp. 1–52). Manchester: University Press.

Goffman, Erving. (1959). *The presentation of self in everyday life.* New York, NY: Doubleday.

Goldhaber, Dale E. (2000). *Theories of human development: Integrative perspectives.* Mountain View, CA: Mayfield Publishing.

Goldstein, Kurt. (1939). *The organism.* New York: American Books.

Graham, Linda. (2013). *Bouncing back: Rewiring your brain for maximum resilience and well-being.* Novato, CA: New World Library.

Grant, A. M. (2012). *An integrated model of goal-focused coaching: An evidence-based framework for teaching and practice.* International Coaching Psychology Review, 7(2), 146–164.

Griffith, James L., & Griffith, Melissa E. (1993). Language solutions for mind-body problems. In Reese Price & Stephen Gilligan (Eds.), *Therapeutic conversations* (pp. 309–329). New York, NY: W.W. Norton.

Griffith, James L., & Griffith, Melissa Elliot. (1993). Language solutions for minds–body problems. In Stephen Gilligan & Reese Price (Eds.), *Therapeutic conversations* (pp. 309–329). New York, NY: W.W. Norton.

Haidet, Paul, & Paterniti, Debora. (2003). "Building" a history rather than "Taking" one: A perspective on information sharing during the medical interview. *Archives of Internal Medicine, 163*, 1134–1140.

Halifax, Joan. (1993). *The fruitful darkness: A journey through Buddhist practice and tribal wisdom*. New York: Grove Press.

Hall, Douglas T. (1971). A theoretical model of career subidentity development in organizational settings. *Organizational Behavior and Human Performance, 6*, 50–76.

Hänninen, Vilma. (2004). A model of narrative circulation. *Narrative Inquiry, 14*(1), 69–85.

Harris, Russell. (2006). Embracing your demons: An overview of Acceptance and Commitment Therapylaw. *Psychotherapy in Australia, 12*(4), 1–8.

Hayes, Steven C. (2004). Acceptance and Commitment Therapy and the new behavior therapies: Mindfulness, commitment, and relationship. In Steven C. Hayes, Victoria M. Follette, & Marsha M. Linehan (Eds.), *Mindfulness and acceptance: Expanding the cognitive tradition* (pp. 1–29). New York, NY: Guilford Press.

Hebb, Donald O. (1949). *The organization of behavior: A neuropsychological theory*. New York: Wiley.

Heidegger, Martin. (1927/1996). *Being in time* (Joan Stambaugh, Trans. Vol. 2). London, UK: State University of New York Press.

Hellinger, Bert. (1998). *Love's hidden symmetry*. Phoenix, AZ: Zeig, Tucker & Theisen.

Heron, John. (2001). *Helping the client: A creative practical guide*. London, UK: Sage.

Hewson, Daphne. (1991). From laboratory to therapy room: Prediction questions for reconstructing the 'new-old' story. *Dulwich Centre Newsletter, 3*, 5–12.

Hillman, James. (1975a). The fiction of case history: A round. In James B. Wiggins (Ed.), *Religion as story* (pp. 123–173). New York, NY: Harper & Row.

Hillman, James. (1975b). *Re-visioning psychology*. New York, NY: Harper & Row.

Hillman, James. (1983). *Healing fiction*. Woodstock, NY: Spring.

Hillman, James. (1996). *The soul's code*. New York, NY: Random House.

Holland, John H. (1995). *Hidden order*. Reading, MA: Addison-Wesley.

Hollis, James. (2004). *Mythologems: Incarnations of the invisible world*. Toronto, Canada: Inner City Books.

Hollis, James. (2013). *Hauntings: Dispelling the ghosts who run our lives.* Asheville, NC: Chiron.

Holmes, Jeremy. (1999). Narrative, attachment and the therapeutic process. In Chris Mace (Ed.), *Heart and soul: The therapeutic face of philosophy* (pp. 147–162). London, UK: Routledge.

Holmes, Jeremy. (2001). *The search for the secure base: Attachment theory and psychotherapy.* London, UK: Routledge.

Horney, Karen. (1945). *Our inner conflicts: A constructive theory of neurosis.* New York, NY: W.W. Norton.

Hoyt, Michael F. (1996). Introduction: Some stories are better than others. In Michael F. Hoyt (Ed.), *Constructive therapies* (Vol. 2, pp. 1–32). New York, NY: Guilford Press.

Husserl, Edmund. (1931). *Ideas: General introduction to pure phenomenology.* London, UK: George Allen & Unwin.

Ibarra, Herminia, & Linebeck, Kent. (2005, January). What's your story? *Harvard Business Review, 65–71.*

Ibarra, Herminia, & Petriglieri, Jennifer Louise. (2010). Identity work and play. *Journal of Organizational Change Management, 23*(1), 10–25.

Ihde, Don. (1977). *Experimental phenomenology: An introduction.* New York: Putnam.

Illeris, Knud. (2004). *Adult education and adult learning.* Malabar, FL: Krieger Publishing Company.

James, William. (1890/1950). *The principles of psychology* (Vol. 1). New York, NY: Dover.

James, William. (1892/1927). *Psychology: Briefer course.* New York, NY: Henry Holt.

Johnson, Robert. (1986). *Inner work.* New York, NY: Harper & Row.

Johnstone, Keith. (1981). *Impro: Improvisation and the theatre.* New York, NY: Routledge.

Johnstone, Keith. (1999). *Impro for storytellers.* New York, NY: Routledge.

Jung, Carl G. (1964). *Man and his symbols.* New York, NY: Doubleday.

Jung, Carl G. (1967). *Alchemical studies* (R.F.C. Hull, Trans. Vol. 13). Princeton: Princeton University Press.

Jung, Carl G. (1969). *The structure and dynamics of the psyche* (Vol. 8). Princeton: Princeton University Press.

Jung, Carl G. (1970). *Psychological reflections.* Princeton: Princeton University Press.

Jung, Carl G. (1972). *Two essays on analytical psychology* (Gerhard Adler & R.F.C. Hull, Trans. Vol. 7). Princeton, NJ: Princeton University Press.

Kailo, Kaarina. (1997). Integrative feminist pedagogy, C.G. Jung, and the politics of visualization. In Sharon Todd (Ed.), *Learning desire: Perspectives on pedagogy, culture, and the unsaid.* New York, NY: Routledge.

Kaplan, Allan. (2002). *Development practitioners and social process: Artists of the invisible.* London, UK: Pluto Press.

Kay, John. (2010). *Obliquity: Why our goals are best acheived indirectly*. New York, NY: Penguin Group.

Kegan, Robert. (1994). *In over our heads: The mental demands of modern life*. Cambridge, MA: Harvard University Press.

Kelly, G.A. (1955). *The psychology of personal constructs* (Vol. 1). New York, NY: W.W. Norton.

Kenyon, Gary M., & Randall, William L. (1997). *Restorying our lives: Personal growth through autobiographical reflection*. Westport, CT: Praeger.

Kolb, Alice Y., & Kolb, David A. (2010). Learning to play, playing to learn: A case study of a ludic learning space. *Journal of Organizational Change Management, 32*(1), 26–50.

Kolb, David A. (1984). *Experiential learning: Experience as the source of learning and development*. Englewood Cliffs, NJ: Prentice-Hall.

Kolodziejski, Karin. (2004). The organization shadow: Exploring the untapped, trapped potential in organizational setting. *Dissertation Abstracts International, 66, DAI-B*, (UMI No. AAT-3166383).

Kramer, Gregory. (2007). *Insight dialogue: The interpersonal path to freedom*. Boston, MA: Shambhala.

Kramer, Gregory, Meleo-Meyer, Florence, & Turner, Martha Lee. (2008). Cultivating mindfulness in relationship. In Steven F. Hick & Thomas Bien (Eds.), *Mindfulness and therapeutic relationship* (pp. 195–214). New York, NY: The Guilford Press.

Kraus, Wolfgang. (2006). The narrative negotiation of identity and belonging. *Narrative Inquiry, 16*, 103–111.

Labov, William. (1982). Speech actions and reactions in personal narrative. In Deborah Tannen (Ed.), *Analyzing discourse: Text and talk*. Washington, DC: Georgetown University Press.

Lane, David A., & Corrie, Sarah. (2006). *The modern scientist-practitioner: A guide to practice in psychology*. London, NY: Routledge.

Langer, Ellen J. (1997). *The power of mindful learning*. Reading: Addison-Wesley.

Lave, Jean, & Wenger, Etienne. (1991). *Situated learning: Legitimate peripheral participation*. Cambridge: Cambridge University Press.

Law, Ho C. (2007). Narrative coaching and psychology of learning from multicultural perspectives. In S Palmer & A Whybrow (Eds.), *Handbook of coaching psychology* (pp. 174–192). East Sussex, UK: Routledge.

Lawley, James, & Tompkins, Penny. (2000). *Metaphors in mind: Transformation through symbolic modeling*. London: Developing Company Press.

LeCompte, Margaret D. (1993). A framework for hearing silence: What does telling stories mean when we are supposed to be doing science? In Daniel McLaughlin & William G. Tierney (Eds.), *Naming silenced lives: Personal narratives and processes of educational change* (pp. 9–27). New York, NY: Routledge.

Lefebvre, Henri. (1980). *La presence et l'absence*. Paris, France: Casterman.

Leonard, George. (1992). *Mastery: The keys to success and long-term fulfillment*. New York, NY: Penguin Group.

Levine, Peter. (2010). *In an unspoken voice: How the body releases trauma and restores goodness*. Berkeley, CA: North Atlantic Books.

Lewin, Kurt. (1951). *Field theory in social science: Selected papers on group dynamics* (G.W. Lewin Ed.). New York, NY: Harper & Brothers.

Linde, Charlotte. (1993). *Life stories: The creation of coherence*. New York: Cambridge University Press.

Locke, Edwin A. (1996). Motivation through conscious goal setting. *Applied and Preventative Psychology, 5*, 117–124.

MacIntyre, Alasdair. (1981). *After virtue*. New York: University of Notre Dame Press.

Maddi, Salvatore R. (1988). On the problem of accepting facticity and pursuing possibility. In S. Messer, L. Sass, & R. Woolfolk (Eds.), *Hermeneutics and psychological theory*. New Brunswick, NJ: Rutgers University Press.

Madigan, Stephen (1996). The politics of identity: Considering community discourse in the externalizing of internalized problem conversations. *Journal of Systematic Therapies, 15*(1), 47–62.

Mahony, Michael J. (2003). *Constructive pyschotherapy: A practical guide*. New York, NY: Guilford Press.

Main, Mary. (1995). Recent studies in attachment: Overview, with selected implications for clinical work. In Susan Goldberg, Roy Muir, & John Kerr (Eds.), *Attachment theory: Social, developmental, and clinical perspectives* (pp. 407–474). Hillsdale, NJ: Analytic Press.

Mainemelis, C., & Ronson, S. (2006). Ideas are born in fields of play: Towards a theory of play and creativity in organizational settings. *Research in Organizational Behavior, 27*, 69–81.

Mancuso, James C., & Sarbin, Theodore R. (1983). The self-narrative in the enactment of roles. In Theodore R. Sarbin & Karl E. Scheibe (Eds.), *Studies in social identity* (pp. 233–253). Westport, CT: Praeger.

Mandler, Jean. (1984). *Stories, scripts, and scenes: Aspects of schema theory*. Hillsdale, NJ: Lawrence Erlbaum.

Mar, Raymond A. (2004). The neuropsychology of narrative: Story comprehension, story production and their interrelation. *Neuropsychologia, 42*, 1414–1434.

March, James G. (1976). The technology of foolishness. In John G. March & J.P. Olsen (Eds.), *Ambiguity and choice in organizations* (pp. 81). Bergen: Universitetsforlaget.

Markus, Hazel, & Nurius, Paula. (1986). Possible selves. *American Psychologist, 41*(9), 954–969.

Marshak, Robert J. (1993). Managing the metaphors of change. *Organizational Dynamics*(Summer), 44–56.

Maslow, Abraham H. (1954). *Motivation and personality*. New York: Harper.

Mattingly, Cheryl. (1998). *Healing dramas and clinical plots: The narrative structure of experience*. New York: Cambridge University Press.

McAdams, Dan P. (1985). *Power, intimacy, and the life story*. Belmont, CA: The Dorsey Press.

McAdams, Dan P. (2003). Identity and life story. In Robyn Fivush & Catherine A. Haden (Eds.), *Autobiographical memory and the construction of a narrative self* (pp. 187–207). Mahweh, NJ: Lawrence Erlbaum.

McKee, Robert. (1997). *Story: Substance, structure, style and the principles of screenwriting*. New York, NY: HarperCollins.

McKee, Robert (2004, September 10–12). [Story seminar].

McLaren, Peter. (1993). Border disputes: Multicultural narrative, identity formation, and critical pedagogy in postmodern America. In Daniel McLaughlin & William G. Tierney (Eds.), *Naming silenced lives: Personal narratives and processes of educational change* (pp. 201–235). New York, NY: Routledge.

McLeod, John. (2004). The significance of narrative and storytelling in postpsychological counseling and psychotherapy. In Amia Lieblich, Dan P. McAdams, & Ruthellen Josselson (Eds.), *Healing plots: The narrative basis for psychotherapy* (pp. 11–27). Washington, DC: American Psychological Association.

McLeod, John. (2006). *Narrative and psychotherapy*. London, UK: Sage.

McMahon, Mary L., & Patton, Wendy A. (2006). The systems theory framework: A conceptual and practical map for career counseling. In M. McMahon & W. Patton (Eds.), *Career counseling: Constructivist approaches* (pp. 94–109). London, UK: Routledge.

McNamara, Olwen, Roberts, Lorna, Basit, Tehmina N., & Brown, Tony. (2002). Rites of passage in initial teacher training. *British Educational Research Journal, 28*(6), 863–878.

McWhinney, Will, & Markos, Laura. (2003). Transformative education: Across the threshold. *Journal of Transformative Education, 1*(1), 16–37.

McWilliams, Nancy. (1994). *Psychoanalyic diagnosis: Understanding personality structure in the clinical process*. New York, NY: Guilford.

Mead, George Herbert. (1934/1967). *Mind, self, and society* (Charles W. Morris Ed.). Chicago: University of Chicago Press.

Meade, Michael. (2006). *The water of life: Initiation and the tempering of the soul*. Seattle, WA: Greenfire Press.

Mehl-Madrona, Lewis. (2010). *Healing the mind through the power of story: The promise of narrative psychiatry*. Rochester, VT: Bear & Company.

Mellou, Eleni. (1994). Play theories: A contemporary review. *Early childhood development and care, 102*, 91–100.

Merleau-Ponty, Maurice. (1945/2013). *Phenomenology of perception*. London, UK: Routledge.

Metzger, Deena. (1992). *Writing for your life: A guide and companion to the inner worlds.* New York: HarperSanFrancisco.

Mezirow, Jack. (1991). *Transformative dimensions of adult learning.* San Francisco, CA: Jossey-Bass.

Mezirow, Jack (Ed.) (2000). *Learning as transformation: Critical perspectives on a theory in progress.* San Francisco, CA: Jossey-Bass.

Mikulincer, Mario, & Shaver, Phillip R. (2007). *Attachment in adulthood: Structure, dynamics, and change.* New York, NY: Guilford Press.

Mink, Louis A. (1969). History and fiction as modes of comprehension. *New Literary History, 1,* 556–569.

Mishler, Eliot G. (1992). Work, identity, and narrative: An artist-craftsman's story. In George C. Rosenwald & Richard L. Ochberg (Eds.), *Storied lives: The cultural politics of self-understanding* (pp. 21–39). New Haven, CT: Yale University Press.

Mishler, Eliot G. (1999). *Storylines: Craftartist's narratives of identity.* Cambridge, MA: Harvard University Press.

Mishler, Eliot G. (2000). *Narrative and the paradox of temporal ordering: How ends beget beginnings.* Paper presented at the Discourse and Identity Conference, Clark University.

Moore, Margaret, Drake, David B., Tschannen-Moran, Bob, Campone, Francine, & Kauffman, Carol. (2005). Relational flow: A theoretical model for the intuitive dance. In Francine Campone & John Bennett (Eds.), *Proceedings of the Third ICF Coaching Research Symposium* (pp. 79–91). San Jose, CA: International Coach Federation.

Moore, Robert L. (1987). *The liminal and the liminoid in ritual process and analytical practice.* (diplomate paper), C.G. Jung Institute, Chicago.

Moore, Thomas. (2000). *Original self.* New York, NY: HarperCollins.

Morgan, Stephanie P. (2005). Depression: Turning toward life. In Christopher K. Germer, Ronald D. Siegel, & Paul R. Fulton (Eds.), *Mindfulness and psychotherapy* (pp. 130–151). New York, NY: Guilford Press.

Morton, Nelle. (1985). *The journey is home.* Boston: Beacon Press.

Muller, Michael J. (2001). *Participatory design: The third space in HCI.* Retrieved from Cambridge, MA.

Nachmanovitch, S. (1990). *Free play.* Los Angeles, CA: Jeremy P. Tarcher.

Nouwen, Henri. (1998). *Reaching out.* Grand Rapids, MI: Zondervan.

Novitz, David. (1997). Art, narrative, and human nature. In Lewis P. Hinchman & Sandra Hinchman (Eds.), *Memory, identity, community* (pp. 143–160). Albany, NY: State University of New York Press.

O'Hanlon, Bill. (2000). *Do one thing different: Ten simple ways to change your life.* New York, NY: HarperCollins.

O'Hanlon, William. (1998). Possibility therapy: An inclusive, collaborative, solution-based model of psychotherapy. In Michael F. Hoyt (Ed.), *The handbook of constructive therapies: Innovative approaches from leading practitioners* (pp. 137–158). San Francisco, CA: Jossey-Bass.

Ochs, Elinor, & Capps, Lisa. (1996). Narrating the self. *Annual Review of Anthropology, 25,* 19–43.

Ogden, Thomas A. (1999). The analytic third: An overview. *fort da, 5*(1).

Oldenburg, Ray. (1989). *The great good place.* New York, NY: Marlow.

Ollerenshaw, Jo Anne, & Creswell, John W. (2002). Narrative research: A comparison of two restorying data analysis approaches. *Qualitative Inquiry, 8*(3), 329–347.

Ordóñez, Lisa .D., Schweitzer, Maurice E., Galinsky, Adam E., & Bazerman, Max H. (2009). Goals gone wild: The systemic side effects of overprescribing goal setting. *Academy of Management Perspectives, 23*(1), 6–16.

Osatuke, Katerine, Glick, Merideth J., Gray, Michael A., Reynolds, Jr., D'Arcy J., Humphreys, Carol, Salvi, Lisa M., & Siles, William B. (2004). Assimilation and narrative: Stories as meaning bridges. In Lynne E. Angus & John McLeod (Eds.), *Handbook of narrative and psychotherapy: Practice, theory, and research* (pp. 193–210). Thousand Oaks, CA: Sage.

Oyserman, Daphna, & Markus, Hazel. (1993). The sociocultural self. In Jerry Suls (Ed.), *Psychological perspectives on the self* (Vol. 4, pp. 187–220). Hillsdale, NJ: Lawrence Erlbaum.

Page, Steve. (1999). *The shadow and the counsellor: Working with darker aspects of the person, role and profession.* London, UK: Routledge.

Paris, Ginette. (2007). *Wisdom of the psyche: Depth psychology after neuroscience.* London, UK: Routledge.

Paris, Ginette. (2011). *Heartbreak: New approaches to healing.* Minneapolis: Mill City Press.

Pearce, W. Barnett, & Pearce, Kimberley A. (2001, 2001). [Transcendent storytelling: Abilities for systemic practitioners and their clients].

Penuel, William R., & Wertsch, James V. (1995). Vygotsky and identity formation: A sociocultural approach. *Educational Psychologist, 30*(2), 83–92.

Perls, Frederick S. (1992/1969). *Gestalt therapy verbatim.* Gouldsboro, ME: The Gestalt Journal Press.

Perls, Fritz S., Hefferline, R. , & Goodman, P. (1994/1951). *Gestalt therapy: Excitement and growth in the human personality.* Gouldsboro, ME: The Gestalt Journal Press.

Petriglieri, Gianpiero, & Petriglieri, Jennifer Louise. (2010). Identity workspaces: The case of business schools. *Academy of Management Learning & Education, 9*(1), 44–60.

Phillips, Adam. (1994). *On flirtation.* Cambridge, MA: Harvard University Press.

Piaget, Jean. (1954). *The construction of reality in the child.* New York, NY: Basic Books.

Piaget, Jean. (1962). *Play, dreams and imitation in childhood* (C. Gattegno & F.M. Hodgson, Trans.). New York, NY: W.W. Norton.

Picard, Max. (2002). *The world of silence*. Wichita, KS: Eighth Day Press.

Pinker, Steven. (2009). *How the mind works*. New York, NY: W.W. Norton.

Plett, Heather. (2015). What it means to 'hold space' for people, plus eight tips on how to do it well. Retrieved from http://heatherplett.com/2015/03/hold-space/

Poincare, Henri. (1952). *Science and method*. Mineola, NY: Dover.

Polkinghorne, Donald E. (1988). *Narrative knowing and the human sciences*. Albany, NY: State University of New York Press.

Polkinghorne, Donald E. (1991). Narrative and self-concept. *Journal of Narrative and Life History, 1*(2&3), 135–153.

Polkinghorne, Donald E. (1995). Narrative configuration in qualitative analysis. In J. Amos Hatch & Richard Wisniewski (Eds.), *Life history and narrative* (pp. 5–23). Washington, DC: The Falmer Press.

Polkinghorne, Donald E. (2001). The self and humanistic psychology. In Kirk J. Schneider, James F.T. Bugental, & J. Fraser Pierson (Eds.), *The handbook of humanistic psychology* (pp. 81–99). Thousand Oaks, CA: Sage.

Polkinghorne, Donald E. (2004). Narrative therapy and postmodernism. In Lynne E. Angus & John McLeod (Eds.), *Handbook of narrative and psychotherapy: Practice, theory, and research* (pp. 53–67). Thousand Oaks, CA: Sage.

Post, Robert M., Weiss, S.R.B., Li, H., Smith, M.A., Zhang, L.X., & Xing, G. (1998). Neural plasticity and emotional memory. *Development and Psychopathology, 10*, 829–856.

Prochaska, James O., & Norcross, John C. (2002). Stages of change. In John C. Norcross (Ed.), *Psychotherapy relationships that work: Therapist contributions and responsiveness in patients* (pp. 303–313). New York, NY: Oxford University Press.

Propp, Vladimir. (1968). *Morphology of the folktale* (Laurence Scott, Trans.). Austin: University of Texas Press.

Raff, Jeffrey. (2000). *Jung and the alchemical imagination*. Berwick, ME: Nicolas-Hays.

Randall, William L. (1995). *The stories we are: An essay on self-creation*. Toronto: University of Toronto Press.

Rappaport, Julian. (1995). Empowerment meets narrative: Listening to stories and creating settings. *American Journal of Community Psychology, 23*(5), 795–807.

Rennie, David L. (1994). Storytelling in psychotherapy: The client's subjective experience. *Psychotherapy, 31*(2), 234–243.

Ricoeur, Paul. (1984). *Time and narrative* (Kathleen Mclaughhlin & David Pellauer, Trans. Vol. 1). Chicago: University of Chicago Press.

Ricoeur, Paul. (1988). *Time and narrative* (Vol. 3). Chicago: University of Chicago Press.

Ricoeur, Paul. (1992). *Oneself as another* (Kathleen Blamey, Trans.). Chicago: University of Chicago Press.

Riessman, Catherine K. (1993). *Narrative analysis* (Vol. 30). Newbury Park, CA: Sage.

Riessman, Catherine K. (2002). Analysis of personal narrative. In Jaber F. Gubrium & James A. Holstein (Eds.), *Handbook of interview research* (pp. 695–710). Thousand Oaks, CA: Sage.

Rimmon-Kenan, Shlomith. (1983). *Narrative fiction: Contemporary poetics.* London: Methuen.

Rogers, Carl R. (1961). *On becoming a person.* Boston, MA: Houghton Mifflin.

Ross, Michael, & Conway, Michael. (1986). Remembering one's own past: the construction of personal histories. In R. Sorrentino & E. Higgins (Eds.), *Handbook of motivation and cognition.* New York, NY: Guilford Press.

Rossiter, Marsha. (1999). Understanding adult development as narrative. *New Directions for Adult and Continuing Education*(84), 77–85.

Rubin, Harriet. (2000, October). Living dangerously. *Fast Company,* 340.

Russell, Robert L., & van Den Broek, Paul. (1992). Changing narrative schemas in psychotherapy. *Psychotherapy, 29*(3), 344–354.

Rycroft-Malone, Jo, Seers, Kate, Titchen, Angie, Harvey, Gill, Kitson, Alison, & McCormack, Brendan. (2004). What counts as evidence in evidence-based medicine? *Journal of Advanced Nursing, 47*(1), 81–90.

Sarbin, Theodore R. (1986a). The narrative as a root metaphor for psychology. In Theodore R. Sarbin (Ed.), *Narrative psychology: The storied nature of human conduct* (pp. 3–21). Wellesley, MA: Praeger.

Sarbin, Theodore R. (Ed.) (1986b). *Narrative psychology: The storied nature of human conduct.* Westport, CT: Praeger.

Satir, Virginia, Banmen, John, Gerber, Jane, & Gomori, Maria. (1991/2006). *The Satir model: Family therapy and beyond.* Palo Alto, CA: Science and Behavior Books.

Schachtel, Ernest G. (1959). *Metamorphosis.* New York, NY: Basic Books.

Schank, Roger. (1990). *Tell me a story: A new look at real and artificial memory.* New York, NY: Scribner.

Schank, Roger, & Abelson, Robert P. (1995). Knowledge and memory: The real story. In Jr. Wyer, Robert S. (Ed.), *Knowledge and memory: The real story* (pp. 1–86). Hillsdale, NJ: Lawrence Erlbaum.

Scharmer, C. Otto. (2007). *Theory U: Leading from the future as it emerges.* Boston, MA: Society for Organizational Learning.

Scholes, Robert, & Kellogg, Robert. (1966). *The nature of narrative.* London, UK: Oxford University Press.

Schön, Donald A. (1983). *The reflective practitioner.* New York, NY: Basic Books.

Schwartz-Salant, Nathan. (1998). *The mystery of human relationship: Alchemy and the transformation of the self.* New York, NY: Routledge.

Schwartz-Salant, Nathan. (2007). *The black nightgown: The fusional complex and the unlived life.* Wilmette, IL: Chiron.

Scott, Susan. (2002). *Fierce conversations.* New York, NY: Viking.

Seel, Richard. (2003). Story & conversation in organisations: A survey. Retrieved from http://www.new-paradigm.co.uk/story_&_conversation.htm

Sennett, Richard. (2008). *The craftsman.* New Haven, CT: Yale University Press.

Sheldrake, Rupert. (2009). *Morphic resonance: The nature of formative causation* (4th ed.). South Paris, ME: Park Street Press.

Sherman, Howard, & Schultz, Ron. (1998). *Open boundaries.* Reading, MA: Perseus Publishing.

Sherman, Steven J., Skov, Richard B., Hervitz, Esther F., & Stock, Caryl B. (1981). The effects of explaining hypothetical future events: from possibilty to probability to actuality and beyond. *Journal of Experimental Social Psychology, 17,* 142–158.

Siegel, Daniel J. (2007). *The mindful brain: Reflection and attunement in the cultivation of well-being.* New York, NY: W.W. Norton.

Silsbee, Doug. (2008). *Presence-based coaching: Cultivating self-generative leaders through mind, body and heart.* San Francisco, CA: Jossey-Bass.

Singer, Jefferson A. (1996). The story of your life: A process perspective on narrative and emotion in adult development. In Carol Magai & Susan H. McFadden (Eds.), *Handbook of emotion, adult daevelopment, and aging* (pp. 443–463). San Diego, CA: Academic Press.

Singer, Jefferson A. (2001). Living in the amber cloud: A life story analysis. In Dan P. McAdams, Ruthellen Josselson, & Amia Lieblich (Eds.), *Turns in the road: Narrative studies of lives in transition* (pp. 253–277). Washington, DC: American Psychological Association.

Singer, Jefferson A. (2005a). *Memories that matter: How to use self-defining memories to understand & change your life.* Oakland, CA: New Harbinger.

Singer, Jefferson A. (2005b). *Personality and psychotherapy: Treating the whole person.* New York, NY: Guilford Press.

Sitkin, Sim B. (1992). Learning through failure: The strategy of small losses. *Research in Organizational Behavior, 14,* 231–266.

Slingerland, Arthur. (2014). *Trying not to try: The art and science of spontaneity.* New York: Crown.

Sorell, Gwendolyn T., & Montgomery, Marilyn J. (2001). Feminist perspectives on Erikson's theory: Their relevance for contemporary identity development research. *Identity, 1*(2), 97–128.

Spence, Gordon B., Cavanagh, Michael J., & Grant, Anthony M. (2006). Duty of care in an unregulated industry: Initial findings on the diversity and practices of Australian coaches. *International Coaching Psychology Review, 1*(1), 71–85.

Spinelli, Ernesto. (2010). Existential coaching. In Elaine Cox, Tatiana Bachkirova, & David Clutterbuck (Eds.), *The complete handbook of coaching* (pp. 94–106). London, UK: Sage.

Spolin, Viola. (1999). *Improvisation for the theater* (3rd ed.). Evanston, IL: Northwestern University Press.

Stadter, Michael, & Scharff, David E. (2000). Object relations brief therapy. In Jon Carlson & Len Sperry (Eds.), *Brief therapy with individuals and couples* (pp. 191–209). Phoenix, AZ: Zeig, Tucker & Theisen.

Stanislavsky, Konstantin. (1936/1989). *An actor prepares*. New York, NY: Routledge.

Stein, Jan O., & Stein, Murray. (1987). Psychotherapy, initiation and the midlife transition. In L.C. Mahdi, S. Foster, & M. Little (Eds.), *Betwixt & between: Patterns of masculine and feminine initiation* (pp. 287–303). La Salle, IL: Open Court.

Stein, Nancy L., & Glenn, Christine G. (1979). An analysis of story comprehension in elementary school children. In Roy O. Freedle (Ed.), *New directions in discourse processing* (Vol. 2, pp. 53–120). Greenwich, CT: Ablex.

Stelter, Reinhard. (2007). Coaching: A process of personal and social meaning making. *International Coaching Psychology Review, 2*(2), 191–201.

Stelter, Reinhard. (2009). Coaching as a reflective space in a society of growing diversity: Towards a narrative, postmodern paradigm. *International Coaching Psychology Review, 4*(2), 207–217.

Stelter, Reinhard. (2013). Narrative approaches. In Jonathan Passmore, David B. Peterson, & Teresa Freire (Eds.), *The Wiley-Blackwell handbook of the psychology of coaching and mentoring* (pp. 407–425). London, UK: Wiley.

Stelter, Reinhard. (2014a). *A guide to third generation coaching: Narrative-collaborative theory and practice*. New York, NY: Springer.

Stelter, Reinhard. (2014b). Reconstructing dialogues through collaborative practice and a focus on values. *International Coaching Psychology Review, 9*(1), 51–66.

Stern, Daniel N. (1985). *The interpersonal world of the infant*. New York, NY: Basic Books.

Stevens-Long, Judy. (2000). The prism self: Multiplicity on the path to transcendence. In Polly Young-Eisendrath & Melvin E. Miller (Eds.), *The psychology of mature spirituality: Integrity, wisdom, transcendence* (pp. 161–174). Philadelphia, PA: Routledge.

Stevenson, Herb. (2005). Gestalt coaching. *OD Practitioner, 37*(4), 35–40.

Strauss, Anselm L. (1997). *Mirrors and masks: The search for identity* (Second ed.). New Brunswick, NJ: Transaction Publishers.

Strupp, Hans H., & Binder, Jeffrey L. (1984). *Psychotherapy in a new key: A guide to time-limited dynamic psychotherapy*. New York, NY: Basic Books.

Stryker, Sheldon. (1987). Identity theory: Developments and extensions. In K. Yardley & T. Honess (Eds.), *Self and identity*. New York: Wiley.

Sull, Donald N., & Eisenhardt, Kathleen M. (2012). Simple rules for a complex world. *Harvard Business Review*, (September), 6. Retrieved from http://hbr.org/2012/09/simple-rules-for-a-complex-world/ar/1

Swann, William B., Jr., & Read, Stephen. J. (1981). Self-verification processes: How we sustain our self-conceptions. *Journal of Experimental Social Psychology, 17*, 351–372.

Tammi, Pekka. (2005). *Against narrative: A boring story*. Paper presented at the Narrative as a way of thinking: International symposium in honor of Shlomith Rimmon-Kenan, Jerusalem, Israel.

Thaler, Richard, & Sunstein, Cass. (2008). *Nudge: Improving decisions about health, wealth and happiness*. New Haven, CT: Yale University Press.

Tillich, Paul. (1965). Frontiers. *Journal of the American Academy of Religion, XXXIII*(1), 17–23.

Todorov, Tzvetan. (1971/1977). *The poetics of prose*. Oxford, UK: Blackwell.

Tompkins, Penny, & Lawley, James. (1997). Less is more...The art of clean language. *Rapport: The Magazine for NLP Professionals, 35*, 36–40.

Tompkins, Penny, & Lawley, James. (2011). Self-nudge: Unconscious decision-making and how we can bias the future self. Retrieved from http://www.cleanlanguage.co.uk/articles/articles/312/1/Self-nudge/Page1.html

Turner, Victor. (1967). Betwixt and between: The liminal period in rites of passage. *The forest of symbols* (pp. 93–111). Ithica, NY: Cornell University Press.

Turner, Victor. (1969). *The ritual process: Structure and anti-structure*. New York: Aldine Publishing Co.

Turner, Victor. (1974). *Dramas, fields and metaphors*. Ithica, NY: Cornell University Press.

Turner, Victor. (1978). [Foreword]. In B. Meyerhoff, *Number our days* (pp. xiii–xvii). New York, NY: Dutton.

Turner, Victor. (1982). Liminality and the performative genres. In F. Allan Hanson (Ed.), *Studies in symbolism and cultural communication* (Vol. 14, pp. 25–41). Lawrence: University of Kansas.

Turner, Victor. (1986). *The anthropology of performance*. New York: PAJ.

Turner, Victor, & Turner, Edith. (1978). *Image and pilgrimage in Christian culture: Anthropological perspectives*. New York, NY: Columbia University Press.

van Eenwyk, J.R. (1997). *Archetypes & strange attractors*. Toronto, Canada: Inner City Books.

van Gennep, Arthur. (1960). *The rites of passage* (Monika B. Vizedom & Gabrielle L. Caffee, Trans.). Chicago: The University of Chicago Press.

Vogler, Christopher. (1998). *The writer's journey: Mythic structures for writers* (2nd ed.). Studio City: Michael Wiese Productions.

Vygotsky, Lev S. (1934/1987). Thinking and speech (N. Minick, Trans.). In R.W. Rieber & A.S. Carton (Eds.), *The collected works of L.S. Vygotsky* (Vol. 1: Problems of general psychology, pp. 39–285). New York, NY: Plenum Press.

Vygotsky, Lev S. (1934/1998). Infancy (M. Hall, Trans.). In R.W. Rieber (Ed.), *The collected works of L.S. Vygotsky* (Vol. 5: Child psychology, pp. 207–241). New York, NY: Plenum Press.

Vygotsky, Lev S. (1978). *Mind in society: The development of higher psychological processes* (Michael Cole, Vera John-Steiner, Sylvia Scribner, & Ellen Souberman, Trans.). Cambridge, MA: Harvard University Press.

Watkins, Mary M. (1976). *Waking dreams*. New York, NY: Gordon and Breach.

Weick, Karl E. (1984). Small wins: Redefining the scale of social problems. *American Psychologist, 39*(1), 40–49.

Wheatley, Margaret J. (1994). *Leadership and the new science*. San Francisco, CA: Berrett-Koehler.

White, Hayden. (1981). The narrativization of real events. *Critical Inquiry,* 793–798.

White, Michael. (1988). The process of questioning: A therapy of literary merit? In Michael White (Ed.), *Collected papers* (pp. 37–46). Adelaide, South Australia: Dulwich Centre Publications.

White, Michael. (1989). The externalising of the problem and the reauthoring of lives and relationships. In Michael White (Ed.), *Selected Papers* (pp. 5–28). Adelaide: Dulwich Centre Publications.

White, Michael. (2004). Folk psychology and narrative practices. In Lynne E. Angus & John McLeod (Eds.), *Handbook of narrative and psychotherapy: Practice, theory, and research* (pp. 15–51). Thousand Oaks, CA: Sage.

White, Michael. (2007). *Maps of narrative practice*. New York, NY: W.W. Norton.

White, Michael, & Epston, David. (1990). *Narrative means to therapeutic ends*. New York, NY: W.W. Norton.

Wiener, Daniel J. (1994). *Rehearsals for growth: Theater improvisation for psychotherapists*. New York, NY: W.W. Norton.

Wilkinson, Margaret. (2010). *Changing minds in therapy: Emotion, attachment, trauma & neurobiology*. New York, NY: W.W. Norton.

Winnicott, Donald W. (1965). *The maturational processes and the facilitating environment*. New York, NY: International Universities Press.

Winnicott, Donald W. (1971). *Playing and reality*. New York, NY: Basic Books.

Woodman, Marion. (1987). From concrete to consciousness: The emergence of the feminine. In Louise Carus Mahdi, Steven Foster, & Meredith

Little (Eds.), *Betwixt & between: Patterns of masculine and feminine initiation* (pp. 201–222). La Salle, IL: Open Court.

Yalom, Irving D. (2000). *The theory and practice of group psychotherapy* (4th ed.). New York, NY: Basic Books.

Yanno, Drew. (2006). *The 3rd act: Writing a great ending to your screenplay*. New York, NY: Continuum.

Yontef, Gary. (1980). Gestalt therapy: A dialogic method. In K. Schneider (Ed.), *Therapy and Neurose*. Munich: Pfeiffer Verlag.

Zadra, Dario. (1984). Victor Turner's theory of religion: Towards an analysis of symbolic time. In R. L. Moore & Frank E. Reynolds (Eds.), *Anthropology and the study of religion*. Chicago: Center for the Scientific Study of Religion.

AUTHOR

David B Drake, PhD is Director of Center for Narrative Coaching & Leadership in the San Francisco Bay Area, with partnerships in Sydney and Amsterdam.

He is the founder of narrative coaching and the creator of the Narrative Design Labs he has run in 12 countries. The Labs provide an experiential introduction to narrative coaching focused on the personal development of practitioners.

David has also designed and delivered narrative-based change, coaching and leadership projects and programs for over 70 organizations on four continents. Clients include: Commonwealth Bank of Australia, Google, Nike, PwC, and the US and Australian federal governments. He has taught coaching skills to over 10,000 leaders, managers and professionals.

He is an Associate Editor for *Coaching: An International Journal of Theory, Research and Practice*, and the author of over 40 publications on narratives and coaching. He is the editor of *The Philosophy and Practice of Coaching* (2008, Jossey-Bass). His next books are as author of *Integrative Development: Rethinking How People and Organizations Change* (Routledge) and as co-editor of *SAGE Handbook of Coaching* (Sage).

CONTACT

For more information

www.narrativecoaching.com

You can find out more about this work, which includes our:

- Narrative Coaching and Narrative Leadership Programs in organizations;
- New online course for practitioners, based on this book;
- Narrative Design Labs, our immersive introductions to this work; and
- Narrative Design Partners program, which enables select graduates to license the material to create new applications.

CONNECTING WITH US

If you would like to (1) interview David or have him speak to your network, (2) present ideas for a potential collaboration or (3) support this book, please contact us via the form on our website. We would love to hear from you.

TRANSLATIONS

If you have contacts who would be interested in translating this book into another language, please contact admin@cncpress.com. We welcome opportunities to bring this work to people in their native tongue and learn more about the work in the process of translating it.

64245587R00200

Made in the USA
Lexington, KY
02 June 2017